Politics
in Everyday Life

BLACKWELL'S SOCIOLOGY SERIES

Politics
in Everyday Life

H. VICTOR WISEMAN

OXFORD
BASIL BLACKWELL
1966

C

233841 Polit

Printed in Great Britain
in the City of Oxford
AT THE ALDEN PRESS
and bound at the Kemp Hall Bindery

To Susan, Monica, Peggy Ann,
Andrew and John,
who have tolerated
their father's mania for politics
and to their Mother
who has none the less
kept them and him
reasonably sane

Preface

This is not intended to be a simple book on civics or citizenship which takes a journey through parliament, ministries, local authorities and courts with patience and a simplicity of description bordering upon the naïve—an A.B.C. of politics. It does, however, aim to bring home the immense importance of politics, political processes and government to our everyday lives and problems in such a way as to destroy the escapist-myth that 'the bomb' makes everything useless, and even the feeling that things are 'too big for us' and that we have no option but to leave it to 'them'.

In the first part, after arguing the necessity of politics and, hopefully, that they are interesting as well as inevitable, an attempt is made in general terms to state one theory or concept of how the political system works. This is not an easy part of the book, but it is essential if politics is to be studied as more than a collection of facts enlivened by anecdotes and scandal. It will be better appreciated if returned to *after* reading the description of British political processes in the second part; though, equally, the second part should take on some shape if studied against the general framework suggested in the first.

The analysis of the British political system does not profess to contain all the details required for complete knowledge of British Government. This can be obtained only from some of the stock text-books and factual studies which are recommended in the bibliography. This includes only relatively inexpensive and readily accessible books which any serious student of politics should wish to buy. Apologies are offered for the repetition of such phrases as 'we cannot pursue the details of this further here': reasons of space as well as design make this inevitable.

No one will pass an examination merely by reading this book.

Indeed, it is a matter of regret that no examinations below the level of first-year university courses (and not many of these) cater for the kind of approach offered in Part I. And Part II, as explained, is not a complete study of every aspect of British Government. But our hope is that first-year university students, students in technical and commercial colleges, in teacher-training colleges and even in Sixth Forms, will be capable of getting something worthwhile from the book and may even be impelled both to read further and—equally important—take an interest in the day-to-day working of the political system of which they are a part. Perhaps even teachers and examiners may be enticed into a little more originality and liveliness in their approach to politics. I have used this approach for many years with first-year university students; indeed, in one sense, they, not I, have made the book what it is. I am grateful to them and hope my readers will be.

A book which attempts to concentrate in narrow compass something of the knowledge and ideas acquired over many years of teaching and reading inevitably owes much to a very wide variety of sources. Indeed, it is not possible to trace all these sources and relate them to particular statements and expressions of opinion which to a large extent have become part of oneself. Where certain sections of the book are clearly a re-presentation of parts of someone else's work references are shown in the footnotes. The bibliography is intended as a 'short-list' for students and has been selected solely with this purpose in mind. It is to be regarded as a minimum—but probably also a maximum!—reading list for examination purposes of books which will stimulate the reader's interest in politics and in the study of politics.

Apart from names specifically mentioned in the text, notes, or bibliography, my gratitude goes to an unnumbered host of writers, fellow political scientists, students, politicians, civil servants, local government officers, and ordinary citizens, with whom the author has enjoyed a lifetime of contacts. That they have not induced greater wisdom in the author is to be attributed not to their shortcomings but to his own deficiencies.

Contents

SECTION II: *Government Institutions*

PART ONE

POLITICS AND
THE POLITICAL SYSTEM

I

Political Problems

On 5 November 1965 Parliament was adjourned to make possible its speedy recall if the month-old Rhodesian crisis exploded in a Unilateral Declaration of Independence. The Prime Minister, Mr Harold Wilson, travelling to a party meeting and then to his niece's wedding, was kept in touch throughout his journey and transport stood by at every stopping place in case circumstances demanded a swift return to London. This is the stuff of which politics is made. Yet one must ask to how many people it was of great personal significance as they attended countless football matches or awaited the results which might bring a fortune on the pools? The never-ending din of foreign events probably deafens rather than penetrates the hearing. Civil rights in the U.S.A.; E.F.T.A. and E.E.C. talks on European trade; De Gaulle wins a second term; the cease-fire in Kashmir; problems in Aden, Malaysia, Indonesia, Cyprus, Turkey, Greece, Vietnam, Iran, Portugal, China, Canada, Ghana, Nigeria, British Guiana and, of course, N.A.T.O. and the U.N.: perhaps many were more interested in the Queen's appearance at the Royal Variety Show or Princess Margaret's breathtaking tour of Hollywood than in any of these events. And how many attached significance to the fact that Mr Brown saw the Queen—'it is understood that she wanted information about the Department of Economic Affairs, the National Plan and the economic situation generally'—; or to the impending discussions on 'Politics on T.V.' which may govern the extent to which the politicians may enter our drawing-rooms to the annoyance of Steptoe, Ena Sharples and 'Avenger' fans or even of those who prefer their politics as dressed up by B.B.C. 3; or to the fact that a new society was seeking a bill to end 'secrecy' in local government and that 'a drive was on to get a local

Ombudsman launched'; or to the protest of the Council on Tribunals that its powers were inadequate? How many people read carefully the Queen's Speech? Yet here in small compass were innumerable illustrations of the fact that politics is not just about war and foreign policy and not just a game played by politicians but something which vitally affects our everyday lives. A brief glance at the Gracious Speech must have convinced even those who do not like politics that no one can escape its consequences.

There were to be rate rebates for people with low incomes, provision for the payment of rates by instalments, and a more drastic overhaul of grants to local authorities. Housing subsidies were to be remodelled and a substantial increase in aid to be offered especially to larger authorities with big housing programmes. A Land Commission was to acquire land and to take part of the increased value arising out of development. The leasehold system was to be reformed and, in particular, there was to be 'enfranchise-ment' for residential property. There was to be a building control Bill to regulate by licence projects costing more than £100,000. A Public Schools Commission was to seek means of 'integrating' such schools with the state system. Teachers' Superannuation was to be looked into, particularly in relation to pensions for widows and dependants. Studies were to continue of the problems of 'transport co-ordination'. Safety on the roads was to be enhanced by making it an offence to drive with more than a given concentra-tion of alcohol in the blood—four pints of beer or six to eight single whiskies seemed to be the norm!—and by making annual inspection of heavy goods vehicles compulsory. There was to be legislation to compel 'advance warning' of price and wage in-creases with power to compel their deferment until after con-sideration by the Prices and Incomes Board. Investment incentives were to be examined. Port modernization was to be speeded up. Social insurance benefits were to be related to earnings, whether paid for unemployment or sickness. Pensions for retired members of the public service were to be improved. There were to be better working conditions and bases of remuneration for general practitioners. Further measures were to be taken to control immigration and to integrate immigrants already here into the community. Like or dislike these measures—and nearly all of them would have been seen in much greater detail during the session in which they were to be placed before Parliament—it is impossible to deny their impact on the lives of probably every citizen in the community. What the citizen might be able to do about them is, in large part, the concern of the rest of this book.

Politics is also about the protection of the citizen. A court calls for an investigation of the behaviour of certain police officers who visited a hotel in the course of their duty. The Association of Child Care Officers expresses doubts concerning the proposals for Family Councils to deal with young offenders. An M.P. presses for a special detention centre for teenage girls in London who may spend weeks in Holloway awaiting trial or treatment. The case of a father of a cyclist of seventeen, killed when his machine struck a telegraph pole, who was presented with a bill for £11 8s. 6d. must be investigated. The Home Office, the Scottish Offices, and 121 police forces in England and Wales promote a publicity campaign 'to encourage citizens to adopt at least simple measures to stop the casual and opportunist thief'.

It is not always the politicians who 'obtrude' into other people's lives; the people frequently demand action—about houses, transport, recreation or the livelihood of the people—which can be taken only after a 'political decision'. Promise of full employment, higher standards of living, social justice and the rest appear from time to time in the most homely terms. A 'power chief' is told to cut back expansion plans for the electricity industry. There will be 'no rise in coal prices before April' and a £15,000,000 subsidy will make up for resultant losses. A Government Industrial Training Scheme may meet with opposition from the shopkeepers. The British Egg Marketing Board establishes centralized accounting and begins to pay the 200,000 egg producers by cheque each month. (Patterns of life may be changed through payment by cheque as many workers have come to know.) Doctors' pay proposals may be put before a Review Board—part of the political machinery now inevitably involved in settling wage and salary disputes. And, perhaps the nicest touch of all, politics penetrates the tea table when an enquiry is commissioned to discover why, under the new Weights and Measures Act, housewives are paying the same price for a twelve ounce jar of jam as they previously paid for a one pound jar; A far cry from jam jars to mushroom clouds—but they are all 'the stuff of politics'.

Yet there are those who are bored with politics and those who deplore them. The first category may merely represent in the political as in other fields those who lack interest in most things outside their own immediate concern or who just lack the capacity or stimulus to think beyond today and its immediate needs. Or they may feel that the problems are just too difficult and complicated for ordinary understanding. Or they may be the 'deferentials' whom Bagehot found predominant in England in the nineteenth century, who leave these things to their 'betters'; perhaps this is one reason for the large number of working-class Tories, though Karl Marx would have described them less politely as *Lumpen-proletariat*! The bored are perhaps not as dangerous as those who deplore and denigrate politics; a certain degree of apathy helps to reduce political tension, although too much—particularly if it leads to a feeling of 'alienation' from the society in which one lives—may equally well produce some form of totalitarianism. The denigrators, however, are more dangerous—partly because their dislike of politics may at first sight appear to be based on plausible rational grounds.

It is curious that while no one would deny the importance of the fact that we live in a society and participate in its manifold activities, that is, that we perform many roles and enter into many different relationships, many are unwilling to accept the necessity for political roles and relationships. Before examining the nature of the social system and the political sub-system which must, we hold, exist in every society, we glance briefly at the arguments which have been used against 'politics'. We shall then seek to prove the necessity of politics. Our conclusion will be that there are certain kinds of decisions which can only be made politically, whatever political system may exist or be preferred. Man has to be a *political* as well as a social animal. Yet as we have stated, there are both theorists and practical men who have denied, or at least deplored this.

We are more concerned with the practical men. But the theorists are interesting, partly because their ideas, sometimes in garbled form and sometimes almost without awareness of their origin, frequently influence less sophisticated attitudes. Hobbes, for example, suggested that those who had studied 'the science of justice and equity'—broadly, political science—might be unwilling to pass on their knowledge because they might offend 'those who have power to hurt'. A simple aspect of this is the attitude of those who claim to have 'no politics' for fear they offend their employers, their customers, or even their friends and families. A more recent political theorist has suggested that political reflection can be subversive of political institutions and undermine that certainty which is essential to effective action. This kind of argument is heard not only in war-time but in peace-time also from those who believe that rational thought may call in question accepted values and practices. New ideas may always be dangerous; once it was religion which ought not to be questioned, now it is frequently 'the American way of life' or the 'traditional wisdom'. In fact, it is doubtful whether even so-called fundamental principles ought never to be questioned. Such questioning is 'political' even if those who indulge in it pretend otherwise, just as acceptance of things as they are is 'political' however much the attitude may be justified in other terms.

As to the practical men, the men who want to 'get on with the job', there are some technologists and administrators who want to get away from politics, at least 'party politics' (as though the alternative to 'party' politics is not either individualism run riot or tyranny). So, we have demands for a business-man's government, a 'ministry of all the talents', government by experts. Or, at the very least we are urged to take certain things 'out of politics' —education, housing, the health service, these, and many others have from time to time been suggested as candidates. This is usually a plea to accept a particular point of view which, of course, it is claimed is 'non-political'.

Finally, there are the human reactions to politics. 'A reaction against politics', Professor Miller has written, 'is the rage of Caliban at seeing his face in the glass; politics is all too human'. Adam

B

Smith referred to 'that vulgar and insidious animal called statesman or politician' and did not distinguish between the two. Sir
Toby Belch had 'as lief be a Brownist as a politician'. So often the
term becomes derogatory: how often does one hear a churchman,
a trade unionist, even a university professor say scathingly of a
colleague, 'oh, he's a politician'! Yet man is a political animal,
political activity is part of human activity, political behaviour is
derived from the nature of man.

In every society there are conflicts between demands made for
certain satisfactions; such conflicts, indeed, are the flesh and blood
of all political systems. Politics, it has been said, is about 'who
get what, when, and how'. A political act is something more than
a piece of agreed routine; political situations arise out of disagreement about the allocation of scarce resources among unlimited
needs—which, as we shall see, cannot be done solely through the
'higgling of the market'. No society can meet all the wants, needs,
and desires of its members. Nor is any society in the twentieth
century likely to be content with the distribution of its resources
in accordance with the relative bargaining power of its members
measured only by their capacity to pay in a competitive economy.
The members, either as individuals or in groups, must call upon
the decision-making machinery of society to settle disagreements.
Some one or some group must be in a position to say 'this' or
'that' must be done, that it should be done in 'this way' rather
than in 'that way'; and be able to obtain acceptance of its decisions,
subject to the continuous right to attempt to modify them. Alternative ends and means are constantly being suggested; how is a
decision to be made between them?

Not all problems can be resolved by the application of simple
'principles' or absolute values. With Bernard Shaw we are tempted
to say that the golden rule is that there is no golden rule. Indeed,
the decision to adopt a particular moral code, ideology, set of
principles for a whole society, as opposed to an individual, is
itself a political decision. The moral principle of the 'divine right
of kings' could be replaced by the moral principle of 'the social
contract' only by the most political of all means—a civil war and
a revolution. Even more is the practical application of such a moral

code to a given set of circumstances political. Patriotism may not always be the last refuge of a scoundrel but it may be used as an excuse or justification for ignoring certain facts, as with the demand in the twentieth century for Lord Palmerston's type of gun-boat diplomacy and some of the arguments used to justify the invasion of Suez in 1956. Even where facts are not ignored or distorted by ideological prepossessions, there is no one 'factual' answer to each problem discoverable either by pure reason or computer techniques. (With the latter, everything depends on the questions asked—the 'programming'.) We may agree, for example, that economic assistance to backward countries is desirable, but there is still room for argument as to the most effective means of helping—large-scale industrialization, smaller projects based on 'intermediate technology' agricultural improvements, aid or trade? We may decide on pure engineering principles what kind of road or bridge to build, but where to put them demands a political answer—witness the suggestion in 1965 that the new Regional Economic Planning Councils should act as pressure groups on the national government to get their 'fair share' (a political concept if ever there was one!) The decision to provide assistance for Ghana's Volta River Dam and to withhold it from the United Arab Republic's Aswan dam was certainly not based on technical reasons. Further, even if all the facts were clear and agreed and the means of achieving the ends revealed as desirable by the facts were equally clear and agreed, there would still remain the question of priorities; a decision would have to be made between alternatives in the face of limited resources. Finally, there is the choice between methods of deciding between such alternatives—since the Quaker 'sense of the meeting' is clearly inappropriate and consensus will not, so to speak, descend from the skies—whether by dictatorship, by expert decision-making, by democratic decision, or even by consulting the oracle!

This argument may be pursued still further. It would seem to follow that every social organization requires that some people have some power over other people (acquired and used by whatever means) which is recognized by a sufficiently large number of the latter as legitimate, acceptable to them. Competition for

such power must be regularized or institutionalized if society is
not to break down. Politics is a striving to share such power, or
to influence its distribution, as well as the actual exercise of power.
The criterion of a political question is its concern with the distribution, maintenance, or transfer of such power. We shall see
later that some people inevitably have more power than others,
and that many may exercise power largely by influencing the
actions of others. Further, there will be some who, armed with
the authority of the State, will be able to exercise legitimate compulsion over others.

Not all the members of a society will, as we have seen, agree
upon the goals which are to be pursued. Many, indeed, may be
unaware of precisely what goals are being pursued. The goals of
the leaders may differ from those of their followers and, indeed,
they may use resources for purposes which might be rejected if
they were made public. But whatever the proportion of members
who know what goals are set or how they are arrived at, politics
implies conflict about how the facilities and the personnel of
government shall be used. If force and compulsion were used to
decide such conflict by each and every individual or group in his
or its own interest, there would be the 'war of each against all'
described by Hobbes. So, some people must occupy what may be
called political statuses which entitle them, because such statuses
are recognized by the rest, to settle such conflicts.

Some of the basic issues of politics, at least in general terms, are
reasonably clear. First, which of the innumerable claims and
counter-claims should be established as rights by the State and the
Government—with the corollary that such rights imply enforce-
able obligations, and which should be left to the arena of bargaining
between individuals and groups. This is the perennial question of
the functions of the state which has been answered differently in
different communities and differently in the same community
at different times. It should be emphasized that this broad decision
is itself a *political* one, despite attempts of political philosophers
from time to time to enunciate eternal rules or even basic criteria
such as John Stuart Mill's (untenable) distinction between self-
regarding and other-regarding actions, the former of which, he

suggested, ought to be immune to state regulation. Indeed, it is not unknown for ordinary citizens to attempt to answer each problem on the basis of some such principle as *laissez-faire*, socialism, natural justice, or individual freedom. The last is an example of how far one may be led astray by such principles: freedom of the person came to be applied to fictitious 'persons' such as corporations which then become endowed with legal freedom to invade the freedom of individuals!

When rights have been determined, there is the further question as to who should bear the corresponding obligations; for example, if the 'right to education' (at what level?) is established, how should its cost be met—out of taxation, out of rates, through some parental contribution, etc.? So, it is necessary to define goals, allocate values and costs and, of course, exercise controls. We shall see later that there is also the important problem of how the statuses which give power to decide such questions shall be defined and filled, of how the occupants of the political roles shall be chosen.

Some of the most likely sources of political conflict in society, conflicts which appear impossible of satisfactory mutual practical compromise between the individuals and groups involved may be further illustrated. For example, should the resources of the southern states of the U.S., or of the Republic of South Africa, or—of concern especially to Britain in 1965—of Rhodesia be used to protect white supremacy or to achieve equality? Should overseas aid be given in such a way as to ensure the spread of free enterprise or to help the recipient countries to industrialize by any means—a constant source of argument in the U.S. but of significance in Britain also at least in the minds of those who equate the slightest degree of state enterprise or of interference with traditional liberal freedoms with 'communism'. On such questions there are no logical, reasoned, quantifiable, solutions, only political ones. Even on less basic issues than these, as we have seen, rights are inherently scarce and involve placing obligations on others. The choice between let us say education or defence (or within education, the choice of primary, secondary or higher) and the balance between both can be made only by a political decision. For example, the cost of social change involved in automation will not fall evenly on everyone; society must make a decision as to how it shall be allocated, even if that decision be to do nothing and thus repeat something like 'the long drawn-out agony of the handloom weavers'. This kind of decision is particularly difficult where social costs are involved: should the 'natural' distribution of industry be controlled in order to minimize the social cost of concentration in areas vulnerable to attack in war or of a flight from 'depression' areas? How should the cost of capital development or war be shared between present and future generations, that is between present taxation and interest on long-term loans (paid out of taxation levied on future generations)? Furthermore, there is a constant division between those who get more of their demands satisfied and those who get less, which is a matter not merely of economic satisfactions but of other values such as status, respect, honours. A balance between these conflicting interests cannot be achieved by the unregulated pursuit of self-interest, with due respect both to Adam Smith and Mr Enoch Powell. Individuals and groups are likely to view most problems from the point of view of their own position in the social structure. Some have argued that there is no such thing as the 'public interest' but someone must at least have the power to compromise conflicting interests; at its lowest the public interest consists in the peaceful solution of such conflicts. Such compromise is, again, the function of those who occupy political statuses.

Behind all these there are, as we have seen, the prior question as to *which* conflicts should be settled politically. In some historical periods religious conflict has been regarded as within the sphere of politics until in most western states at least the principle of *cuius regio eius religio* (subjects must accept the ruler's religion) gave way to the principle of toleration (still barely accepted in some theocratic states). Indeed, even in countries like the U.S. where the Constitution protects religious freedom religious issues cannot always be avoided as witness the argument over federal aid to Catholic schools. There is continuous argument about whether economic issues are the concern of the State and the answer to this question is constantly changing. This appears to be a good example of the impossibility of deciding purely on the facts if there be any truth in the gibe that wherever two or three economists are gathered together there will be three or four opinions! The list might be extended: medicare in the U.S.—with arguments still heard in Britain about the national health service; education—comprehensive schools, the future of the public schools; the proper basis of social insurance; not to mention equally controversial arguments about defence and foreign policy. To repeat, it is a political decision whether the State should intervene—even if the decision be not to intervene. It is equally a political decision as to how resources should be allocated between competing demands. Finally, it is a political decision—though one in which 'expert' opinion may become more significant than in the two previous cases—as to *how* the State should act, what means it should use, once a decision is arrived at that it should 'do something'.

Is it possible then clearly to establish the limits of the 'political' or when a political problem is being raised? A simple answer might be that an individual or group is a political actor when he or it is concerned to obtain authoritative decisions from the leaders or those who occupy official roles in the political system. But if this implies that certain individuals or groups are political actors always while others never are, it is misleading. *No* individual or group is likely *never* to raise problems which are relevant to the political system. None can escape the influence of the political system nor avoid supporting or running down by his attitudes the political decisions taken by governing bodies. In a sense *any* person or institution may become political or change its aspect, at least at times. At any moment problems may arise which concern a variety of individuals or groups and which the subjects or citizens, left on their own, would be unable to solve or could only try to resolve by putting the unity of society in jeopardy.

If we pursue briefly again the question as to *why* certain social problems are raised by governing bodies while the solution to other problems, apparently quite as important, is left to the subjects or citizens themselves, we find that the key to the answer is the attitude of those subjects or citizens. A social problem becomes a political one when the actual or potential disturbances produced by a given situation which engenders such problem lead all, or a section, of the subjects or citizens to turn to the governing bodies to ask for its settlement. In addition, of course, the governing bodies themselves may be in a position to suggest or even insist that a problem be settled politically—by the authoritative decision-making process of the society. There is intrinsically no political problem; a political problem exists by convention. The decisions of the governing bodies about such problems are solutions or elements of solutions to such problems. With this general idea in mind we now turn to a detailed examination of the political system.

2

The Political System[1]

In order to understand the necessity of a political system and the contribution which it makes to the solution of the problems raised in a society, it is first necessary to understand society—the most inclusive social system—itself. Man is a social animal. Aristotle, whose famous statement is thus better translated than 'political' animal, added that any man able to live outside society is either a god or a beast. Basically, the term 'society' is a shorthand way of describing the social behaviour of a group of biological persons regarded in their totality. The term 'social system' identifies some narrower aspect or part of the social interactions or relationships in which these biological persons engage. The broadest social system for our purposes is a whole society (whose geo-political boundaries are defined in terms of the State, as for the purposes of international law) with all its various interactions between individuals and groups, all the various social roles which are played. It is a social system comprehensive and differentiated

---

[1] This account of the political system is a much simplified version of that contained in two books by David Easton: *A Framework for Political Analysis*, Prentice-Hall, 1965, and *A Systems Analysis of Political Life*, Wiley, 1965.

enough to be self-sufficient with respect to the various functional needs of its members; it meets the needs of long-term persistence from its own resources, including, of course, those from exchanges with other similar social systems.

We must all be aware of the existence of interrelated acts of people, starting with our awareness of the family and extending as our contacts widen, and that there is some degree of regularity or recurrence in these acts; we ourselves acquire early the expectation of certain kinds of behaviour from those around us. The processes of interaction between these people, the actors, the structure of relations between the actions involved in an interactive process—relations with each other—constitute the structure of the social system, its pattern of interactions. The system is a network of such relationships; each actor is involved in a large number of such interactive relationships—in family, church, school, workplace, club, trade union, political party etc.—each with one or more partners in a complementary role—parent and child, pastor and flock, teacher and pupil, employee and employer as well as fellow employees etc. The most significant *unit* of a social system is this participation of an actor in a patterned or regular interactive system.

The participants are occupants of roles; in permanent groups these roles persist beyond their occupancy by any one person as monarch, prime minister, civil servant—or referee etc. Further, the groups within the larger system persist longer than individual persons e.g. cabinet, parliament, the judiciary—or the Football Association, the M.C.C. etc. These 'collectivities' as well as individuals concern us when we examine the working of any social system. A role is socially conceived i.e. it cannot exist except in a social setting in relationship to other roles. It is, of course, played by individuals (or groups) but it is analytically separate from them; for example, we can think of a 'legislature' or of the United Nations without visualizing any *particular* people at the time. Individuals (or groups) play a variety of roles, or engage in a number of institutionalized (or regular) forms of behaviour. Their behaviour is related to a position in the social structure; it involves 'expectations' about their own and about other people's behaviour; it conforms to certain 'norms' or standards which imply obligations to other people. Within the 'total social system' which we call society there are a number of sub-systems which involve different kinds of social roles with different norms, expectations etc.; for example, the newly-elected M.P. soon discovers that in the House he is not expected to make the same demagogic speeches which he made on the hustings or a businessman turned civil servant soon discovers that he is expected to make different kinds of explanations of his conduct than would be expected by his business associates or board of directors—or even a meeting of share-holders. The various sub-systems include the religious, the economic, the fraternal, the educational, the cultural, and, of course, the political.

Although sociologists do not always agree either in definition or in classification, we shall now present a widely-accepted simple description of the basic functional problems which, it seems, every social system must face. *Firstly*, there is pattern-maintenance and tension-management: members of the system must learn certain patterns of behaviour which are acceptable in society and must be 'socialized' into such patterns; where conformity to such patterns creates tensions, means must be found to alleviate such tension if the society is not to be faced with the possibility of breakdown. Values and norms must be established, absorbed, and accepted ('internalized' from the point of view of the individual) by members. *Secondly*, every society must adapt to its environment both physical and social; it must be able to draw upon this environment for the resources which it requires and be able to make the best use of them. *Thirdly* it must possess means of defining its goals and of achieving them—the function of goal-attainment or goal-gratification. *Fourthly*, it must achieve and maintain integration; it must regulate the interaction of its various units, must provide an acceptable pattern of decision-making, establish and maintain procedural consensus and provide an hierarchy of authority which in some way is accepted as representative, but with means of control over those who deviate too far from acceptable patterns of behaviour.

To meet these functional problems there are in every society

functional sub-systems. There is no one-to-one relationship between such sub-system and functional problem, since all the structures in society are to a greater or less degree multi-functional.
Indeed, the sub-systems are abstracted or analytical concepts;
concrete structures are not confined to any one sub-system. The
'economic system' includes structures which may have functions
also outside that system; so, too, with the 'political system'. But
there is some degree of specialization in modern developed societies. Pattern-maintenance is largely the function of the family,
religious groups, peer or age groups, work-place groups, although
the political sub-system or polity plays a part in this function also,
especially in tension-management. Adaptation is largely the
function of the economic system, though again the polity becomes
increasingly concerned with this function, either directly (nationalization) or by control and supervision; in some societies such as the
U.S.S.R., the polity may appear to have taken it over altogether.
The integrative function is performed by virtually every structure
in society, though considerable importance attaches to the constitution, the system of law and the law courts. We shall see that
symbols such as the flag, ceremonies, public holidays also share in
this function. Once again the polity is of great significance both as
providing for a representative system which must be generally
acceptable if it is to be integrative and as a means of control over
deviants who are inadequately integrated.

Although, as indicated, the political system is thus concerned
with all the three above functions, it is pre-eminently concerned
with goal-attainment for the whole society. It is the focal point
and organizing centre for the most important aspects of the co-
operative effort of society to achieve its goals and may, indeed,
play a considerable part in defining such goals. It—or at least
that part of it known as the State and the Government which is
in charge of the machinery of the State—wields power and regulates the struggle between proponents of competing demands.
Through it members are allocated to political roles, and the goods
and services of society are mobilized; it provides generalized
leadership in the setting and attaining of collective goals and
deciding between the different policies of individuals and groups.

On the basis of these generalizations about the functions of the political system in and for the total social system or society, we now turn to a more detailed consideration of what exactly the political system or polity is. In it, a number of political roles —of which the *official* roles are only a part—are played. In some of these roles pretty well the whole 'biological' person seems to be engaged; for example, ministers, M.P.s (though not all are full-time), administrators, judges (though not the unpaid justices of the peace), some political leaders, perhaps even the leaders of some pressure groups. But there is a vast complex of political activities outside these formal and virtually continuous roles. Many individuals and groups are engaged more or less intermittently in arguing with, making demands upon, or supporting candidates for office; in criticizing or advising public officials either directly or through the medium of the press; in seeking advantages, for themselves as businessmen, educators, employers etc. Such political activities are not always easily identified or isolated from other activities. Even where there are specialized structures such as parliaments, executives, administrative agencies, political parties and pressure groups, much behaviour on the part of other individuals and groups is also directed towards political objectives. Such behaviour, such interactions between individuals and groups, are political if they are predominantly directed towards influencing 'the authoritative allocation of values for a society', towards authoritative decision-making. Such allocation and decision-making are, of course, carried out in a large number of groups and institutions. But we are concerned with those relating to society as a whole; those involving the widest range of responsibilities and, of course, the widest scope of legitimate compulsion.

The office-holders in the political system have special powers, within the limits of the constitution and the accepted machinery of the State, to mobilize the resources and the energies of the members of society and to bring them to bear upon broad or specified objectives in the name of society and with its authority. They are possessed of special instruments to reinforce these powers and to enable them to fulfil the general expectation in society that they will assist in bringing about a settlement of differences which cannot be resolved by autonomous bargaining—as in the field, for example, of industrial relations. Besides the ultimate right to use compulsion, these instruments include the notion of legitimacy, tradition, custom and other integrative and pattern-maintenance factors. No society could survive without providing for some processes through which authoritative allocations or decisions can be made if and when differences arise with regard to values.

The political system, then, consists basically of a set of inter-actions which are 'abstracted', so to speak, from the total behaviour of the members of society, as being interactions through which values—benefits, rewards, deprivations—are authoritatively—i.e. by methods which are generally accepted by the vast majority of members—allocated for the society. The persons involved in such interactions or relationships, that is, those performing political roles (which may be any or all of us at times and in certain cir-cumstances), may be regarded as the members of the political system. We shall see later that their behaviour in these political roles may be influenced by external (i.e. external to the political system) factors such as human personality, culture, and the social structures. The only practical way, vague and uncertain though it may be at the margin, in which we can define the boundaries of the political system is to identify the latter by the criteria which enables us for each interaction or relationship between persons and groups to determine whether it falls inside or outside the political system; that is, whether such interaction or relationship is more or less directly related to the authoritative allocations of values for the society, or to authoritative decision-making.

Since many changes may take place in a political system, changes in the way in which authoritative allocations or decisions are made, it may help at this point to refer briefly to what we mean when we speak of the continuity of the British political system. Clearly this system has not remained unaltered over the centuries; it has been radically modified in a number of ways. Yet it has retained its basic identity as a system continuing through time. Its geographic scope has expanded; indeed, if we think in terms as wide as those as Empire and Commonwealth, it has also con-tracted. It has a variety of political arrangements, from the Anglo-

Saxon Kingdoms, through the Tudor Monarchy, and on to the present system of cabinet government. It is just worth reminding ourselves, incidentally, that we have not been completely free from revolutionary changes; although our present system has largely evolved—'freedom slowly broadening down from precedent to precedent'—it was found necessary to cut off the head of one King and send another about his business! There have been fundamental transformations; if later Reform Acts seem to have emerged almost imperceptibly, that of 1832 was produced only by near-revolution. Yet it is meaningful as well as useful to interpret the history of British political life in terms of the persistence of broadly the same way of making authoritative allocations of values or authoritative decisions—even though those who shared in such allocations and decisions changed from time to time. Members of the present British political system feel for and believe in their historical identity with the earlier political systems; there is genuine national continuity.

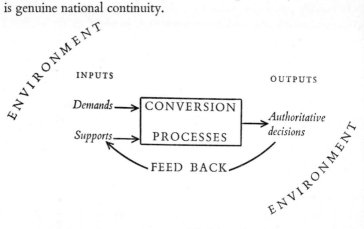

A Simple Input-Output Model of the Political System

We may sum up the argument so far by saying that the political system involves four processes, or serves four interrelated functions. *Firstly*, it is a set of interactions through which valued things are authoritatively allocated for a society in accordance with the wants expressed in that society, which, as inputs, become demands about which issues are formulated, debated, and decided. *Secondly*, it is a means for resolving differences which cannot otherwise be resolved, for example, by autononous bargaining. *Thirdly*, it is a set of interactions through which demands are processed into outputs i.e. authoritative decisions; we shall examine this 'conversion process', as it has been called, in detail later. *Fourthly*, it is a means through which the resources and energies of society are mobilized and directed towards the pursuit of the goals of the society.

Let us examine in more detail the first of the four above aspects of the political system, of which the above diagram is a simplified model. In this aspect, political life consists of a complex set of processes through which certain kinds of inputs are converted into the type of outputs which may be called authoritative policies, decisions, and implementing actions. The political system must be able to allocate values for society and manage to induce most of its members to accept these allocations as binding at least most of the time. Inputs are the exchanges or transactions which cross the boundaries of the political system; they are outputs from the other sub-systems in society or from the extra-societal environment.

A simplified analysis of these inputs would divide them into demands and supports. These may then make their way into the authoritative decision-making part of the political system—in which it will be necessary later to examine the pattern of power relationships and the institutions involved—and emerge as political outputs i.e. the decisions and actions of the authorities. It is important, further, to understand that these outputs help to determine each succeeding round of inputs through what has been called the feedback process. Each output flows back to influence later demands; to each output there will be some kind of response from members who made the original demands, or from those who were affected by the way in which such demands were met. Information about such responses will flow back to the authoritative decision-makers and possibly lead to further action by these authorities. So, we may regard the political process as a continuous and inter-linked flow of behaviour; it has been said that 'the political process looks like a vast and perpetual conversion process'. The inputs provide the raw materials on which the system acts to produce outputs. The conversion processes naturally move towards the authorities who, alone, can make authoritative decisions. But the outputs of these authorities feed back upon the political system, and also influence its environment.

Clearly, the political system does not always work smoothly; it has problems to cope with which may arise either within the system itself—for example, a struggle between Lords and Commons, or between Executive and Legislature, or between political parties; or within society—for example, worsened industrial relations, demands for new social services, protests against comprehensive schools; or from the environment—for example, international crises, balance of payments problems. Demands arising from such factors may impose strains on the system, especially if they consume an excessive amount of time in their processing i.e. in deciding how to meet them, or if they increase in number at any given time. A demand is basically an expression of opinion, or an outcome of circumstances, that necessitates consideration whether an authoritative allocation or decision should, or should not be made by the responsible authorities. A demand may be narrow, specific, and relatively simple in nature e.g. for improved hospital services, larger grants to students, more places in universities; or may be general, vague, and complex like a demand for 'more socialism' or a return to 'true Conservatism'. Demands may be directed to the existing authorities for action to be taken; or they may be directed to the replacement of the authorities as for the replacement of a particular Minister or for a general election. Demands may be expressed or implied as for example a firm demand for the abolition of capital punishment or for unilateral disarmament, or an expression of general opinion by voting for a particular party or joining a particular organization. Again, demands may be concerned to achieve self-centred aims e.g. higher remuneration for doctors or dentists, or to impose duties on all (or most) members of the system e.g. for greater expenditure on education, or defence, or for 'curbing' trade unions. In the case of self-interested demands those making them are almost certain to claim that they also are in the 'public interest', at least in those political systems where values and norms impose an expectation of such attitude.

It is useful to distinguish briefly between demands and other similar phenomena. Expectations, as indicated above, may involve a general feeling that certain kinds of behaviour should be required e.g. that people should use their vote or that sit-down demonstrations in Trafalgar Square are to be deplored; but expectations do not necessarily constitute a demand for public regulation. (Should the vote be made compulsory, as, for example, in Australia?) Public opinion does not necessarily involve public demand; for example, there may be certain attitudes on matters of public importance such as adultery, homosexuality, but those who hold such attitudes may not necessarily hold that the authorities should be pressed for particular action. Motives are not necessarily identical with demands, though they may provide an incentive to the latter. Nor need demands necessarily evidence very strong sentiment; for example, leaders may press the cause of the unemployed, or the case against immigration as a political tactic without feeling very strongly about it. On the other hand, if an unpopular case is pressed say for *not* restricting immigration, it is pretty certain that strong sentiments do lie behind the demand. Ideologies are more than sets of concrete demands (the 'true socialist' is not content with moderate gradual methods and ameliorative measures) though they may also include a programme of immediate demands. Interests are clearly the basis of demands, whether they are personally (subjectively) felt by individuals or merely attributed by observers of the political scene to groups, because of a belief that (objectively) they would be in the interest of the group. But if groups are not aware of their interests (as some would argue is the case with 'working-class Tories' or with those who refuse to join professional associations or trade unions) clearly they will not make demands. Moreover, even if the interests are subjectively felt, the individual concerned may not consider that the best way to pursue such interests is by political action. Apparently business-men would feel like this if they followed Mr Enoch Powell's advice—except, of course, negatively i.e. to *prevent* political action which might affect them.

C

Finally, many individuals have certain preferences but they need not necessarily demand authoritative action to enforce them. We repeat that only *demands* for such action are of direct political significance, though we shall see that whether preferences, interests, expectations are expressed as demands will depend to a large extent on the political culture of the society.

If a demand is expressed the implication is that there is support for it. Further, if a political party, for example, formulates demands it then seeks support for such demands; it may seek to convert supporters of rival political parties or to obtain the support of the 'floating voter', or to interest the apathetic likely non-voter. Other groups besides political parties, of course, formulate demands and may seek support for them. But in advanced industrial societies like Britain there is usually some institutional difference between those who seek to formulate and propose alternatives for action and those who build up support. More important, however, is the question as to when a demand is 'put into' the political system. Political demands may arise as a result of experiences in those sectors of society which are not directly concerned with politics. If, however, they lead to a demand for authoritative action then they are 'put into' the political system. So long, for example, as the National Union of Students merely debates the problem of student grants there is no demand for action; the moment, however, that they ask the Secretary of State to receive a deputation, this is a political demand. Sources which stimulate the output of demands may, however, derive not merely from the society itself; they may arise within the political system as for a demand for proxy votes for sick M.P.s or for specialist committees to enable back-bench M.P.s more effectively to perform their function of scrutinizing and controlling the administration. Or they may derive from other political systems e.g. the United Nations, N.A.T.O., or the European Economic Community— witness E.F.T.A.'s protest against Britain's import levy in 1964. Or, finally they may derive from other single political systems or States; for example, Rhodesia in 1965 with its threat of U.D.I. which required not merely a response from Britain but which threatened also to set up further repercussions such as the sense of protest which caused Tanzania and others to break off diplomatic relations with Britain.

Demands, as we have stated, may be a source of stress on the political system. If demands remain unsatisfied this may lead to a decline of *support*. Such failure to satisfy may result either from inadequate resources e.g. the inability of the Labour Government fully to implement its social service proposals in 1964 because of balance of payments problems; or from the fact that the authorities are unresponsive. The kinds of demands made, as well as their quantity may affect the degree of support for the political system. With excessive unsatisfied demands *output* failure may occur i.e. outputs may fail to hold even the minimal support of the politically significant members—those who 'count' when it is a question of maintaining the existing authorities. We shall see later that such loss of support may affect merely the political incumbents of the day, or the whole regime.

In a democracy there is inevitably a great increase in the number of demands which become *issues* for decision. This taxes the machinery for organizing the agenda for public discussion and it becomes difficult to bring public attention to a focus on critical issues. In part, of course, such difficulty depends on the nature of the issue. In 1962 it was possible briefly to concentrate on a concrete issue such as entry into the Common Market—though this is not necessarily to say that the issue was understood by all those whose attention was directed to it. As one character in 'Coronation Street' said to another, 'what does the trade gap mean to you?' On the other hand ideologies—or basic general approaches to political problems—and stable party loyalties may help to structure or simplify attitudes on specific issues. In any event, authorities must find some way of regulating demands if they are not to be overwhelmed, whether it be by the number of demands or the frequency with which similar demands are voiced. Politics is more than the technique expressed by one French Premier— 'my business is not to solve problems but to prevent people from raising them'—but it includes this technique.

We may regard demands in one sense as information or messages which flow through political channels to the authorities. The 'carrying capacity' of such channels is clearly important or, in other words, the problem of the rate of input. To understand this we may examine the notion of the *conversion* of wants to demands. Expectations, opinions, motivations, ideologies, interests, preferences, are all expressions of wants. Demands consist of those wants which the members of society wish to see met through political *outputs*. The conversion of wants to demands involves some preparatory or pre-processing phases. When wants are converted into demands, the volume of such demands may then be reduced through the combination of some of them (probably with some compromises), through their modification or even through their elimination. By one or other of these processes demands, if not eliminated altogether, are thus transformed into *issues* i.e. they will then be seriously entertained by members of the political system as the possible subject-matter of binding decisions. A demand which becomes an issue may thus enter the political system, but it may then 'wither on the vine' (or, in Britain, be referred to a Royal Commission!) At the other extreme, it may move at once to the output stage i.e. action will at once be taken by the authorities. More likely, however, than either of these two immediate fates is that demands will be combined with other demands, or will be modified e.g. by political parties, and then become issues. So, a demand is preceded by a want; such want may or may not be articulated in some form. If the former it is converted into a demand; it then becomes 'politicized'. Then, the various stages of 'regularization' outlined above—conversion into issues—will be governed partly by the political structure (who converts wants to demands to issues etc.); partly by cultural norms (the rules of behaviour which deal with what is permissible in any given system).

Structural mechanisms for regulating the flow of demands and the responses to them are made up of the more or less differentiated roles which are performed in such institutions as interest groups, political parties, legislatures, executives, administrative agencies, and by opinion-leaders and the media of communication. These operate at various stages as check-points on the channels of communication. There are, so to speak, gateways and gatekeepers, though many of them may be by-passed if there are strong popular demands or even upheavals. On the other hand, such popular outbreaks may be inspired and manipulated. The degree of structural differentiation both between the political system and the rest of society, and within the political system itself, will determine the overall distribution and the numbers of the 'gate-keepers'. There will also be generally accepted rules within which the gatekeepers operate. In democratic systems there are a large number of gatekeepers; even so, much of the conversion activity is carried out by the holders of well-defined political roles, the opinion-leaders, politicians, legislators, administrators, interest groups, political parties, the intelligentsia and newspapers. Demands may, of course, be initiated by the governmental bureaucracies, the political leaders in the executive, influential members of legislative committees etc., whether because of pressures which affect their views about what ought to be done or because of outside circumstances.

As to *cultural mechanisms*, there are in every society norms which regulate the conversion of wants into demands. There are, as we have seen, vast areas of social life where wants are met through other than political means. We are 'socialized' (influenced by our contacts, surroundings etc. in ways which are discussed later) to inhibit automatically the utterance of demands with regard to large segments of life; for example, the religious, although there may be exceptions like the Lord's Day Observance Society or the Roman Catholics in Massachusetts who have succeeded in enforcing on non-catholics by political means their own particular views about birth control. There is, so to speak, a general idea as part of the political culture about the purposes for which political pressures may be used, though these change, for example from the views of the classical economists who persuaded at least the politically relevant members of nineteenth century Britain that it would be 'wrong' to interfere with wages, to the present general belief in a National Incomes Policy. Some cultural norms may, of course, encourage demands e.g. the norm of democratic participation. Not all the members of a society agree on all the norms, though usually certain norms which serve to reduce the flow of demands likely to produce fundamental cleavages in society, together with certain central values such as freedom of speech, may be generally accepted in democratic societies. But democratic norms do encourage the output of demands, since they stress involvement in the political process, and this tendency is increased because of the existence of competing elites seeking for suitable inputs to encourage. On the other hand, in successful democratic systems, leaders generally show a sense of responsibility in promoting demands; they exercise a degree of self-restraint (and restraint over their followers, as, for example, the 'platform' over the 'floor' at a Labour Party Conference); they try to avoid fundamental controversy.

These structural and cultural mechanisms, then, regulate generally the flow of demands. This regulating process, however, must be examined in somewhat more detail. Clearly, the articulators of demands must direct their efforts towards those who are able to make authoritative decisions. The channels which lead to such holders of official roles include interest groups, parties, opinion leaders, the mass media, political leaders, legislators, and the relevant unorganized publics who must be influenced. Each of these 'subchannels' may, in fact, modify the demands which flow into them. In a democracy the network of channels must be large and extensive enough to ensure that demands are brought before the relevant publics for discussion as well as to the attention of political leaders and authorities. Structural differentiation within the political system helps to regulate this process. In Britain and similar countries there has been a growth of specialized political institutions in which the actors adopt politics as a major vocation. There is also differentiation and specialization among the political roles themselves; for example, a separation of the administrative apparatus from the legislature, and specialization within the legislature itself. More channels and alternative channels are thus made available; as a result, more time is made available for the processing of demands.

In addition, there are what we have called the reduction processes, through which, firstly demands are subject to 'pre-processing'. Demands may be modified in order to mobilize and maximize support for them, or so that at least some part of a particular demand can enlist sufficient support. In this way the volume of demands may be reduced and their content modified. A process of collection and combination of demands also takes place. For example, a number of almost identical demands relating to industrial conditions may be collected and pooled by trade union organizations. Different demands in the same general area may be negotiated and combined; for example, various proposals for extended and more effective health services. Such combination and amalgamation may be carried out by interest groups, parties, or even administrative agencies. After such pre-processing, at a later stage, we have seen that such demands may expire through lack of continuous or ultimate support, or they may, in exceptional circumstances, get through to the authorities because thay are virtually uncontested. Or, they may meet with further difficulties and have to undergo further processing when, as issues, they reach the key areas of the decision-making process.

The British system may be briefly examined from this point of view. Many demands are made by the politically relevant members. They may then diffuse outwards to all the members of the system without intermediaries. But more usually they will meet such gatekeepers as opinion leaders, interest groups, political leaders, parties, the mass media, legislators etc. At this stage some demands may find no further support. Others may be collected or combined. In this process they may go through many hands; the 'political agenda' is under continuous development and is at some stage consulted by the authorities (or perhaps even in part compiled under their influence) in order that they may obtain help in the performance of their tasks. Thus the authorities themselves, the legislators, administrators and executives, also participate in the gate-keeping process.

A demand may begin simply with a letter to the newspapers or to a public representative, or by a complaint to a friend or acquaintance. If the member concerned belongs to an organization such as an interest group, or if the organization senses the existence of needs, it may act so as to combine the overlapping demands of a large number of members. Thus there may emerge a programme or set of objectives of an interest group, usually restricted to a limited number of purposes. Next, these demands may reach the political parties and if they seem relevant to a political campaign a party (or parties) will try to incorporate in its 'appeal' both the demands which it thinks it perceives as significant and also the demands which have already been incorporated in the less inclusive demands of interest groups. Thus parties regulate the flow of demands as well as their content. Later, the processes of combination will be continued by Parliament and Cabinet, assisted by the bureaucracy.

A further possible stage is the reduction of these demands through issue formulation. After the above processes of combination of demands there is the question of which demands are the subject-matter of the greatest controversy; the question of priorities (though, as we have seen, some demands may become issues immediately and then either lapse or be directly dealt with by the authorities). Some issues, of course, may embrace a number of demands. Some may become part of what has been called an orientation or ideological issue e.g. socialism. Or, the issue may become merely one of who can best be trusted to do the job e.g. modernization in mid-twentieth century Britain or the harnessing of science and technology to the service of government. The closer the major political parties approach each other in policy the more likely is the issue to be one of 'who can do it best?' This produces a state of 'me-too-ism' or of 'anything you can do we can do better'. Voting studies seem to suggest that at election time at any rate issues are 'statements that allege differences between the contending parties or candidates.' These are of two kinds: those which involve differences in the context of policies and those which involve differences in the quality of candidates, parties or leaders. There is some evidence that in Britain in recent years the issue of 'leadership qualities' have become of increasing importance: Sir Alec Douglas Home lost votes for the Conservatives—or on another view prevented an even greater loss!—while Mr Wilson helped to win the election for Labour; Mr Heath's main task is to establish himself as a 'credible leader' able effectively to 'take on' Mr Wilson. But in a democratic system, in so far as votes signify identification with a leader or with a party they do also constitute a stand on particular issues (whether the voter appreciates the issue or not), although the day-to-day working out of the details is left to the leaders and parties. This is not to say, as we shall see later, that votes are given to a party primarily or even predominantly because of its policies or that a 'mandate' to do certain things can be deduced from the overall pattern of voting at an election; nor, on the other hand, that leaders can do nothing except what they are supposed to be empowered to do by the voters or by some interpretation of the 'mandate'. We must add here that a demand which has not been transformed into an issue, though not a matter of immediate controversy, may yet continue to be debated primarily for 'educational purposes' like the question of Britain's entry into the Common Market, at present (1965) surely an 'academic question';[1] or that of 'integrating the public schools into the state system'. It may, of course, be debated for 'political' reasons i.e. to stimulate a sense of difference between the parties even though no effective action could be taken by whatever party came into power e.g. to stop the war in Vietnam or end apartheid in South Africa.

Finally, on demands, we may examine a little more closely the question of who are the 'gate-keepers', who are those in critical positions of control or power. Popular issues are probably far less numerous and 'popular demand' therefore a far less frequently used mechanism for regulating demands than other modes of conversion of demands into issues, even in a democracy. Only a limited range of subject-matters lend themselves to popular campaign dispute or popular discussion between electoral campaigns—still less to a popular referendum. (Some subjects may not thus be discussed at all e.g. the possibility of devaluation or an increase in the Bank Rate, or even such questions as the precise terms upon which a compromise might be reached between the British and Rhodesian Governments.) There are more likely to arise administrative issues, based on demands which arise in the administrative organizations; or legislative issues, which arise from certain members of the legislature—in Britain, notably

---

[1] During the 1966 Election this became an issue again.

those who hold governmental positions; or from the advisers of the executive leaders. Nevertheless, in a democracy all, or most, of such issues may arise indirectly from public opinion or from what leaders think is public demand, and they can be brought out for public discussion.

Up to this point we have concentrated our attention largely on demands. We now turn to the question of *supports*. These may be considered in relation to the authorities at any given time; to the regime or the constitutional order; and to the political community. Before examining these in more detail one or two preliminary explanations are necessary. Firstly, support may be overt, whether intentional or otherwise; or it may be covert or consist of supportive states of mind. Overt support may be estimated by the numbers belonging to various organizations which favour the political system; the regularity with which citizens perform their obligations; the manifestation of open hostility. Covert support may rest upon blind faith, unquestioning loyalty, uncritical patriotism ('my country right or wrong' or 'if my party put up a pig in my constituency I'd vote for it') or on mere acquiescence. It has been suggested that 'apathy' might be regarded as a separate input, on the grounds that a lack of interest in politics may make it easier for the authorities to carry out certain decisions and policies. On the other hand, too much apathy may become 'negative support'. It is not easy to know the point at which the one aspect may merge into the other. However that may be, as regards support in general it is important to try to discern the number of supporters, the intensity of their support, their capacity i.e. their potential or actual effectiveness, and their willingness to put their attitudes and power to work. Can all the known supporters of a party for example, be persuaded to come out and vote? We now examine the notion of support for the three objects listed above and first for the *political community*.

This term is used here to describe just one particular aspect of a political system, one of the basic political objects towards which support may be extended or from which it may be withdrawn. It implies some kind of affective solidarity between members of the system. In a political community thus viewed a group of persons are for one reason or another joined together in a common political enterprise; the way in which this common enterprise is conducted may vary with respect to the degree of cohesion or sense of community the members feel. The political community is thus the aspect of the political system which consists of its members seen as a group of persons bound together by a political division of labour. This forms the structural connection among the members of the system that gives minimal linkage to political activities which might otherwise be isolated or independent. Each system provides certain criteria of membership through territorial presence, legal definition, blood, kinship, subjection etc. In any political community thus defined there will be some sense or feeling of community—more technically, some degree of solidarity—which is the 'affective' aspect of the political division of labour. This is related to a feeling of belonging together as a group which, because it shares a political structure also shares a political fate; participation in a common political unit demands the existence of at least minimal affective political bonds. Incidentally, a political community may precede and become a condition for the growth of a *sense* of community; this was true of Europe in the seventeenth, eighteenth and nineteenth centuries and of Africa, for example, in the twentieth century. Of course, these mutual bonds are not of themselves sufficient; coercion is a 'hard fact of participating collectively in a community.' The simple point to make here is that loss of support for the political community might prevent the system from continuing effectively to process demands through to binding outputs.

Next there is the question of support for the regime or the constitutional order. In every political system there is need for some regularized method for ordering political relationships, some basic procedures and rules. These are needed to ensure relatively stable expectations with regard to the range of matters which can be handled politically; rules or norms must govern the way in which matters are processed and the filling of the positions through which binding action may be taken. They constitute a set of formal or operating constraints which are generally accepted through quiescence or consensus by both rulers and ruled; they relate to goals, practices, and structures. Such aspects of the constitutional order include more than the formal constitution; indeed Britain has no 'written constitution' in the American or Continental sense, though her rulers have written a large number of constitutions for other members of the Commonwealth! They amount, as a whole, to the established expectations of political life and include three broad components.

Firstly, there are principles: ideologies, doctrines, or just more or less inarticulate assumptions. For example, in Britain the effect of the alternation of Labour and Conservative Governments (though not, as is sometimes suggested, by an automatic 'swing of the pendulum') is moderated by a general commitment to the 'welfare state' and to some kind of 'middle road,' however defined; also by the convention that succeeding Governments do *not* undo all the work of their predecessor. There may be variations within the political community but certain dominant political values give tone and direction to political practices, norms, and structural arrangements. Not all the members of the system necessarily share all these; the politically relevant members matter most in this connection. But they do set outer limits to political behaviour; they are the silent assumptions of behaviour rather than articulate ideologies but they do impose broad constraints. As we have said, no Government ever comes into power with the express intention of undoing everything which its predecessors have done: witness the attitude of the Conservatives in 1951 to the welfare state and even to nationalization. More fundamentally, as Lord Simon has said, democracy can work only if all parties prefer to see their opponents win rather than subvert the constitution.

In addition to basic principles there are norms—operating rules, rules of the game—both customary and legal. As to the former, in most democratic systems members expect to be able to act through political parties and interest groups and to 'enter the political market' with relative ease. There is an expectation of tolerance and authorities are expected to be responsive to demands. There are limits of virulence and accusation and a preparedness to negotiate and compromise. Neither a description of Tories as 'lower than vermin' or of Labour voters as 'bonkers' is generally regarded as a contribution to the art of democracy. It has even been said that no democrat has the right to assert that he is right; he may say only that he thinks he is. He must be prepared for discussion and argument during the course of which he must accept the obligation to explain and justify his beliefs. And in such argument he must eschew dogmatism. He must recall the famous debate between Cromwell and Ireton and the Levellers in the seventeenth century, during which Cromwell, having listened to the Levellers' arguments and dogmatic assertions, was finally constrained to burst out, 'I beeseech ye in the bowels of Christ to think that ye may be mistaken'. As to the legal rather than the customary norms, we think of such as due process of law (or the rule of law), freedom to vote, freedom of speech and association, constitutional safeguards, legal codes, judicial decisions and, in Britain especially, of conventions. Both customary and legal norms constitute the cultural expectations about how members ought to behave in a system; they provide one of the conditions necessary for a system to be able to convert demands into binding outputs.

Still speaking of the régime, there is also the question of support for its structure. There is need for acceptance of the processes of decision-making, for compliance with decisions, and for means of their effective implementation. There must be an organizational concentration of power, at least a minimal division of political labour, more or less stable sets of political roles possessed of an adequate degree of authority. We refer here, of course, to the roles of political authorities, not to their occupants at any given time. 'Authority' implies special powers, formal or otherwise, together with moral responsibility, and capacity to give direction, order or command. The right to command involves the duty to obey, which is necessary as the basis of agreement that authority is legitimate. It must be emphasized, however, that cultural expectations also involve certain corresponding limitations on the authorities. The political roles, if effectively structured, stand in some determinate order in relation to each other, and also to the excluded set of non-authoritative political roles such as opinion leaders, interest groups, 'influentials' etc. through which political activities are also performed though they are not included in the 'régime'. Support is necessary for the whole pattern or system of authority-roles if, again, demands are to be processed through to binding outputs.

Finally, there is the question of support for the *authorities*, the occupants of political roles for the time being, including the 'government'. So much of the next part of this book will be concerned with this aspect of the political system that it needs only brief treatment here. There will normally be at least two strata of authorities of which the first is politically superior to the second. In Britain, for example, we may distinguish between the Government (including the legislature) and the administration or civil service; in a somewhat different position from either are the holders of judicial office. All these must be supported in the appropriate manner and to the necessary degree. Again it must be noted that these strata do not constitute the whole of the political structure, nor need they be the most influential. The authorities need not be co-extensive with the politically relevant members—and, indeed, are unlikely to be; but they must perform the task of governing i.e. of processing demands through to binding outputs, with the support or acquiescence of these politically relevant members.

Having examined the element of support for political community, régime, and authorities, we turn to the question of the kinds of stress which may result from an erosion of such support, and the measures which may be taken to deal with it. Minimal support from the politically relevant members—who they are in Britain will be discussed later—is clearly essential to any political system. Apathy, inertia, inadequate opposition leadership, and similar factors may, of course, help to account for the persistence of support for the authorities. Further, support may be mediated through sub-groups or intermediate leaders; it may also depend on the relationship between potentially rival elites.

Output failure, whether in the form of omission to take action to meet the demands of relevant members, or to anticipate further conditions, or to take appropriate action, may lead to a decrease in support. Such failure may derive either from the poor qualities of the authorities or from shortage of resources. In addition, there may be cleavages which divide the politically relevant members who may be unable to cooperate, negotiate, or compromise their differences. Such cleavages may be based upon social diversity, but the latter does not offer a complete explanation of likely political behaviour. Classes and social strata are not necessarily internally united (a fact which tends to weaken such theories as those concerning ruling classes, the Establishment, or the power *élite*). There may be group conflict between interest groups or political parties which is not directly related to social structure. There may be patterns of conflict rather than mere differences of opinion. Social diversity (the basis of attitude cleavage) and political cleavage may cut across each other. On the other hand, adequate opportunity to express conflicting points of view and to align one's-self in competing groups may contribute to the unity and persistence of the political systems; this may have cathartic effects. As a result, demands may be formulated in such a way as to make possible compromise and even benefit others than those making the conflicting specific demands. While freedom to mobilize support or to join others exists the system as a whole may benefit. Competing groups may trade with each other for mutual support. Nevertheless there is need for some consensus. Too much and too fundamental cleavage may reduce the capacity to negotiate and compromise. Rigidities in the structure of potential coalitions of groups e.g. Extreme Right and Extreme Left which can combine to overthrow the Centre but not to form an alternative government, make such structure less apt for promoting and processing any proposed output. The hostilities engendered among various groups may leave such scars over time that finally, the participating members, profoundly dissatisfied with the total situation, may find themselves unable to accept a common régime or political community. They may then add to the already existing centrifugal forces in the system by offering alternative points of emotional attachment. The American Civil War is a case in point.

But it is important to understand that a political system is not just a passive recipient of outside stresses; it is not entirely without means of responding to strains on support. *Diffuse support* may be elicited from a 'reservoir' created for such contingencies; or *specific support* may be elicited by appropriate responses to demands. As to the first, the rules of the régime may be modified so that each group obtains institutional recognition in the political sphere and self-expression as a unit e.g. by an extension of the franchise, the establishment of separate rolls for each community or the institution of a federal system. The last solution has not been adopted in Britain except in the form of independence for (Southern) Ireland and devolution for Northern Ireland. But Britain has certainly modified her representative structures so as to provide a means of expressing and accommodating differences, of affording access to the centres of authority so that all groups may meet in a common forum. Extended representation in the legislature is not the only way. Bureaucracies may be recruited from wider circles (*N.B.* the current concern with the over-representation of 'Oxbridge' in the Administrative Class of the Civil Service). Specialized functional bodies such as economic councils, advisory bodies, a National Economic Development Council and 'little Neddies' may be established. The executive—the cabinet—may be made more representative.

There are also possible informal responses. The various groups may be offered more opportunities of consultation, more representation on committees, a greater share in the 'honours' system. They may even penetrate the administrative structures themselves through changed recruitment processes. Where a political system establishes norms which permit the permeation of political structures on the part of representatives of conflicting points of view in society, it may be assumed that such attempts constitute an effort to cope with cleavage. There may also be positive action to invite the overlapping of various groups; for example, parties of maximum inclusiveness may be created. It is also possible to use the election rules to achieve such ends: it is often argued that single-member constituencies like those in Britain compel candidates, or parties, to appeal to a wider spectrum of opinion, though current argument is diverted to the possibility of some form of proportional representation in order to remedy the under-representation of certain groups e.g. the Liberals. Another possible way of reducing cleavage is to attempt to take certain issues out of politics; this is particularly true of some issues which persist over time and which, if mixed up with other issues, exacerbate controversy. There may be tacit agreement between the politically relevant strata; for example, no party in Britain is prepared to bid for the Roman Catholic vote by seriously offering to alter basically the terms on which voluntary schools are given state aid. Nor is religion the only issue frequently to be taken out of politics; basic values such as freedom of speech or (where relevant) the recognition of certain languages as official are other examples. This may be done either by the constitution or by the norms of the political culture. Other issues may be left to special channels for discussion; for example, adjudication processes rather than (more obviously) political processes are applied to certain kinds of disagreement, although the experience of the U.S. suggests that to leave some emotionally charged issues to the Courts (such as desegregation of schools or the redrawing of the boundaries of political constituencies) may rather bring the Courts into the political arena than take the issues out of it. This is perhaps one reason why in recent years the Courts have been reluctant to seem to interfere in discretionary administrative decisions; hence the demand for an Ombudsman. Nevertheless, in Britain an attempt has been made to subject monopolies and restrictive practices as well as resale price maintenance to judicial or quasi-judicial decisions.

In addition to structural changes in the régime there are other methods of seeking to increase diffuse support. There are many reasons why individuals or groups may be persuaded to accept compromise. The motive may be pure self-interest or expediency. But there is also a prevailing attachment to the régime as such, especially to its procedures for settling disputes. Moreover, there may be a general or diffuse attachment both to the constitutional order and the political community. This kind of generalized goodwill may rest upon a notion of legitimacy, upon certain symbols of the common interest, or upon the degree to which members identify with the political community.

There is a need to establish a stable relationship between the

D

authorities and the general membership of the system. This is a matter of gradual and imperceptible 'socialization' into a belief in the *legitimacy* of the régime and the manner and degree of its achievement depend upon a number of factors, ideological, structural, and personal. The first of these relates to the acceptance of the goals and principles of the system, of an articulated set of ideals, ends, or purposes. The second we have already discussed; it is the attachment to the structures and norms of the system. The third, the personal, relates to the moral approval—for whatever reason—which members may feel for the régime.

So far as a belief in a *common interest* is concerned, the authorities come to be regarded as the main spokesman for these. Such belief regulates and limits any disposition towards divisive behaviour. It may become an 'internalized' norm i.e. accepted as part of one's personal outlook and attitude, and not just as something emanating from outside one's-self. Various kinds of symbols may be used to foster such belief. (Though their effect may be somewhat problematical; just what do the young enthusiasts feel who join in 'Land of Hope and Glory' and 'Rule Britannia' on the last night of the Proms?)

As for diffuse support for the *political community*, again modification of the régime may help to create such support. But the sense of political community in part appears as 'an automatic product of existing sets of interlocking roles, groups, and institutions'. The longer such interactions continue and the more comprehensive they are, the greater the increase in the mutual responsiveness of members. Men would rather bear those evils which they know than fly to others of which they know not; though this is to place the attachment at its lowest.

To diffuse support for authorities, régime, and community we added (above) the generation of *specific support*. This brings us at last to the *outputs* of the political system. We shall see later that these outputs are not a terminal point in the political process; they constitute a transaction between the political system and its environment and one part of a continuous chain of activities by means of the feedback process. To elaborate this notion further we may once more look at the political system from a slightly different point of view. The system constitutes a goal-oriented pattern of relationships through which the members are capable of adapting to the environment, using it as a source of resources, physical, financial, human; and, if necessary, of transforming the system as well. The political system adapts by using, acting on, and shaping the conditions to which it is exposed. The authorities react, by outputs, to the problems of demands and supports. They intervene positively in the course of events; they recombine, reassess, assimilate or reject demands. They also create demands and turn them into issues. Of course, 'outputs' (authoritative decisions) are directed also to objects within the political system itself; for example, changes may be made in the methods of election or there may be changes in administrative actions and methods.

Outputs, defined generally, are authoritative allocations of values, binding decisions and actions. They involve transactions or exchanges between the system and its environment and constitute a stream of activities flowing from the authorities in the system. However influential or powerful other members of the society (or of the political system outside the realm of official or authoritative roles) they must process their demands through the authorities, and information necessary to influence or produce outputs also tends to converge towards the authorities. Of course, not all *political activities* which have consequences for a system (or its environment) are political *outputs:* witness, for example, a political strike or a protest march. Outputs are *one kind* of political behaviour, that of the authorities. They are, broadly, those activities through which the resources and energies of the members of a society may be organized, focused, and committed. Again, not all the *consequences* of outputs are constituent (or deliberate) parts of outputs; there are also *outcomes*. For example, a constitution may provide for a one-party system; the decision may have historic-remote-effects. An increase of interest rates to rectify an unfavourable balance of payments may have secondary and tertiary effects—even to the loss of an election, scarcely to be described as a (conscious) output of the authorities. The establishment of a linguistic state, as in India, may lead to general social tension rather than merely settle one immediate source of tension.

No set of authorities can possibly have complete foresight, though it is arguable that they ought to arm themselves with better information than is sometimes the case, and that they ought more frequently to consider long-term effects.

The different types of outputs may be very briefly categorized. They may be divided into (1) formal outputs or authoritative decisions and (2) associated outputs: policy decisions, statements of policy etc. In each case the category may be subdivided into (i) verbal statements such as laws, decrees, delegated legislation etc. and (ii) performances or actions such as taxation or the provision of services; or (i) associated statements such as ideologies, policy statements like the Queen's Speech with its proposals for legislation and (ii) associated performances such as informal benefits, advantages, favours etc., e.g. those provided through M.P.s' 'surgeries' or replies to letters.

Let us now turn to the *feedback loop* which completes the circle of a continuous political process. We may start with the assumption that the objectives of the authorities include the matching of outputs to demands. The effectiveness of this operation will depend in large part on the information available to the authorities about the general state of the system and its environment and about the effects of their specific actions. The notion of 'feedback' (feedback loop or feedback processes) includes the 'property of being able to adjust future conduct by past performances'. The authorities may explore and discover new ways of dealing with problems or they may change their goals and objectives or the structures and processes of the system. We may describe this as a process of 'error regulation' combined with 'purposive redirection'. In a political system there are a large number of feedback loops, providing linkage among the producers of demands and supports; between individuals and interest groups; between interest groups and political parties; between parties and some part of the administrative services or of the executive; between the administration and the executive, between the outputs of the executive (and legislature) and the individual or the group—and then back to the beginning again. All these feedback loops may, in practice, be interlocked in various ways.

Looking at the last stage in the political process (in the order used above, though in fact the process is continuous and may be broken analytically at any point) outputs and outcomes are perceived as *stimuli*; they may lead to a modification of demands and supports. The response to these stimuli is then fed back as information to the authorities who may then produce 'follow-up' outputs. The precise effect of outputs will depend on (1) whether they *do* in fact, modify circumstances—even though members may be unaware of the connection between outputs and changes, and the opposition may wish to convince members that there is no such connection! and (2) whether they modify the way in which members *perceive* the connection between outputs and changes. The former has been called 'circumstantial', the latter 'perceived'.

The authorities may, of course, anticipate future events and act so as to modify them, while members are unaware that things might have been different but for such acts. Again, authorities (like the opposition above) may *induce* a perception or misperception by manipulation of perceptions. On the other hand, misperceptions may be unintended or autonomously generated. The way an output is perceived or presented may lead to the substitution of 'symbolic gratification' in place of genuine fulfilment of demands, especially through the means of verbal statements. For example, 'honour' may be satisfied by the presence of British Ministers at the 'top table' even though they exercise little influence on decisions. A perception or a misperception may, of course, be assisted by the factor of 'causal indeterminacy'. Did a particular decision really produce a particular result? If 'experts' cannot always be certain of cause and effect members can be even less certain. This fact is often traded on by parties, leaders etc. through ideological statements, persuasion and propaganda etc. There is also the time-factor to be considered; this makes both necessary and possible 'informed guesses'. In addition, many outputs cannot be perceived at all.

Nevertheless perceptions cannot always or permanently be manipulated. Abraham Lincoln put it more simply: 'you may fool all the people some of the time; you can even fool some of the people all the time; but you can't fool all of the people all of the time'. Rival *élites* and competitive groups propose different interpretations and attempt to prove that 'the emperor has no clothes'. Assuming that there was a trade deficit of £800 million in 1964, was this due to Conservative ineptitude or to Labour's mishandling of the situation? And was the improvement of 1965 attributable to Conservative foresight or to Labour's effective coping with the situation? Doubtless in a few years' time objective students of economics may be able to clear this up, but this is unlikely to happen in time to influence the next election! But to return to the point that the results of outputs cannot forever be hidden, the *actual* (as opposed to the manipulated) results of any output are likely to be felt eventually, though the implication of our example above is that if outputs are carefully planned, this may happen too late to affect the choice between parties. Further, members do not necessarily make their own interpretations of results; they lean on others—leaders, experts, interest groups, parties, newspapers— to mediate them. Finally, it is the aggregate of outputs over a period of time which really matters. This is an obvious explanation—though not necessarily the only one—of Prime Minister Wilson's determination to avoid an election within the first twelve months of his period of office.

However the stimuli may be perceived, there is a *response* to them. We now examine this matter of response to outputs by the politically relevant members who perform the gate-keeping function over the input of support. Such response will depend upon a number of factors such as the general levels of satisfaction ('you never had it so good'); specific satisfactions; and a general feeling that may be quite unrelated to outputs e.g. that the economic situation is not really the fault of the authorities or that the (new) Government ought to be given a chance to prove itself, especially after a long period of rule by the other side. If the output stimuli succeed in meeting current demands or in averting the emergence of future demands there will be a reduction in the pressure of demands leading to broad satisfaction which nourishes supportive attitudes through contentment in general. Such results will depend in part on the cultural expectations of members. In older, well-established systems particularly there is a degree of self-restraint.

Ideological demands may be softened or postponed by acceptance of practical realities.

But what will happen if the culturally sanctioned expectations are not met? Here we must refer again to the distribution of sentiments of support or otherwise over the whole membership. Only the politically relevant members are important. Even here, it may be necessary to meet the demands of only a certain percentage of such members; and of these, only to meet their demands for some of the time. In the end, much will depend on the degree of *diffuse* support available, together with the acceptable degree of coercion which is a last resort weapon in the hands of the authorities, at least against a minority in the face of general consensus and acceptance of their legitimacy.

In all this, information both about supportive attitudes and about satisfaction of demands, may be vital. There is the problem of the accuracy and the distortion of information. Ideology, prejudice and indifference, lack of skilled judgment on the part of the rulers; the length, complexity, and fidelity of the transmission of information through the press, surveys, parties, leaders, administrators, interest groups, public opinion polls etc.—all these are important factors. No one single channel of information is reliable and when conflicting information is received the authorities must use their judgment and intuition. There are time factors—whether the time lag is too long or too short. Channels may lead direct to rulers or be mediated. The number of those who receive feedback responses is important. Gatekeepers may collect, store and discharge responses (in most complex systems according to certain rules); they may space out the flow of communications whether as representatives or as public officials. We may note the interesting comment, for example, that the Permanent Secretary may act as a selective sieve allowing what he wishes to filter through to his Minister! Moreover, there is a pre-processing of support and preliminary storage by interest groups, party leaders etc. who may control its release.

Whatever the degree of reliability of information may be, however, it is important to remind ourselves that the politically relevant members do not put in demands or supports which are unrelated to what has already been taking place. Nor do outputs just appear in reaction to demands which are independently introduced by the input units. They are a reaction by the authorities to the responses made to previous outputs. What precisely this reaction will be will depend upon the degree of responsiveness by the authorities; the time lags in their reaction to feedback response; the competence of the authorities; the resources available to them. Further, the reaction will depend in part on the kinds of sanctions which the politically relevant members can exercise. If a demand from a group is met, can the group in return 'deliver the vote'? On the other hand, since power relationships are not always clear, the authorities can exercise some independent control, the more so because members are not always sure of their influence or of the sanction they possess. Can an anti-nationalization campaign by e.g. 'Aims for Industry' or the Institute of Directors, really sway votes, as opposed to getting out the vote which is anyway anti-nationalization?

Nor, of course, are authorities infinitely adaptable and flexible, swayed by every pressure exerted on them. They work within traditions and a frame of references. Beyond this, the sympathies of the authorities, their capacity to understand and appreciate the problems and demands put to them, their intuitive ability to forsee emerging wants, their ability to comprehend the situation—all these are factors which influence authority-response. There may be some social and political distance separating the authorities from the input units, due perhaps to constraints on the circulation of leadership into positions of authority or to the fact that only those who conform—in British terms, join the Establishment—are admitted. All authorities are 'attuned' to different segments of society. They may also seek to circumvent rather than satisfy the demands of members.

The output lag—the time between the expression of a demand and an attempt to satisfy it by appropriate outputs—may be due either to resistance by the authorities or to circumstances. Authorities lack time to deal with everything and must establish some system of priorities. The norms of the régime may regulate the output process—use may be made of Royal Commissions, Committees etc.; there may be a convention of consulting all interested parties; a small majority may be interpreted as forbidding radical action—it certainly will be by the opposition; or a Second Chamber may impose delay or, as in the U.S. the separation of powers may do likewise. Resources, whether external or internal, are limited and there is need to strike a balance between resources and demands, between the present and the future. The internal resources, of course, include the talents of the authorities themselves, their personal ability and organizational skill, the administrative structures available, the rules which govern decision-making, the storage of 'know-how' etc. These are some of the general factors which must be taken into account when the inevitable question is raised by politically-immature members of society: 'why don't *they* do something about it?'

Among these factors we have from time to time referred to the influence of the environment in which the political system has to work and the way in which it may limit the alternatives which the system can entertain in its allocation of limited resources between unlimited ends, or its capacity to take authoritative decisions. This requires further consideration.

3

The Environment of the Political System

We have seen that the political system is a sub-system of the total social system or society. Its environment, therefore, consists in part of the other sub-systems of the society of which it is a part, its 'inter-societal' environment as it has been called; in part of the other societies and various organizations of an international kind outside the society itself, the 'extra-societal' environment. In each case we must take into account both the physical and the social or human aspects of the environment.

Looking first at the intra-societal environment, both human

and physical, it is clear that the political system is affected by the ecological, bibliogical, personality and social systems. The last may be subdivided into the cultural, social structural, economic, and demographic sub-systems. So far as the extra-societal environment is concerned, the same four aspects are important; similarly the social system has the same four sub-divisions. Clearly, the international society and its units (U.N., N.A.T.O. etc.) are of extreme importance; though, especially in the case of Britain the international economic system is of pre-eminent significance. We shall see later the extent to which the policies and decisions of any British Government are limited by such external factors. But recent problems such as those associated with the war in Vietnam; disturbances in Aden; the confrontation of Malaysia by Indonesia; Indian-Pakistan relationships; French attitudes to Britain's entry into the Common Market; West German and American views on matters connected with nuclear weapons; Afro-Asian attitudes to the problem of Rhodesia; the response of international bankers including the notorious 'gnomes of Zurich'; the willingness or otherwise of institutions to extend loans—the list might be extended—are a sufficient reminder of international limitations on freedom of action. Internal or intra-societal limitations will appear even more clearly in our later account of the working of British government. For the moment, we merely add some general points about the relationship between the political and other (sub) systems, particularly the intra-societal systems.

We must first remind ourselves that the notion of sub-systems is basically *analytical* i.e. if there are four broad functional problems facing each society there must be structures to cope with these problems. Analytically, this presupposes, for example, an 'economic system' and a 'political system' among others. But *concretely* the structures which make up such systems or which cope with the functional problems in question are *not* confined to the system; in other words, they are not completely specialized to any one system or functional problem. For this reason it is not always easy to discern what we have called *exchanges* or transactions between one system and another, despite the fact that the starting point of our study of the political system is, as we have seen at some length, the notion of inputs from and outputs to society which pass through the political system. It is worth noting briefly, therefore, the conditions under which such exchanges may be most clearly discerned.

Four such conditions have been suggested. The notion of exchanges is clearest (1) when there is a high degree of structural differentiation of political roles, or regularized patterns of expectations associated with behaviour in such roles; (2) when the occupants of political roles—or, at least of official roles—form a well-defined separate group and possess a sense of internal solidarity and cohesion; (3) when to a great extent the political roles are arranged in some hierarchy which is distinguishable from other hierarchies in society such as those based on wealth, prestige, status etc.: (4) when to a large extent the recruitment processes and the criteria of selection for political roles differ from those for other roles.

This analysis may be applied in somewhat more detail to Britain on the basis of some suggestions made by Richard Rose.[1] He defines the political system in general terms as consisting of all kinds of social institutions in so far as they have political functions (or in our terms, are connected with authoritative decision-making for a society). At once, however, it is clear that the boundaries between this political system and other systems cannot always be easily discerned. For example, the Cabinet may be influenced by bankers, trade unionists, those possessed of 'superior social status'. There may be family and personal connections between those who occupy national roles in government, in the economic system or in the social status hierarchy. There are, of course, different patterns of authority in such spheres as politics, economics, the arts and sport. Every individual plays many roles which involve him in a variety of authority patterns. *Theoretically,* any one pattern of authority could dominate the political system as, indeed, in some societies the priests and the military have done.

But within these patterns of authority there are important distinctions concerning the direction, channels, weight, and scope

[1] *Politics in England,* Faber, 1965.

of authority. In Britain it is expected that the electors shall determine which party shall govern; incidentally, a possible explanation of the preference for single-member constituencies and the 'first past the post' voting system is that this normally produces an overall party majority and government in the House of Commons, whereas with other systems there is a greater likelihood that governments may have to be formed by bargaining between parties and groups *after* the elections, as in the Fourth French Republic and in Western Germany in 1965. It is also expected that the party in government shall decide what new laws the electorate must obey; though this, of course, leaves open the question to be discussed in more detail later as to who really decides what laws shall be proposed and what their content shall be. The channels of political power and influence in the British system are more or less institutionalized; the weight of authority differs in the political system e.g. 'money' counts for less than in the economic system; the scope of authority or the area over which it operates is defined with reasonable clarity, though there is always argument about the extension of state activity.

Each of the chief systems in Britain, on the other hand, contains a variety of patterns of authority; no single set of values, interests, or institutions commands complete allegiance within the economic, social, or political systems. In the economic system, for example, trade unions, employers, the Government (both in respect of the nationalized industries and in relation to various forms of control and planning), the cooperatives and other retailers (divided into large and small), the City, the industrialists, the agricultural interest etc. all share power and influence; each has its own leaders and patterns of authority and they constrain each other. The status system is based on the value of prestige; it is more heterogeneous than the economic system, being related to such criteria as birth but also to a large number of new and emerging criteria such as education and expertise. High status alone rarely carries with it clearly defined groups of followers; prestige must be joined with other forms of power—economic or political—as Lord Salisbury found once he resigned from the formal inner councils of the Conservative Government and party. In the political system

itself there are divisions of values and institutions; two major
political parties, party leaders and specialized groups, politicians
and senior civil servants, central and local authorities. Again
mutual influences operate between all these.

More important, however, in considering the political system
and its environment is the relationship between the different
systems. In Britain, political and economic leaders move very
little between roles in separate systems. Business-men, city mag-
nates, commercial leaders, trade unionists, co-operative leaders
seldom become major political leaders. Between 1900 and 1963, of
forty Prime Ministers, Foreign Secretaries, and Chancellors of the
Exchequer, only seven were business-men and two trade unionists.
There were three business-men in Sir Alec Douglas Home's
Cabinet of 1963. Several have joined Mr Wilson's Cabinet although more have moved temporarily into the civil service, a
practice much more prevalent in the U.S. than in Britain. The
interchanges between status leaders and the political system is
more noticeable, at least in certain segments of the latter. In the
1959–64 Parliament three-quarters of the M.P.s came from
public schools and clearly benefited from some diffuse social
prestige. Mr Macmillan's Cabinets were based largely on a combination of his 'extended family' and the Etonian old school tie,
while Lord Baldwin is on record as having determined to form a
Government of which Harrow would be proud. On the other
hand, despite some disquiet in certain circles about the narrow
social and educational origins of the higher civil service, at least
there is no patronage; civil servants must qualify and specialists
must possess 'expertise'. The status system, in fact, helps to move
people *out* of effective political roles—to the House of Lords.
In general, very few people occupy leading roles both in the
political system *and* outside it; a great deal of adjustment to new
roles is required, as both business-men and university dons who
were recruited into the civil service in war-time discovered.

The relations between the various sub-systems may be based on
hierarchy, bargaining, autonomy, or democratic rules. A combination of bargaining and autonomy is particularly true of the
economic system *vis-à-vis* the political system and democratic

rules do not necessarily have the last word. For example, the iron
and steel industry may be legally nationalized but its leaders
cannot be compelled to serve on government boards. So far as the
social status system is concerned it 'enjoys' virtual autonomy
from the political system (except in so far as 'honours' confer
status), though there is some element of integration especially in
relation to the Conservative Party. Sir Alec Douglas Home
clearly had other claims to leadership of that party, but the fact
that he was a 'belted earl' was not unimportant, especially to the
rank and file members of the party. But there are few *necessary*
points of contact between the status and political systems. In
summary, Britain shows a marked degree of autonomy in the
major sub-systems. Political leaders are constrained from influencing the other systems by accepted norms, but they also
enjoy autonomy in relation to the other systems. Nevertheless the
holders of political influence are widely dispersed and the holders of
political roles cannot ignore those occupying roles in other systems
i.e. in the environment, from the point of view of the political
system.

4

Political Democracy

We continue this examination of the political system in general
with an account of what has been seen as a model for 'political
democracy'. It will be of interest to consider how far Britain fits
this model. Political Democracy, according to Edward Shils[1] on
whose analysis this account is based, presupposes a régime of
civilian rule through representative institutions and with public
liberties guaranteed. The legislative body is periodically elected
by universal suffrage; it is empowered to initiate legislation through
private members, committees, or the executive leaders (over-

---

[1] *Political Development in the New States*, Mouton, 1962.

whelmingly the last in Britain), and to enact or repeal legislation initiated by the Executive. The Executive carries out its policies through an hierarchically organized non-political bureaucracy, answerable to its political heads and through them to the legislature. Candidates for the legislature are normally members of contending political parties and the party which wins an overall majority of seats or achieves one in coalition (though, as Disraeli remarked, 'Britain does not love coalitions') dominates the legislature of which its leaders may be members. In Britain they *must* be members. Executive and legislative action is subject to periodic review through free elections (though in Britain the Prime Minister can, within limits, choose the time to go to the country, as Sir Alec Douglas Home did in 1964 and Mr Wilson was able to do in 1966). It is also continually scrutinized by the free organs of public opinion, and, in Britain, by a large number of advisory committees. Within the legislature opposition and minority rights are guaranteed by the rules of procedure. Elsewhere the Speaker is not always the impartial chairman as in Britain and governments can be changed by the regularized procedures of elections. An independent judiciary exists to protect the rights of citizens against the Government as well as against each other (though in Britain the courts have for various reasons been frustrated in this, hence the decision in 1965 to establish an Ombudsman or Parliamentary Commissioner). There may be a written constitution (though not in Britain) but in any case traditions and conventions regarding the conduct of the executive, the legislature, the civil service; the army, and the police, as well as the judiciary, are well-known and generally respected.

What are the necessary pre-conditions for this kind of political system? The ruling *élite* must be stable, coherent, and effective. Governments must receive sufficient support to give them confidence that their policies are likely to be approved and effectively carried out; their authority will in large measure depend upon reasonable effectiveness in the promulgation and execution of policy. Coherence and organization are essential in both the alternative parties or groups, between whom mutual and fundamental trust is also essential. The political leaders must be attached to representative institutions and regard themselves as generally answerable to the electorate. The legitimacy of the *élite* must be accepted by a very substantial proportion of the population, particularly those sections who are politically conscious. Both competence and integrity in the rulers are essential for this. Nor should the outside party or its bureaucracy be able to turn the parliamentary party into its mouthpiece—a problem of continuous interest in Britain owing to an alleged danger that the Annual Conference, especially of the Labour Party, might be able to dictate to the Parliamentary leaders. The point is that responsibility should be maintained through Parliament, the 'centre of gravity' of the system.

A fairly coherent and responsible opposition must be accepted as a necessary part of the political system; it would appear to follow that too long a period of continuous power for one party is 'not good' for democracy. But opposition criticism should be constructive and not merely obstructive, which, again, is not easy to maintain if opposition appears to be a permanent role; the party should certainly eschew all methods which involve conspiracy and subversion. Together, the majority and the opposition should form a preponderant block over against extremists of either right or left.

There must be adequate machinery of authority, which requires a well-trained and organized civil service, detached in its political orientations, loyal to any constitutional government yet independent enough to offer strong and objective advice which politicians feel compelled to take into account. Conversely, the civil servants must never despise politicians. Freedom from corruption is, of course, essential to the 'rule of law', especially that aspect of it which insists upon an independent judiciary. There must be an effective police force, a reliable military force, and other organs of law and order—but all with a binding obligation to the prevailing political authority.

Outside the more formal or 'official' roles there must be a self-confident and self-sustaining set of institutions of public opinion—press, university, civic and independent associations, professional bodies, trade unions, and local government bodies, widely spaced throughout the regions and the classes of the country. Information must be available from sources other than governmental and there must be freedom of expression and association. There should be a 'modern civilian intelligentsia' and a fairly numerous moderately educated and reasonably politically concerned section of the population. There should also be a fairly comprehensive and elaborate system of private and voluntary associations though none should be sufficiently powerful to be able to hold the rest of society to ransom. This ensures 'an infrastructure of decision and authority which reduces the amount of authority exercized or decisions made by the organs of the State . . . (and) also keeps in check tendencies towards the "politicization" of life (i.e. the turning of every issue and every relationship into a political matter) which are inimical to a régime of civilian rule, representative institutions and public liberties.'

Continuity is essential to civil order. There must be a sense of community, a sufficient degree of interest in public affairs, a general acceptance of the legitimacy of the existing political order, a sense of dignity and rights as well as of obligations on the part of the citizens, and a sufficient degree of consensus regarding existing values, institutions and practices. No part of society must be excluded from access to the polity. On this, it may be added that democracy is basically a political system in which all, or the most significant groups in the population, participate in the political process and have access to effective representation in the process of making government decisions i.e. of allocating scarce resources. Parties, elections and the rest are more or less reliable *symptoms* of the existence of democracy rather than factors producing it.

This description of a 'model' political democracy has, without specific detailed reference, involved us in the notion of political culture, and to this we now turn.

E

(5)

Political Culture[1]

It is proposed here first to look briefly at the general notion of political culture and then to summarize a few of the most important analyses of the political culture of Britain. Every political system is embedded in a set of meanings and purposes related to *attitudes* to politics, political values, ideologies, national character and ethical standards; the whole makes up a certain kind of 'orientation' to political action which involves three aspects; the cognitive, or how people actually see the political scene or 'map'; the affective or emotional, or what people's feelings and beliefs are; and the evaluative, or what people's ethical standards are. Political culture may be embodied in signs, symbols and rituals as much as in institutions or practices. Unlike general culture, which is the concern of sociologists who study whole societies, political culture is concerned with specifically *political* orientations, with attitudes to the political system and its various parts and to the role of the *self* in the political system—one's sense of obligation, competence etc. It is convenient to distinguish orientations or attitudes to the general political system or community, to the roles or structures (or régime) in the system, to the incumbents of those roles (the authorities) and to public policies (outputs).

Since Almond holds that Britain is an outstanding example of what he and Verba call the *civic culture* it is interesting briefly to examine this. What has been called the rationality-activist culture, he says, postulates that a successful democracy requires that its citizens be involved and active in politics, informed about them, and influential. Their decisions, including that of voting, should be based on a careful evaluation of the evidence and a careful weighing of alternatives. The passive, non-voting, poorly

[1] *The Civic Culture*, Gabriel S. Almond and Sidney Verba, Princeton U.P., 1963.

informed, or apathetic citizen may weaken democracy. This model emphasizes the *participant* orientation to politics and especially to political *inputs*, and minimizes or ignores the *subject* orientation, which encourages willing acceptance of authoritative decisions, as well as the *parochial* orientation, which encourages scepticism about government, maintains centres of interest and influence as counter-balancing forces and prevents what earlier we described as the excessive 'politicization' of life.

The rational-activist citizens as described above are undoubtedly to be found in greater number in successful than in unsuccessful democracies. But the civic culture adds to this category the *allegiant-participant* who is not only oriented to political *input* but also positively to the *input structures* and the *input process* of the particular system in which he lives. Further, participant orientations do not replace the subject and parochial orientations. The former ensures the acceptance of authoritative decisions and co-operation with the authoritative decision-makers; the latter limits the individual's commitment to politics and makes the commitment milder. We may note here Lord Balfour's comment that in Britain 'it is evident that our whole political machinery presupposes a people so fundamentally as one that they can safely afford to bicker, and so sure of their own moderation that they are not disturbed by the never-ending din of political conflict'. In the civic culture, traditional attitudes are maintained and fused with participant attitudes, while subject attitudes produce a ready acceptance of political outputs and the role-structures involved in them.

To this we add a description by Professor S. E. Finer[1] of what he calls 'a high level of political culture'. This exists when the 'political formula' i.e. the beliefs or emotions by virtue of which the rulers claim the moral right to govern and be obeyed is generally accepted; or when the complex of civil procedures and organs which jointly constitute the political system are recognized as authoritative i.e. duty-worthy, by a wide consensus; or when the public involvement in and attachment to the civil institutions is strong and wide-spread. The criteria by which the existence of

[1] *The Man on Horseback*, Pall Mall, 1962.

these attitudes can be judged are the degree of public approval of the procedures for transferring power and of the corresponding belief that no exercise of power in breach of these procedures is legitimate; the degree of public recognition as to who or what constitutes the sovereign authority and of the corresponding belief that no other person or centre of power is legitimate or duty-worthy; the size of the public involved in the above sentiments and beliefs and the extent to which it is well mobilized into private associations such as cohesive churches, industrial associations and firms, labour unions, political parties.

Almond[1] finds that in Britain modern and traditional attitudes are well combined to produce a homogeneous political culture which is both secular and traditional. It includes a variety of different values, is rational-calculating, bargaining and experimental. There is a wide sharing of both political ends and means; the great majority of actors accept as the ultimate goals of the system some combination of freedom, mass welfare and security, though at times some groups stress one value at the expense of another, while at times one value is stressed by all. Such balancing often occurs below the surface and is not explicit. There is considerable specialization and a measure of autonomy among the various roles; arm's-length bargaining takes place and there is the atmosphere of the market. There are groups of electors with votes to 'sell' for policies. The holders of office in the formal-legal role structure tend to be regarded as agents, instrumentalities, or brokers. Policies are viewed as 'hypotheses' and their consequences, like those of legislation, are rapidly communicated within the system as crude tests of those hypotheses. There is the atmosphere of 'a game'.

Richard Rose[2] has pursued this kind of analysis in somewhat more detail and we draw freely on his observations in the following passages. First, he looks at the broad social structures and at the history of the British system. The basis of the system is clearly a popular choice between competing élites through elections.

---

[1] *The Politics of the Developing Areas*, Gabriel S. Almond and James Coleman, Princeton, U.P., 1960.
[2] Op. cit.

These take place among a people which shows a degree of insularity but not of isolationism. There has never been a successful invasion since 1066 and no occupation; there is no large standing army and no officer caste. There is a strong sense of national identity and an absence of major cleavages along the lines of ethnic groups, language and religion and, with only five per cent of the employed population engaged in agriculture, no significant 'peasant' group. There are many points of contact between the economic and political systems. While government expenditure accounts for over forty per cent of the gross national product and the government is not only the country's largest single employer but exercises, through such means as the National Economic Development Council, the 'little Neddies', the Prices and Incomes Board, and the National Plan, great influence over economic activities, yet Britain has a mixed economy. Economic pressure groups have a large share in decision-making. Political parties are broad-based and inclusive and have a great deal in common despite the connection between the trade unions and the Labour Party and the concern of the Conservative Party for big business. Both parties draw wide support from all sections of the community. According to one poll, more than half of those interviewed thought that there was a conflict of interest between classes. Yet if occupation be taken as an indication of class it is clear that members of the same class do not necessarily share a common outlook on life. Occupationally, about two-thirds of the population belongs to the working class, but one poll revealed that slightly less than half of a representative sample placed themselves in this class. Put another way, one-third of them 'subjectively' assigned themselves to a class different from that to which 'objectively' they would be regarded as belonging. Finally, as regards religion, another poll showed that Nonconformists disproportionately supported either the Liberal or Labour Party; Anglicans divided two to one for the Conservatives and those admitting to no religious affiliation divided two to one for Labour. Yet 'the chief feature of the British political system in this sphere is the *absence* of the significance of religion in voting habits'.

Against this background we may look more closely at the political

culture of Britain. The norms of the régime are very generally
shared: the fundamental constitutional principles such as elections
as a means of choosing governments; the legitimacy of competing
political parties; the acceptance of the existing political roles,
including those of the office-holders; the general expectations as
to which individuals are likely to participate in politics; the kinds
of things which governments are expected to do and the level of
performance they should reach; the high level of agreement or
consensus; the broad fundamental political principles such as those
affecting the rights and duties of citizens. Consensus is, of course,
not necessary on specific questions such as the sharing of economic
benefits or the distribution of social welfare, but it is necessary and
it does exist on the procedures whereby such specific differences
are resolved.

This general sharing or acceptance of norms is closely related to
the continuity of political development in Britain. Many norms
have survived from pre-industrial times: early on, a single, strong
centralized government was established; the political community
was clearly defined; religious differences were gradually composed;
modernizing tendencies were in evidence long before the industrial revolution. There were no caste barriers: the younger
sons of the aristocracy were commoners, unlike their counterparts in France; they entered into trade, while the new industrial
groups were themselves linked with the landed gentry; there was
no immediate pressure for complete 'democracy', largely because
of fears aroused by the French Revolution. Despite the early emergence of *laissez-faire* doctrines they were never completely predominant because of the countervailing influences of the nobility
and the landowners with their paternalistic outlook. The Reform
Act of 1832 began a gradual adaptation of political institutions, a
slow and partial process not entirely completed until more than
one hundred years later and which preserved the fundamental
framework of the existing system. The trade unions and labour
movements obtained access to channels of political influence
before the emergence of Marxism and their leaders, partly through
the influence of Christianity—'the Labour Party owes more to
Methodism than to Marxism'—were sufficiently moderate to

support parliamentary methods. A period of unrest and violence between 1906 and 1914—Ireland, the suffragettes, strikes—was brought to an end by the outbreak of war, just as earlier class divisions had been blurred by a widespread acceptance of the new imperialism which provided unifying 'symbols' even for the working class. It is true that between the two wars there was considerable social, economic, and political unrest but 'the co-existence of moderate trade union leaders and people like Mr Baldwin—particularly after the General Strike of 1926, prevented the emergence of fundamental cleavages which occurred in other countries.' During World War II tremendous social changes took place as a response to circumstances not to divisive ideologies, and a Labour Government had full power to build on these changes without a semblance of the 'capitalist unconstitutional reaction' which some had prophesied in the nineteen-thirties. With a change of government in 1951 there was a period of consolidation but little retrogression. The bulk of the innovations made between 1945 and 1951 were accepted during the long Conservative rule until 1964, when a Labour Government was returned to power ready to resume its own particular variation of social and economic change. The continuous rise in the standard of living and the general contentment had, of course, caused considerable re-thinking in the Labour Party; it came to power in 1964 in conditions which made it certain that the Conservative Party also would indulge in some re-thinking. In 1965 it was still uncertain how far the policies of the two major parties would tend to come closer together in an effort to win 'the centre'. Yet it was clear at the Party Conference in that year that the Conservatives were as unlikely to move to the extreme right as the Labour Party was to move to the extreme left. If either move took place it seemed likely that the main beneficiaries might be the Liberal Party—which is probably one reason why such polarization remained unlikely.

Other more general features of the political culture appear to include a strong determination to preserve essential liberties despite the absence of statutory guarantee such as those contained in the American Constitution and embodied in various Bills of Rights

which Britain included in the constitutions of her colonial terri-
tories as they become independent. There has also been a continuous reduction in certain kinds of social inequalities despite
some regression during Conservative rule and the Conservative
determination to maintain such underpinnings of this social
inequality as the public schools. England remains, as Bagehot
described her, a deferential nation, deferential to both birth and
wealth, but with an increasing deference also to *revealed* superiori-
ties resulting from greater equality of opportunity, and possibly
leading to Michael Young's 'meritocracy', more popularly expressed in Mr Quintin Hogg's statement that Britain would
inevitably be ruled by her graduates. Despite this feeling for
educational opportunity however, the private sector of education
remains a major influence on recruitment into political offices;
moreover, new recruits from outside appear to acquire at least
some of the social characteristics and therefore some of the advantages of the traditional political leaders. In general, political
leaders are expected to possess diffuse qualities that are not clearly
specific to the political system. Britain still appears to devalue
technical accomplishments despite the new realization that scientists
and technologists possess qualities as essential as those 'generalists'
who have hitherto been so respected.

But however leaders are recruited and from whatever sectors
of society they come, the cultural attitudes expect that those
leaders will pay heed to the needs and desires of their followers
as expressed, primarily, at election time, although in certain
circumstances they must risk temporary unpopularity; there is
little respect for the notion, 'I am their leader, therefore I must
follow them'. There is a general sense of trust in the *élite*, which
operates also in the narrower political field. The rulers can make
public policy in considerable privacy without undue concern; yet
they are expected to engage in continuous consultation with those
likely to be affected by their policies. As we shall see in more
detail later, the Government reduces its own authority and freedom of action by the array of committees which it sets up, always
including representatives of groups who will be affected by
governmental decisions.

As has been revealed by a number of inquiries, the great majority of people in Britain believe that the Government has an impact on their daily lives. In one such inquiry seventy-three per cent of those interviewed saw some such impact, and three-quarters of these thought it was for the better. There are, of course, differences of opinion about such matters as defence or the welfare services. Conservatives stress the family, the neighbourhood, religion, the individual, free enterprise, as against *national* politics. Labour stresses the limits of the latter less. But in general there is a degree of scepticism about planning—even in the 1965 National Plan! It is recognized that there are limits to 'rationalism' and there is general acceptance of evolutionary change.

Political symbols are important as a unifying force in all systems. There is a great respect for the position of the monarchy—witness, for example, the care with which the television authorities on the occasion of the first showing of the Queen's Speech emphasized that the Speech in fact represents the *Government's* policy; for the system of honours despite some few critics of awards to the Beatles; for the 'ceremonial' or 'dignified' aspects of the system. An excellent example of this is the publicity given to the summoning of the leader of the party victorious at the polls—to the Palace to 'kiss hands' on forming an Administration: the final scene in the exciting 1964 election, when till early afternoon it appeared uncertain who would actually win, came when Mr Wilson was seen on television going to Buckingham Palace. No one could then doubt who was the First Commoner in the land. In the same way the *panoply* of Parliament plays an important part in maintaining a sense of legitimacy and tradition; indeed, many have suggested that, as with the monarchy in an earlier age, Parliament is in danger of becoming more dignified than efficient!

To sum up, we find a mixed culture, very like Almond's civic culture: universal suffrage was achieved finally only in the twentieth century and double voting did not go until 1948; yet the monarchy remained as an important part of the political system and the House of Lords still symbolized an aristocratic element despite the institution of life peers and the renunciation of titles by those who preferred the Commons. Above all, there remains general agreement that the peaceful compromise of political differences is essential and that change should be gradually assimilated into the existing political system. These, then, are the general features of the political culture in which the political system is embedded. Our next general question is how the members of the system are 'socialized' into these attitudes, norms, and values.

6

Political Socialization and Recruitment

It is obviously no longer true that 'nature doth contrive that every little boy or gal that's born into this world alive is either a little Liberal or else a little Conservative'. But it remains true that a process of 'induction into the political culture', of learning one's social heritage, begins from an early age in the family and continues in church, school, work-group, voluntary association; through the media of communication, political parties and government institutions. This process produces a set of attitudes or orientations to the political system. A further stage, to be examined later, is that of recruitment into political roles, or the process whereby to a greater or less extent individuals come to participate in the political system. All this is generally known as political socialization, with the stage of political recruitment in a sense, beginning where the former leaves off. It should be added that political socialization does not determine adult political behaviour; it merely creates certain dispositions.

In Britain there seems in general to be little expectation of continuous and active participation in political relationships on the part of the vast majority of citizens. The small minority of whom such participation is expected are apparently expected to begin their training early. As regards general political attitudes, the family tends early to establish certain primary loyalties; it has been shown, for example, that by 1960 only fifteen per cent of those whose fathers voted Conservative before the war were voting Labour, while only twenty-eight per cent of those whose fathers voted Labour before the war were voting Conservative. Family patterns may by some extent depend on where one lives and works; it is difficult to be a Conservative in a tightly-knit mining community or a Labour supporter in a deferential rural community. Voting habits may be affected by moving from one community to another; so may party fortunes if there is anything in the notion that party loyalties are affected by place of residence, as is suggested by those studies which relate the possible future of the Labour Party to the fact that its strongholds are declining in population as people move into growing centres which are already Conservative dominated. More obvious is the fact that the tendency to follow the family pattern is strongly associated with the son's remaining in the same social class as the father. The attitude of young people is clearly affected by the period in which they grow up, but in most cases they develop attitudes similar to those of their elders. It appears at present that young people are usually slightly more inclined to Labour. With old people there is a time lag which, of course, tends to strengthen their social conservatism, yet their voting behaviour was apparently volatile in the period 1950 to 1964. As time goes on, of course, more people—proportionately—will have been brought up in the Labour tradition; their commitment may not be as strong as that of the smaller number who grew up when the movement was struggling, since with them it may be no more than a matter of voting Labour, but there will be more of them.

The educational system helps to form certain general attitudes of which the most basic is probably that of patriotism—though not necessarily of the old-fashioned jingoistic style—or at least of strong preference for one's own country and its cultural norms which are, in part transmitted through the schools. There is still general acceptance of inequality in education, or even in 'educability', and of a connection between intelligence and social status. The public schools especially still inculcate the notion of 'leadership' into their products; but the notion of hierarchy and the acceptance of authority is encouraged in most schools to a far greater extent than is the case, for example, in the U.S. though there conformity to the 'American way of life' may be an equally potent form of socialization. Only at the level of the universities, it appears, may education produce disatisfaction with existing norms; but it is a moot point how long afterwards this lasts, and indeed, some evidence to suggest that universities and, especially, other institutions of higher education, today may be tending to produce as many conformists as rebels.

The influence of the work-place tends to confirm the attitudes already developed by family and school, unless there is upward mobility in the social strata. As an example of this kind of influence we may note that a trade unionist is twice as likely to vote Labour as Conservative, although one-third of the forty per cent of employed who are in trade unions vote Conservative. We have already referred to geographic location in a particular community as influencing voting habits and this is clearly related to the factor of work-place. It has been fairly well established that Britain has the highest level of class voting in the group Britain, the U.S., Canada, and Australia. Added to this is the well-known partisan stability of the majority of people, though—as we saw in our reference to working-class Tories—the middle class shows more solidarity than the working class. Within classes there are differences related to job differences: skilled and unskilled; white and blue collar; secure professions and those struggling to be recognized as such.

Political parties are, of course, important agents of socialization as well as of recruitment: the Socialist Sunday school may have disappeared but the Young Conservatives catch them very young. Party members are more likely to be opinion-leaders in their face-to-face contacts with other citizens, they talk politics more and have more definite views. On the other hand, among the voters at large there is apparently a failure to develop a coherent set of attitudes to public policy. From one survey it appeared that judged by their views on issues of public policy only one-third of Labour voters could be classified as pro-Labour, while thirty-nine per cent appeared to be pro-Conservative; Of Conservative voters only four per cent appeared to be pro-Labour but on the other hand, only thirty-eight per cent supported their preferred party on at least three out of four stated issues. Parties, of course, can draw on diffuse, emotional loyalties; it is clear that voters are more likely to endorse a policy if it is identified to them as *their* party's policy; they tend to trust the party leaders and to be attracted to the 'image' of the party rather than to its specific policies.

The socialization experiences of citizens tend to be cumulative and their attitudes to develop some degree of coherence; the differing agencies of socialization with which they come into contact—in the natural course of their life and also, to some extent, by deliberate choice—tend to strengthen their earlier political outlooks. But, of course, these socializing agencies tend to change; family life alters, education becomes more generally available, religion becomes less important, wars have an effect on attitudes. Political parties themselves change. On the other hand, the majority of citizens do not appear to change, whether due to apathy, prejudice, or common-sense. Finally, it must be emphasized that whatever direct attempts at political socialization—or indoctrination—may be made, political socialization is very largely a product of other—more indirect—influences.

We have said that political recruitment, or, more broadly, the emergence of political participation, begins where political socialization leaves off (though, in fact, the latter never really ceases); we therefore attempt a brief examination of this process in the British political system. Richard Rose distinguishes four levels of participation. First, there is national leadership, concerned with the making of policy-decisions and with ready access to all the other policy-makers. It includes the Cabinet, senior civil servants, expert advisers, and spokesmen for the major pressure groups. Secondly, there are the 'political auxiliaries', who work closely with the leaders but who are intermediaries between them and the local political activists, or between the national leaders themselves. They may include M.P.s, party officials and even journalists. Thirdly, there are the local activists, the councillors, branch secretaries of the trade unions, voluntary leaders of various social service groups. Finally, there are those engaged on the periphery who may be nominally involved in a pressure group or a party, or remain outside these and at most vote in elections. It will be clear from this analysis that political roles as thus conceived are not the same as constitutional offices; they include elected representatives, appointed officials and individuals without formal office, all of whom interact politically.

Those on the periphery and those engaged locally are usually only involved on a part-time basis. They are at a great distance from the central government and the great majority do no more than vote. This is a very shallow form of political participation. In one survey it was revealed that only forty-three per cent of those interviewed claimed to get a feeling of satisfaction from voting; the rest claimed to be thinking of nothing special at the time and regarded it largely as a waste of time. Yet, as we have already seen, they generally show a firm attachment to party. One poll revealed that something like eighty per cent of those interviewed were ready to identify with a party, although only fourteen per cent showed themselves to be intensely partisan in their non-political social contacts. A relatively small number described themselves as *very* interested in politics, or, at the other extreme, *not at all* interested. It should, perhaps, be mentioned here that non-voting is not necessarily an indication of lack of interest; it may be due to reasons over which the voter has no control such as absence from home or not being on the electoral register. This limited interest in politics is emphasized by the lack of political information possessed by the interviewees.

In addition to voting there may be indirect participation in the political process as through membership of at least one social organization; but such membership may be purely formal. Those who accept office in such organizations are not typical of the population as a whole; there, is, for example, a highly significant relationship between the level of education and the acceptance of office. In political parties there is a similar pattern of active and passive participation; the majority of members pay their subscriptions (if that) and no more. There are only a few hundred thousand activists in the party organizations at *all* levels; the others are more concerned with local and parochial matters, with their clubs, sporting activities, families, and social engagements. If one defines sustained participation in politics as indicated by the self-assessment 'very interested in politics', about fifteen per cent of the adult population are active participants. If active participation is required in the local party organization, even on a part-time basis, then only one in every two hundred of the electorate is active. On a somewhat different definition of active interest an American author has suggested that in the U.S. there may be two such 'politists', as he calls them, in every one hundred of the adult population.

When we turn to national roles there is a sharp distinction between these and local roles; some locals go into politics—trade unionists, local councillors etc. but for the most part they do not obtain leading positions. Apart from the many spokesmen of the pressure groups, the nationals normally enter national politics as fairly young men and accumulate their political experience. This tendency is strengthened in Britain by the centralization of politics in London and the fact that there is no residential qualification required of a parliamentary candidate. Many M.P.s— and an increasing number—are full-time politicians and so, of course, are the administrative class career civil servants. On the other hand, many pressure group spokesmen are only involved in politics on a part-time basis, as are the members of many kinds of public commissions, committees, and boards.

A few interesting illustrative facts about the origins of these national leaders may be given. Of forty Prime Ministers, Chancellors of the Exchequer, and Foreign Secretaries, nearly one-half were educated at Eton, Harrow, or Winchester. Only six of the forty had an ordinary state school education. Fifteen of them were, in fact, professional politicians and all of these except one inherited money and family connections. In the 1945–51 Labour Government four of the six who held these positions had attended major public schools; Ernest Bevin, the trade union leader, was an outstanding exception. It is clear that entry into the Cabinet in general tends to be confined to a narrow social strata, the hereditary aristocracy and the upper middle class, who constitute only five per cent of the population. Most of them enter the House of Commons at an early age and serve a long apprenticeship. In the House of Commons the Conservative Party consists largely of men from the top five per cent of the social structure; the Labour Party, mainly through its trade union M.P.s who occupy safe seats, may produce some ninety ex-manual workers (mostly a long time away from soiling their hands!). In assessing the significance of attainment to ministerial status, however, it must be remembered that a large number of M.P.s are not interested in high office; they are the 'ballast' which ensures the stability and predictability of parliamentary life. Not all of them are full-time or even approach it. It is also a matter for argument whether a House of Commons or a Government which was a better cross-section of society as a whole would necessarily be a 'better' organization.

As for the Civil Service, only a small percentage of the roughly 600,000 take on a national leadership or auxiliary role. The highest ranks number about 170, or if the whole of the Higher Civil Service is included, about 2,800. The Administrative Class in particular is recruited in its youth and possesses little if any professional or technical skill. In the post-war period the entrants to the Home Civil Services included 171 who read History at the University, but only twelve who read Mathematics and six science or technology. Of 149 recruited by the Foreign Service one had read Mathematics and one Science. The tradition is maintained of a 'generalist' or 'amateur' bias. Methods of recruitment also reinforce the bias in favour of the highest social strata. Between 1948 and 1956 the top three per cent of the population by occupational classification won thirty-eight per cent of the places in the Home Civil Service and sixty-three per cent in the Foreign Service. Families in the bottom eighty per cent of the population won only twenty-two per cent and nine per cent of the places respectively. The picture is, of course, slightly altered by the possibility of promotion from the Executive Class but few such promotees have as yet reached the highest positions. Naturally the public schools and 'Oxbridge' are consistently over-represented. It ought, perhaps, to be emphasized that we are only attempting to show the relationship between social structure and recruitment to the Civil Service. It has to be *empirically* ascertained (but how?) that widening the field of recruitment would, in fact, produce a 'better' Civil Service. However, there does seem to be general agreement that the Civil Service needs more scientists and technologists.

If we consider all the national roles together it is clear that those who hold them undergo a process of 'role socialization' which tends to produce a common outlook and which makes for more effective informal collaboration. Pressure group leaders, committee chairmen, experts, and opinion leaders often have a political role 'thrust upon them' but in most cases they seem to acquire the atmosphere in not too long a time. In general, there are only slow and limited changes in the recruitment processes into national politics; it is thus easy for the 'system' to transmit the informal norms of political behaviour. National leaders expect to be shown some degree of deference and usually are; they are not '*of* the people'; they exercise and are expected to exercise judgment and leadership. Yet they must be able to appeal to the people in general and prove themselves moderate and broadly acceptable to public opinion.

It is important, finally, to note that the relative homogeneity in social origins of the national leadership is not conclusive evidence about the making of policy and the distribution of power.[1] Leaders do not always agree among themselves. Moreover, there are other routes to political influence, through pressure groups, academic institutions, technical knowledge, social status, friendships and so on. All this makes it difficult to assess the significance of such notions as 'ruling class', 'Establishment', or 'power *élite*'. The first can only mean that the governing circle consists of members of one class in an economic or social sense. The second also refers to a socio-economic group but includes a psychological element, the sharing of certain attitudes—the 'traditional wisdom'—and membership of a social network. The third simply implies that power is limited to those (of whatever origin) in certain top positions which, since inevitably 'some animals are more equal than others' is really a tautology. In all three cases it is implied that there exists a separate group of leaders. Government is, of course, bound to be in the hands of a 'ruling circle'; the representative process is bound to separate leaders and followers; moreover,

---

[1] *Voters, Parties and Leaders*, Jean Blondel, Pelican, 1963.

F

politicians, as well as holders of other political roles, are quite unlikely to be drawn proportionately from all social groups.

But there are difficulties in the way of accepting such *theories* of an *élite* as those outlined above. Firstly, the group at the top would have to be a group in the strongest sense; it must be a community with an *esprit de corps* and recognizable attitudes, and different from the mass because of its values. Secondly, its rule would have to be permanent or at least not seriously challenged by outsiders; for example, the difference between parties must in some sense be irrelevant. In Britain, the Labour Party in power would have to preserve the *status quo* or else the ruling group must continue somehow to run things behind the scenes, like Breakages Ltd. in Bernard Shaw's *Apple Cart*. Thirdly, the word 'rule' has to be explained; how much power is implied? Clearly it does not simply refer to administration; it must include decision-making and be more than just 'honest brokerage', acceding to demands as they are balanced between competing groups.

Those who speak of a British ruling circle often begin with a list of leading families, of products of the public schools, of the aristocracy, and those 'new entrants' who have been 'accepted'. They go on to speak of the links between influential families, the Conservative party, the financial houses, the Foreign Office, the Armed Services, and those whose education was in common. But this group is clearly not isolated from the rest of the community; it is only an inner circle and there is no complete gap between it and the rest. Movement takes place both ways. Some newcomers are admitted, though Ramsay Macdonald with his boast that every duchess in England would want to kiss him was probably the *reductio ad absurdum* of this category. Some leave the circle and are hated more than the 'born outsiders': witness the attitude to the late Hugh Gaitskell (Winchester, and New College, Oxford). There is, of course, a certain unity of doctrine and value within the group; they are conservative-minded. Yet this is true of the whole middle and upper-middle class and, indeed, of large numbers of working-class Tories! Within these classes, however, there are conflicts; we may note the differences between Mr Macmillan and Lord Salisbury on matters which again emerged during the

Rhodesia crisis of October, 1965, with similar differences of opinion between Lord Salisbury and Sir Alec Douglas Home. The 'tribes', or even the 'extended family' do not hold together despite a good deal of nepotism and the 'old-boy network'. The establishment is rather a system of selection than one by which ideas are developed.

As to the nature of its power, the group, however defined, possesses no permanent hold on key decision-making positions. The Labour Party is certainly not reduced to impotence; it passed many important measures between 1945 and 1950 and appeared poised once more in 1965 for making inroads if not for mounting a frontal attack on the so-called citadels of power. It *may* have been brought down by a bankers' ramp in 1931 (though this is rather part of the mythology than of the facts of political life); it certainly defeated the 'gnomes of Zurich' and some of its opponents in the City in 1964. The Labour Party is, of course, moderate; some might argue too moderate after the apparent watering-down of the already moderate election programme of 1964. But has such moderation been imposed by the '*élite*'—or, more likely, especially in view of the narrow margin of victory, by the electors? The Labour Government did not eradicate the social prestige of the *élite*: it may be that Sir Alec Douglas Home following upon the Profumo scandal more effectively achieved this; certainly he has been succeeded by a new type of leader of whom it has been said that he was chosen because he was most like Mr Wilson!

Finally, if the '*élite*' rules, it rules only in a very limited way. It is limited by outside forces such as the trade unions and big business (not always in favour of Conservative policies, certainly, for example, not adopting that party's attitude to Mr George Brown's National Plan), by some technocrats and managerial groups, and by the bureaucracy. Neither the inner circle nor the whole of the establishment is the *sole* repository of political power. Its real strength lies in its social prestige, which may be on the wane. There are, of course, differences between the parties. The Conservatives tend to stress good background and the right education; the Labour Party emphasizes service to 'the cause'— the Movement—and, more than ever now, the managerial-bureaucracy and a 'meritocracy', with the Conservatives also angling for such support. But the establishment cuts across all these groups and can exercise political power only through them.

Political socialization thus operates unevenly and in different ways on different individuals and groups; political recruitment even more so. But while, as we have said, it may be true that 'some animals are more equal than others', there is nothing eternal about which particular animals shall at any given time enjoy this 'greater equality'.

PART TWO

THE BRITISH POLITICAL
SYSTEM AT WORK

Input Functions

I

Introduction

In addition to the kind of general analysis of political systems outlined in Part I there have been many attempts to describe the main functions and institutions of the political system in more detail. Although we shall not use any of these schemes as they stand for our description of the British political system at work, it is worth looking briefly at one such scheme, devised by Almond.[1]

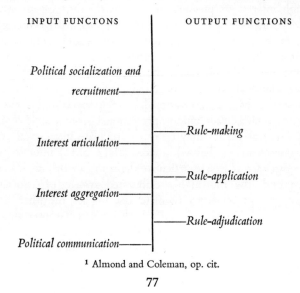

INPUT FUNCTONS   OUTPUT FUNCTIONS

Political socialization and recruitment————

————*Rule-making*

Interest articulation————

————*Rule-application*

Interest aggregation————

————*Rule-adjudication*

Political communication————

[1] Almond and Coleman, op. cit.

This 'seven-function' scheme refers to four input and three output functions, but does not consider in detail the 'conversion processes' which operate so as to turn the former into the latter. The first of these functions, *political socialization and recruitment*, has been discussed in Part I. It is necessary only to add that, as we have seen, this is not only an input but also an output function, and, indeed, operates within the conversion process, since the political system itself and the holders of official roles within it influence both the socialization and recruitment processes.

The second function, *interest articulation*, refers to the formulation and expression of claims and demands for political action. This may take place during elections, when clearly or vaguely, directly or indirectly, citizens are expressing a choice between alternative policies or, at least, alternative teams committed to different policies, general or specific. We shall examine the electoral process and voting habits in Britain and the candidates who present themselves. The role of political parties is important here since they select both issues and candidates for the electors' choice. But interest articulation does not occur only at election times; there is a continuous interplay between citizen and government, partly through interest or pressure groups, partly through an array of advisory and consultative bodies of all kinds, partly through the press, or by means of campaigns, marches and demonstrations. So far as the groups are concerned, they may be institutional like the army, the churches, the legislature, the bureaucracy; or non-associational as kinship, ethnic, religious, regional, status, or class groups; or associational, as the specialized continuous structures such as trade unions, professional groups, civic organizations. Political parties may serve to articulate interests as well as aggregate them (cf. below); indeed, some broad interest groups may aggregate as well as articulate demands. In Britain, according to Almond, the thoroughly elaborated system of associational interest groups tends to regulate the impact of other interest structures, to mitigate and moderate their particular interests and to translate them into explicit general and bargaining demands for public policies. The associational groups thus articulate demands in society, seek support for them from other groups, attempt to influence the choice of political personnel and the various processes of public policy-making and enforcement.

Interest aggregation is seen primarily as the function of political parties. It implies the formulation of general policies in which the interests which have been articulated may be combined, accommodated and compromised. It also involves the bringing together of political personnel who are more or less committed to a particular pattern of policy. Aggregation takes place at a more inclusive level of this combinatory process than articulation. But just as interest groups may share in the aggregative function, so may legislatures, executives and bureaucracies. In Britain however, again according to Almond, the aggregative function is distinctively performed by the party system; interest aggregations in the bureaucracy, for example, are controlled and to some extent assimilated into the aggregative processes of the party system from which political leaders, who control the bureaucracy, emerge. The parties are broad-based and can aggregate interests into general policies *before* the performance of the authoritative functions by legislature, executive, and bureaucracy. With certain obvious limitations there is also some degree of free movement of interest groups between the parties.

It is useful at this point to refer to Richard Rose's argument that it is not possible to make an absolute distinction between pressure groups and parties; there is considerable mutual interpenetration. This is, perhaps, most obvious in relation to the Trade Unions and the Labour Party. The unions control about eighty-eight per cent of the votes at the party's Annual Conference and elect eighteen of the twenty-eight members of the National Executive Committee. They sponsor a large number of labour candidates, as we shall see later; in some constituencies the National Union of Mineworkers, for example, *is* the local Labour Party. The Trade Union Congress exercises considerable influence in the party. There is, of course, a close, though less formalized connection between the Conservative Party and business pressure groups. In the sixteen months before the 1959 Election, for example, these groups spent nearly one and a half million pounds in anti-labour propaganda. Many Conservative M.P.s act as spokesmen for certain groups in business and industry; in 1965, Mr Callaghan, the Labour Chancellor of the Exchequer said that he often thought of certain M.P.s not as members for a particular constituency but for an 'interest'. (He was found *not* to have committed a breach of parliamentary privilege by this remark). Further, the boundary between 'interest' and 'principles' may be blurred. The National Farmers' Union seeks to justify subsidies by the social principle that agriculture makes an important contribution to 'the British way of life'. Coal-mining and textile communities often seek support for a distinctive way of life as well as protection for their means of livelihood. On the other hand, resolutions sent to Party Conferences frequently represent pressure group demands e.g. for education, pensions, transportation. Conversely, trade unions frequently submit political resolutions. Parties and pressure groups are, in fact, both parts of a single political system; on particular issues they work together, on others, such as entry into the Common Market, they divide within themselves. The Confederation of British Industries or the Trade Union Congress *aggregate* demands and decide between competing policies. Political parties often demand, as a matter of principle, attention to certain interests. Nevertheless, in Britain at least, there is one generally accepted distinction between interest groups and political parties; the former do not seek to win control of the Government. In addition, pressure groups have extensive non-political activities but usually within a restricted field; parties are more inclusive but are almost entirely political.

The fourth input function is *political communication*. Here, again, it must be emphasized that communication takes place throughout society and in every part of the political system, and is an output as well as an input function. Almond is particularly impressed by the extent to which in Britain there exist autonomous and differentiated media capable of neutral or objective communication. There are 'covert' communications in the bureaucracy, interest groups, and parties; 'overt' but Government controlled communications through public relations officers. But all these can, with certain reservations, be regulated by critical publicity. Latent interests are made explicit; a free flow of information regulates both the articulation and aggregation of interests and the actions of government. There are both general policy or 'good government' pressure groups and a large number of informed citizens free to a considerable extent of previous commitments. How valid this picture is we shall examine later.

Almond's three output functions are *rule-making, rule-application,* and *rule-adjudication.* This is not just another way of expressing the traditional distinction between the legislative, executive, and judicial functions. We shall see that rule-making, even in the form of general laws, is more and more the concern of the political executive, the Cabinet, while at a lower level the vast amount of delegated legislation is in the hands of Ministers and civil servants and sometimes of other government or quasi-government bodies. Rule-application is primarily performed through the administrative machine, though, again, other bodies may have rule-application functions delegated to them while the rules may be applied in ways which are influenced by the various interests likely to be affected. Even in the sphere of rule-adjudication it is not sufficient nowadays to look merely at the courts of law. There is a large number of administrative tribunals, and many adjudications are made by government departments and Ministers, while if a Parliamentary Commissioner or Ombudsman (proposed in October 1965) is appointed, he, too, will have something like adjudicatory functions at least of an informal kind. In our examination of the processes of government we shall look at these complicated and interlocked structures and the many output functions which they perform in greater detail.

With these introductory remarks we turn to our detailed examination of the British political system. The seven functions and various structures to which we have referred will appear again at many points, but we adopt a somewhat different set of headings for this section of our study.

2

Elections, Voters, and Candidates

Four criteria of a satisfactory working system have been suggested. Firstly, it should enable the legislature to embody the opinions of the majority and the minority on the great issues of public interest but not—in this view—the total drift of opinion with mathematical precision if there is to be an effective government. (We discuss this point further in relation to proposals for electoral reform). Secondly, constituencies should be small enough for candidates to be known and to cultivate personal relations with their constituents. Thirdly, there should be some means of checking the drift of opinion between elections, preferably through by-elections in the same constituencies. Fourthly, the voters should be as directly related as possible to the Government in power, which should be seen to be their choice. (This, again, is related to the electoral system and also to the number and nature of political parties). It is obvious that these 'criteria of a satisfactory system' have been derived from what are considered to be the basic features of the British system.

This system is, basically, simple. The winner in each single-member constituency need obtain only a 'plurality' of votes, not an absolute majority; we have what is popularly called the 'first past the post' system. Today there is universal suffrage based upon the principle of one man one vote at the age of 21, though some have argued for a reduction of this to 18; though plural voting disappeared only in 1948. A further principle, one vote one value, depends upon equality in numbers of qualified voters in each constituency. This, however, cannot be achieved in practice. The delimitation of constituencies, though fairly carried out by a neutral Boundary Commission, always lags behind population movements. Although the mean figure to achieve the nearest approach to equality would be about 55,000, in 1959 the smallest constituency had only 25,178 voters while the largest had 87,544. Another reason for such discrepancies is that irrespective of population, of the 630 constituencies, Scotland is guaranteed 71, Wales 35, and Northern Ireland 12. In addition, even in England alone, the Boundary Commission has to allow variations from the mean partly in order to avoid cutting across local government units, partly because with equal populations rural constituencies might be impossibly large geographically. To return to population movements, between 1955 and 1959, two hundred and thirty-six constituencies lost population, but of the ten largest five *grew* by more than twenty per cent and two by more than ten per cent. In general, by 1959 more than one-third of all British constituencies were either over or under-represented; of the former, forty-two were in Wales or Scotland while in England all except four of the one hundred and ten were in the latter category. Further populations movements had taken place by 1964; no general redistribution of constituencies was due for fifteen years after 1955.

What effect does this uneven size of constituencies have upon party fortunes? It has been suggested that in the last four General Elections neither of the two major parties gained added representation because of having a larger proportion of its supporters in sparsely-populated areas. It has, however, often been argued that there is a bias against Labour because the party piles up large majorities in safe seats. In 1955–59 it was estimated that Labour had to gain 1.4 per cent more total votes than the Conservative for the same number of parliamentary seats. This bias, however, disappeared 'mathematically' in 1964, though this may have been due to a larger number of abstentions in strong Labour seats. On the other hand it has been argued that Labour has not, in fact, really suffered from large majorities. In 1959 the Labour Party won thirty-five seats with majorities of over forty per cent as against the Conservatives with twenty-seven. But if majorities of over thirty per cent are considered the Labour Party won only fifty-six as compared with the Conservatives' seventy.

It is deduced from this that the real problem is that Labour strength is not as advantageously distributed as that of the Conservatives; Labour has fewer *effective* votes. Voters who may swing to the Conservatives are so spread that fewer of their votes are needed to turn the tide for that party; more Conservative candidates need a few extra votes to put them at the top of the poll. The two parties therefore have an unequal chance of maximizing an effective proportion of the total vote; the Labour vote is less 'effective' than the Conservative. To pursue this a little further on the basis of an analysis of the 1964 Election, it has been estimated that there are one hundred and twenty-four Labour-held seats where any normal swing could bring disaster to the Party; the keenest danger is in sixty-five 'volatile' seats which changed hands in 1964, 1959, and between.

We can only mention briefly the likely effect of Liberal votes on the fortunes of the two other parties. The Nuffield study of the 1964 Election estimated that although the Conservatives might have gained one additional seat had there been no Liberal candidate there, Labour could well have gained six additional seats in the same circumstances. Even on the most prudent estimate Labour would have gained three extra seats. In general, it seems clear that Labour suffered most from Liberal candidatures in 1964 and that the Conservatives managed to retain their marginal seats more easily where a Liberal stood. In view of frequent speculation to the contrary, especially by Conservative spokesmen, it is interesting to note that a leading Conservative ex-Minister, Sir Edward Boyle, in a review of the Nuffield study in 1965, professed himself 'convinced' by the arguments advanced therein with the conclusion quoted above. There were some signs in by-elections after October 1964, that 'radicals' were voting either Liberal or Labour according to which candidate appeared most likely to defeat the Conservative but, of course, there is no certainty that in another General Election more Liberals would vote Labour than Conservative if no Liberal candidate stood, or if in the previous election the Liberal came third in the poll.

Indeed, it must be emphasized that the kind of analysis briefly illustrated above is extremely complicated and subject to many reservations; we have merely tried to create some interest in this kind of calculation. What, however, can be said of the British electoral system in general? Firstly, a party seldom obtains fifty per cent of the total vote cast and none has done so since 1935. Secondly, the relationship of seats to total votes is not proportionate, but on the other hand, on only two occasions (1929—Conservatives; 1951—Labour) has a party obtained the larger percentage of the votes but fewer seats in the House of Commons. The Liberals, have, of course, been consistently under-represented on this basis; our system is hard on minor parties, although if socio-economic factors are strong enough they can succeed—witness the rise of the Labour Party, although this was helped by a split in the Liberal Party. Thirdly, the system exaggerates party majorities except on those occasions (1950, 1951, 1964) when the electorate is very evenly divided. If any meaning can be attached to the word 'fair' in this context, it may be argued that the system is fair at least to the extent that the party with the largest number of votes normally gets the largest number of seats. One of the main virtues of the British electoral system is that it normally helps to produce clear parliamentary majorities. One of its main weaknesses is that it often produces exaggerated majorities.

Those who interpret 'fair' as meaning a close mathematical relationship between seats and votes, however, will not wholly accept such arguments. It is important, therefore, particularly in view of the current (1965) interest in electoral reform, to look briefly at its possible consequences. One suggested change is the alternative vote; in a three-cornered fight, if no candidate obtained an absolute majority, the candidate at the bottom of the poll would be eliminated and his votes divided between the other two candidates in accordance with the voters' second preferences as indicated on the ballot paper. In order to estimate the possible effect of this system it is clearly necessary to make certain assumptions about how second preferences might be distributed. Looking at this from the point of view of most immediate practical importance, we may ask how Liberal second preferences might be given, for the Liberals came second in only fifty-four seats in 1964 (twenty-seven in 1959); in all other seats they would have been eliminated. Of course, with the new system, more first preferences might go to Liberal candidates and fewer might be at the bottom of the poll. As we saw, above, the Labour Party probably suffered more from Liberal candidates in 1964; but we also remarked that it cannot be assumed that in the absence of a Liberal candidate next time a majority of Liberal votes would be given to Labour candidates. Still less can we assume that a majority of Liberal voters would give their second preference to Labour. Indeed, there has already been an estimate that the alternative vote system might very well benefit both Liberals and Conservatives at Labour's expense. Certainly it could do no harm to the Liberals but how much good it might do them is difficult to estimate.

For what they are worth, we quote various opinions as to what might have been the result of the alternative vote in the past. One expert has suggested that it would have made no difference between 1918 and 1945; another has queried this for 1924 and 1929 (when we had an effective three-party system). More important is likely results since 1945. It is most likely that in 1950, 1951 and 1964 no one party would have had an overall majority in the House of Commons. One's reaction to this will depend on how important one feels it is that there should be such a majority rather than a minority or coalition Government. In general, we may say on the basis of Australian experience, that the system does not prevent a party with less than fifty per cent of the votes cast from obtaining a large parliamentary majority.

The consequences of proportional representation on the single transferable vote system are at once more difficult and more easy to assess. The basis of this system is multi-member constituencies (the larger the better from the point of view of 'proportionality') in which seats are filled by a 'quota' (obtained by dividing the total number of votes cast by the number of seats to be filled plus one and adding one to the result; without going into the technical details of this it may be simply stated that it is then impossible for more than the required number of candidates to obtain the quota). Voters would mark their ballot papers from 1 to X in order of preference for candidates. Any candidate obtaining more than the quota would be declared elected; his surplus votes would be distributed according to second preferences. If this fails to produce a sufficient number of winning candidates the one at the bottom of the poll is eliminated and his preferences distributed among the others. This process would continue until the required number of candidates received the quota and were elected. We shall not comment upon the system in relation to the voters' capacity properly to mark their ballot papers nor upon the process of counting the votes—very simple with the appropriate machine.

But assuming intelligent use of the single transferable vote, we must attempt to assess the possible results. If we assume for the moment that no more than three effective parties contest the election—and it is a fair assumption that the Liberals would contest pretty well every seat—all the experts are agreed that it is highly improbable that any one party would have gained an overall majority in any election in the twentieth century save those of 1918 and 1931. Even if this is queried for 1945, it is certain that in no subsequent election would such a majority have emerged. It is, of course, possible that as the system became better known, more candidates might appear, either of different parties or of rival sections within the same party; that votes would be spread more between different candidates since the 'wasted vote' argument would no longer apply; that, as a consequence, the House of Commons would be more divided than at first sight appears likely.

Strong majority governments, therefore, would be rare. Moreover, the electors would not have decided which party should form the Government nor what general policy it should follow. Governments would be formed by post-electoral bargaining between groups, thus substituting what has been called 'the politics of manœuvre' for 'the politics of policy'. There would, again, be minority government or coalition government. In the former case it may be asked whether a House in which, for example, a small number of Liberals held the balance between Labour and Conservatives would be more or less 'democratic'. In either case it must be asked whether we should have more or less effective government. We need not exaggerate the possible results of P.R. in order to raise pertinent questions. Nor need we argue that the electoral system *causes* certain results; for example, a multi-party system may persist whatever the electoral system though it

G

is less easy to argue that a two-party system might be maintained despite a change in the system. But, as we argued in Part I, any political system must be viewed as a whole and a change in any one part examined for its likely effect on other parts. If we confine our comments to Britain since 1918, we have seen that there would seldom, if ever, have been a one-party majority; there would have been at least three parties, none with an overall majority. Could the rest of the Constitution have remained unchanged? For example, would the convention that defeat on a vote of confidence leads either to the resignation of a Government or—more important—to a dissolution and a general election remain unchanged? Could Governments, liable to frequent defeats, be left with the right to plunge the country into such frequent elections? And would a general election produce a more stable situation? Yet if dissolution was denied, could frequent defeats be avoided in the House of Commons? And if they could not, what would happen to continuity of policy and administration? We shall see later that it is not the function of Parliament to govern the country, yet it might be impossible for governments to govern if they were subject to every chance combination of votes on each specific issue. These are some of the questions which must be seriously pondered before a new electoral system, which undoubtedly would produce in the House a mathematically more accurate reflection of electoral opinion, but which might lead to some of the consequences outlined above, is adopted.

We turn now from the electoral system to the voters themselves. In Part I we suggested that the 'rational-activist' interpretation of democratic politics is limited and misleading. There is considerable evidence in Britain of lack of political interest, and for many voting is the only form of political awareness shown. The nature of even this awareness needs further examination. It has been suggested that about one-sixth of the electorate is clearly interested in and informed about public affairs, while another one-sixth is 'completely clueless'. Between these two, the typical voter is neither particularly ignorant nor well-informed. On the other hand we should not exaggerate the extent to which political views can be manipulated through the mass media, nor assume that the approval of followers can be achieved by mere fiat of the leaders. Nor, as we shall see, does lack of detailed political information necessarily produce political instability; British voters are extraordinarily stable in terms of party preference and most of them appear to retain their party allegiance for life. News and propaganda, including election campaigns, are judged in the light of pre-existing stable preconceptions. Whatever the balance of argument about the intelligence, interest, and openness to rational argument of electors it must be emphasized that elections provide the only chance for what we called 'the peripheral public' to intervene directly in the political process—though it is possible that anticipated shifts of public opinion may influence political leaders between elections. At a general election the mass of the population does intervene significantly in government by making its choice between competing *élites*.

What, then, influences their choice? It has been said that class has a more significant effect on voting in Britain than, for example, in the U.S., Canada, and Australia. Middle-class voters comprise about 30.4 per cent of the total vote, working-class voters 64.6 per cent. But one-third of the working-class vote Conservative and make up one-half of the total Conservative vote, while there is a comparatively high percentage of Conservative votes in the lower middle class of white collar workers. These statements relate to class as objectively defined by sociologists. But subjectively, people who *call* themselves middle class are more likely to vote Conservative than those who *call* themselves working class, though the broad picture of voting is the same on either the objective or subjective basis. We return to this below. It has rightly been suggested that voting Conservative may be the *cause* rather than the *effect* of calling one's-self middle class. Nevertheless, the way in which a person *thinks* of himself and his place in the class structure has a stronger influence on the way in which he votes than the economic interests which are derived from his objective position. Other general influences include sex (which appears to outweigh even class as a voting factor); women in all classes and age-groups vote more conservatively than men; age, which appears to have a conservatizing effect; religion: for example,

Roman Catholics support Labour more than other religious groups, though this may be a class factor in view of the large number of Irish labourers; education: those with only an elementary education (to use pre-1944 terms) are more likely to be Labour; and, finally, the general influences surrounding the voter: it has been said that 'the political opinions of the individual voter's family, friends, and associates have a more powerful influence on how people vote than any other single factor'.

Let us look a little more closely at class voting in recent years. General Elections certainly do not appear to be automatically determined by class loyalties. But most of the middle class are still predominantly Conservative and most of the working class Labour; though the middle class remains much more solidly Conservative than the working class is Labour. In the top twelve per cent of society (as divided into occupational classes) the voters split ten to one in favour of the Conservatives, while Liberal support is roughly equal to that of Labour. In the working class, skilled and unskilled workers split about eleven to seven in favour of Labour. But it is obvious that since there are twice as many working class as middle class voters the Conservatives must always do better among the workers than Labour needs to do among the middle class if the Conservatives are to win. In 1964 it appears that the Conservative Party had managed to hold on to working class support and perhaps slightly increase its share, possibly due to a combination of traditional and deferential reasons and the appeal of prosperity. Labour, however, had made headway with the lower middle class and especially among the 'new owner-occupiers'. The cross-currents of party preferences are thus clearly important. One survey showed that of all voters expressing a party preference sixty-one per cent were either middle class Conservatives or working class Labour, while thirty per cent had party loyalties opposed to their objective occupational class; the other nine per cent were Liberal. Elections are not won by a steady swing of the pendulum; party loyalties are relatively stable.

If we turn again to subjective class, only forty-six per cent of those interviewed called themselves working class while forty per cent said that they belonged to the middle class. Eleven per cent gave answers which made it impossible readily to assign them to a class. Thirty-eight per cent of those interviewed assigned themselves to a category different from their objective class; thirty per cent of the skilled workers called themselves middle class as did twenty-one per cent of the semi- and unskilled workers, while twenty-six per cent of the lower middle class and ten per cent of the middle and upper middle classes called themselves working class. But, as we suggested earlier, the difference between a person's subjective and objective class has only a limited effect upon party preferences: those who called themselves working class divided fifty-nine per cent to twenty-nine per cent in favour of Labour (a five per cent difference from the 'objective' result) while support for Labour among those calling themselves upper middle class was only five per cent higher than the 'objective' figure. Those who refused to classify themselves were slightly more pro-Conservative than on the objective basis. Most significant, perhaps, is that individual assessment of social class had changed little since 1945 despite the strong class antagonisms which emerged during the period of Labour Government up to 1951 and the considerable speculation about changing class allegiances during the period of Conservative Government especially under Mr Macmillan.

This is borne out by an examination of the findings of the public opinion polls over the same period. The graph of party support has been comparatively static since 1945. There was no marked effect of the change of Government in 1951, no dramatic gain in Conservative support or loss of support for Labour in subsequent years. The Conservative lead in the polls in the Spring of 1955 was almost their first since 1951 and the party enjoyed two leads only after 1955—in the Autumns of 1958 and 1959; nor did the party enjoy a lead between 1962 and October 1964. If dramatic political crises such as credit squeezes, strikes, scandals, overseas alarms affect the polls we do not know; certainly their effects are short-lived though, of course, a short-lived effect during an election campaign may affect the result, hence Labour's sensitivity to such things as strikes during that period.

Nor is it easy to see a connection between party preferences and more gradual demographic changes. Affluence, an increase in the number of white collar jobs, movement to new estates, the growth of middle class identification, the emergence of the 'status voter'—all these have been suggested as a danger to Labour, as, more recently, has the outflow of population from Labour strongholds to marginal or Conservative constituencies. Yet so far the level of support for Labour has remained steady. The average Labour support was higher in the period from 1959 to 1964 than between 1945 and 1950. As we remarked earlier, stability of party support is far more evident than change, despite the fact that nearly half the electorate died and were replaced by new voters over a period of twenty years. Labour and Conservative polls have been within five per cent of each other for sixty per cent of the time and within ten per cent of each other for eighty-five per cent of the time. Indeed, Labour has averaged rather more than two per cent over the Conservatives over the whole period. Liberal support has remained almost as stable. In other words, the polls do not seem to have responded much to slow demographic changes nor, in the long term, to political crises. How then is it possible to predict changes in voting habits? It must always be remembered that the key question is 'how would you vote if there were an election tomorrow?' We can only ask with many others, is the result due to luck and a quick electoral calculation by the Prime Minister in calling an election; is which party in power a matter of chance?

Brief mention must be made of two special categories, the non-voters and the 'floating-voters'. The former are usually the most ill-informed of electors and are frequently found to have no opinion on current political issues; they are more likely to be found among women, the very young, the very old, and the poorer section of the community. As we have seen, however, non-voting may also be related to purely fortuitous circumstances such as absence from home on election day. There is also a clear relationship between a high voting turn-out and towns with a stable population i.e. with not a large proportion of newcomers from outside; this is probably due to a combination of a lack of feeling of community outside such areas and of failure to get on the register.

As to floating voters, much nonsense has been written about these and even experienced politicians, who ought to know better, have 'angled' for the floating vote on the assumption that it is more intelligent, better informed and more likely to be swayed by reasoned argument. In fact, there is nothing whatever peculiar about the floating voters; they are a representative cross-section of the electorate as a whole. It must be remembered that they are not the same group from election to election; some have died, moved, or registered for the first time. There are, of course, definite 'changers', though eighty per cent of the electorate do *not* change. The most significant changes, however, take place between elections not during the campaign. The 'changers' show no marked difference from the rest except that a voter in a higher social class is more likely to have changed at some time. Changing is *relatively* more frequent in the lower middle class. There is also some evidence of disintegration of party loyalty after the age of 65, due perhaps to lack of pressure from working and family ties. It has been shown that those whose voting intention was the same as that of the majority of the family and work group were likely to 'stick' on polling day while those who differed from the group were more likely to change or abstain. Abstention is an important factor, though not many commentators are prepared just how it affects a given party. In 1964, for example, there appeared to be more Labour abstainers but since a large proportion were in safe Labour constituencies they do not seem to have affected the overall result. Women are more likely to abstain than change.

Do the voters see elections in terms of issues? One interesting point is that despite stability in party voting the electorate shows a readiness to assimilate the values of both major parties and to bring them together. One poll in 1962 showed that forty-seven per cent of those interviewed thought that the political parties were 'all much of a muchness', though forty-five per cent thought that there were really important differences between them. In 1961 thirty-one per cent of those interviewed thought that the Opposition should support the Government (twenty-one per cent of Labour voters thought thus!) while only forty-one per cent thought that the Labour Party should do everything possible to turn the Government out. Of sixteen statements of characteristics presented sixty-three per cent of the interviewees attributed a particular characteristic to *both* parties. Clearly the electorate does not regard itself as being presented with a choice between two mutually exclusive parties nor as being faced with one set of policies presented under competing labels. There are differences on a number of short-term issues and, in principle, on a number of long-term emphases but there is a common outlook on other issues and principles.

But does the electorate even have a clear view on issues? When voters are presented with a list of the main policy proposals of the parties and are asked whether they agree or disagree complete agreement with one set and rejection of the other is extremely rare. There is sizeable overlapping of opinions although agreement tends to be greater among Conservatives on Conservative issues; Labour voters reveal a much wider set of political views. Attitudes, like party preferences, remain remarkably stable even during an election campaign. Extreme views appear to become modified. In 1959 support grew for Conservative attitudes but the reverse was probably true in 1964. What does happen is a hardening of political attitudes; there is *more* policy support for the elector's own party *after* the election results! They have won so we can confess that they were right?

As previously emphasized, people do not always look at a party in terms of a rational appraisal of the various social, economic and international issues raised by them. They do not even select the most important issues in an election. More influential is what is now called the *image* of the party—a mental set of impressions of 'what the party stands for', gathered from general ideas, propaganda, discussions and so on. For example, there has been, at least in the past (though a successful period of office for Labour following upon doubts concerning Sir Alec Douglas Home's leadership and about Mr Heath's as yet incomplete 'image' could change this) a general impression that the Conservatives 'stand for superior leadership', skill in foreign affairs and 'looking out for the nation'. Labour is seen as working-class (the 'cloth cap' image is, even now, not completely dead), 'for the under-privileged' and in favour of welfare benefits. Where an image is popular such as 'standing for modernization' both parties seek to establish it. This notion of image helps to account for the relative stability in party preference and the striking degree of persistence in attitudes. Images are extremely resistant to change; a party can (up to a point) trade on old issues, while abrupt changes are suspect. Labour supporters appear more likely to rely on a very few commonly held images than Conservatives. We cannot discuss here the question of the extent to which an image can be 'created' for instance by Public Relations Officers and ad-vertising experts.

One thing is certain about the British political system. Although not many voters, perhaps, would go so far as one who is alleged to have said that 'if my party put up a pig in my constituency I would vote for it', yet the party label is more important than any other factor, whether candidates' personality, policy, organization or anything else. Candidates, of course, are selected by the parties and for this reason some attention must be given to the selection processes. How are the men and, relatively, the few women chosen between whom voters must themselves choose?[1]

The selection of Conservative candidates is supervised by the Standing Advisory Committee on Candidates which is attached to the National Union, by the vice-chairman of the party organi-zation who is an officer of the party's top national management and by the various Central Office Area Agents. The first of these three, which includes the Chief Whip in the House of Commons, has 'to assess on the broadest grounds the suitability of men and women who are desirous of becoming approved candidates'. This is done by specifying procedures and criteria for constituency associations to apply, by maintaining a list of approved candidates, and by withholding or withdrawing approval from any locally adopted candidate. But the S.A.C.C. is a ratifying not an initiating body and has far less actual influence on candidate selection than the vice-chairman of the party organization himself. He suggests to the S.A.C.C. who should be included in the list of approved

---

[1] *Pathways to Parliament*, Austin Ranney, MacMillan, 1965.

candidates and also consults with the constituency associations' officers about persons to consider as candidates, as well as watching the associations' selection procedures.

Persons seeking inclusion on the approved list must set out on a form their basic personal data, their social position, nationality, religion, education; their experience both political and non-political, their political views, and the time they are prepared to devote to constituency and parliamentary work. They must give the names of 'three responsible referees', who provide confidential reports. The applicant is interviewed in London by the vice-chairman and two or three others. The questions are primarily concerned with personal qualities, social, educational and occupational background, and party service.

England and Wales are divided into twelve Areas by the Conservative Party. Each has an office under an area agent who oversees the financial, propaganda, electioneering and other activities of the constituency associations in the area and normally accompanies the chairman of a constituency association when the latter goes to London to consult the party's vice-chairman about candidate selection. At such meetings the local chairman may announce a number of qualifications suggested by his selection committee such as 'under fifty, male, not a Jew, with solid business background and strong connections in the constituency'. The vice-chairman usually insists on 'the best possible person available'; he will also produce a list of ten to twenty persons from the cross-indexed files of approved candidates and recommend them for consideration.

The party always has in mind several people whom it would like to see adopted; promising young men without electoral experience, able Central Office employees, former M.P.s and even Ministers. But such names are suggested with great circumspection and usually without special urging. All parties feel that their candidates should be as broadly representative as possible; women as well as men, Jews and Roman Catholics as well as Protestants, trade unionists as well as business-men. The Conservatives are particularly concerned about some of these categories. Yet since 1945 only two trade unionists have been adopted for Conservative-held seats, the number of women candidates fell from seven per cent (excluding women M.P.s) in 1951 to four per cent in 1964. On the other hand, the number of candidates with a public school background (again excluding M.P.s) rose to fifty-six per cent in 1964.

Any individual party member may submit his name or have it submitted to a constituency association. These names are first sifted by a scrutiny or selection committee which draws up a first short list. This screening committee usually includes the associations' principal officers, usually about nine in number; sometimes other representatives are added, bringing the number up to eighteen or twenty. Perhaps fifteen or twenty applicants will then be invited to an interview. After this, a short list is submitted to the executive council, which usually, though not always, accepts it. A date is then fixed for the selection conference, a special meeting of the constituency association's executive council consisting of thirty to one hundred members.

There appears to be little pre-conference lobbying on behalf of candidates so that only members of the selection committee will have first-hand knowledge of the contenders. The chairman reads out the details of each one's background—'to let the members know what sort of stable the chap comes from', as one chairman put it! Each contender delivers a ten to fifteen minutes' speech and answers questions for about the same time. The executive council makes its choice on the basis of this performance (and possibly the appearance of the candidate's wife!) and recommends it to a general meeting of the entire association. Only occasionally does the latter body reject the recommendation.

One point of general interest is the importance of local connections. It seems that only the most outstanding local candidates are selected. Over two-thirds of Conservative candidates from 1951 to 1964 were people who had no discernible personal connections in their constituencies. Only twenty-two per cent of those in seats of 'high-winnability' had any local connections; a large proportion fought hopeless constituencies, doubtless because attractive outsiders could not be persuaded to stand. Interestingly, the strongholds of 'local connection' are not the rural but the metropolitan constituencies.

To sum up, the selection committee undoubtedly has the greatest influence over the choice of candidates. Most of these committees are dominated by a few members who take their lead from the chairman, who has himself been elected as 'the best person' to run the constituency's affairs. He usually ensures that the selection committee includes a majority of 'reasonable and co-operative' colleagues. He also acts as the official channel of communication both with candidates and with Central Office. His opinions weigh heavily with everyone. The constituency agent and the Central Office also sometimes exercise considerable influence since they are the confidants of the Chairman. But the latter 'is the nerve centre of all the association's affairs and as such he usually plays a critical role in the selection of candidates'.

Labour candidates are also selected by local party organizations subject to certain controls from the centre. The constituency Labour Parties (C.L.P.s) adopt somewhat different methods from their Conservative counterparts. An individual cannot formally bring his own name forward; he must be nominated by a body directly affiliated to the C.L.P., e.g. a ward committee, trade union or local socialist society. He may be sponsored by a trade union or by the Co-operative Party and the sponsoring body will contribute to election expenses, and the C.L.P.'s general funds. Finally, the Labour national agencies have greater formal power than the Conservatives.

The National Executive Committee, subject to the Party Conference, is the party's Administrative Authority. Its functions include the selection of parliamentary candidates. Decisions are usually taken on recommendations from the Organization Sub-Committee which is, in effect, the principal national agency dealing with candidates. It includes the leader, deputy-leader, party treasurer, the chairman and vice-chairman of the N.E.C. and ten to twelve other members. The national agent serves as the secretary's chief deputy for organizational matters and is the sub-committee's secretary.

The Labour Party has also twelve regions, each managed by a regional organizer who is an employee of the N.E.C. He exercises the latter's supervisory powers which include authorizing the

C.L.P. to select a candidate, prescribing selection procedures, setting the qualifications for candidature, endorsing selected candidates and laying down special procedure for by-elections. All candidates must be party members and, if eligible, members of a recognized trade union. They must not be members of certain proscribed organizations and must accept the party's constitution, programme, principles and policy, and the Parliamentary Party's standing orders.

Transport House, the equivalent of the Conservative Central Office, assembles the names and other particulars of parliamentary candidates. Two separate lists are maintained. List A includes persons nominated by trade unions and approved by the N.E.C. The national unions assemble their own lists and submit them to the national agent. The organization sub-committee interviews the nominees and makes recommendations to the N.E.C. This list is available to any C.L.P. but the sponsoring union must approve the adoption of anyone from its list. List B consists of candidates not sponsored but whom the N.E.C. considers suitable. Such candidates will at most contribute their own personal election expenses and not more than £50 p.a. to the C.L.P.'s general fund. To get on List B it is necessary to be nominated by the C.L.P. or by some other organization nationally affiliated to the party. Particulars required include some items not included in the Conservative form e.g. length of party service, languages and similar qualifications, publications and experience abroad, but *not* such items as marital status, birthplace, rank etc. and nationality. Two referees must be cited. The applicant will then be interviewed by members of a panel established by the organization's sub-committee for fifteen to thirty minutes. Personal qualities are often of importance but political opinions may also be questioned, especially if the candidate is known to have opposed the party leader's views on public policy. The interviewers recommend the inclusion or otherwise of the name on List B and the sub-committee periodically recommends lists of such names to the N.E.C.

Like the Conservative Central Office, Transport House has a number of individuals they would like to see placed in 'winnable' seats—defeated M.P.s and young men regarded as 'good

front-bench material'. It is also concerned to see that the C.L.P.s
generally adopt the right kind of candidates. A 'truly representative' national list is desired, dons as well as day labourers, Jews as
well as Gentiles, Catholics as well as Protestants. In some respects
this is easier to achieve for the Labour Party but in many C.L.P.s
there is still a feeling for 'the cloth cap' and many years of service
in 'the Movement'.

Selection of candidates is often a battleground between right
and left for 'the policy preferences and fractional loyalties of
the candidates selected determine the kinds of Labour M.P.s
elected and they in turn select the parliamentary party's leaders'.
It has been suggested that right-wing groups are more successful
in achieving their end than left-wing. The leadership has also
used its control of the party machinery to encourage C.L.P.s
to adopt right-wing candidates. Yet Transport House uses its
power of direct nomination to short lists very infrequently and
circumspectly and no candidate can be directly imposed on the
local constituency party. The local parties are as jealous as Conservative associations of their rights and do not wish to have
names 'pushed off on them'. Certain regional organizers, rather
than the N.E.C. or the organization department, have played key
roles in the few cases where the party leader had a firm preference. In the general elections from 1950 to 1959 eighteen Labour
M.P.s of ministerial rank were defeated; eleven were subsequently
adopted in other constituencies and ten returned to the House.
Seven did not stand again. But no evidence exists of the extent
to which success was due to central influence.

All applicants for selection must be formally nominated by one
or more affiliated organization or ward committee. Nominating
bodies are therefore agencies for preliminary screening and in
winnable seats it is common for local aspirants and hopeful contenders to sound out people they know in ward committees or
trade union branches about possibilities of being nominated. In
less popular seats the local executive may often ask candidates on
List B if they would like to be nominated and then request nominating bodies to put such names forward. The constituency executive draws up a short list from, usually, a smaller number of names

than that facing Conservative selection committees; but they may have a wider range of choice between views and attitudes. Again, it appears that right-wing executives, working with right-wing organizers, have been effective in keeping down the number of left-wing candidates. The short list must be submitted to Transport House; this is usually a matter of routine, but occasionally names have been struck out. The local General Management Committee then approves the list, very occasionally altering it, and fixes the date of the selection conference.

At this conference aspirants speak for ten to fifteen minutes and answer questions. The delegates then proceed to ballot until one contender receives an absolute majority of the votes cast. Attendance at selection conferences varies widely according to the desirability of the seat. There may be as few as fifteen or twenty or as many as two hundred or more delegates. It is not unusual for campaigns to be conducted on behalf of aspirants in winnable seats. But merits are not discussed at the conference itself. No delegate may be mandated by his organization to vote for a particular candidate but the rule is apparently not enforced— or is unenforceable. When the N.E.C. has endorsed the candidate selected by the G.M.C. he becomes the official prospective Labour candidate; there is no formal adoption by a general meeting of the whole constituency association.

Labour activists feel strongly associated in a movement and for this reason place a higher value on length of party service than the Conservatives. There is a tendency to feel that it is 'better to lose with a true believer than win with an agnostic'. Again, contenders are expected to 'display devotion to the articles of the true faith'. Yet, as with the Conservatives, most critical decisions are made by a few activists holding key positions. The nominal memberships of the C.L.P.s, like those of the Conservative associations, are usually only five to ten per cent of the party's vote in the constituencies. Individual memberships range from two hundred to six thousand, the average being about twelve hundred. The General Management Committee of a C.L.P. comprises perhaps ten to fifteen per cent of the members of the C.L.P. Nor does more than a small minority of delegates appear to vet the applicants before voting. The affiliated organizations and ward committees, the trade unions and other groups which can mobilize voting majorities at the G.M.C. and, above all, the executive committees who draw up the short lists, really select candidates. In the greatest number of cases Transport House has not intervened.

What kinds of M.P.s result from this selection process? We emphasize M.P.s because more than two-thirds of the constituencies are safe seats; the selection of a candidate in them is virtually the selection of an M.P. For a detailed description of those elected in 1964 *The British General Election of 1964*, by D. E. Butler and Anthony King, should be consulted. Here we select only a few general points. If the occupational categories are divided between (1) professions (2) business (c) miscellaneous and (d) workers, the percentage in each category elected for each of the three main parties was as follows:—

	Conservative	Labour	Liberal
1	48%	41%	50%
2	26%	11%	30%
3	25%	16%	17%
4	1%	32%	3%

This pattern is very similar to that of previous elections. As compared with 1959 the Conservatives doubled their trade union representation from one to two. Labour manual workers increased in number from ninety to one hundred and three but in percentage fell from thirty-five to thirty-two. The professional element in Labour rose from thirty-eight to forty-one per cent, while the business element in the Conservative Party fell from thirty per cent to twenty-six per cent. Trade union sponsored candidates rose from one hundred and twenty-nine to one hundred and thirty-eight, but such candidates included a number of able 'non-manuals' some of which achieved office after the election.

The educational pattern was also almost unchanged as compared with previous years, with a slight decline in Etonians among the Conservatives and a slight increase in the number of graduates in

the Labour Party. Labour candidates claimed more local government experience. As Butler and King conclude, 'the new men
coming in to replace the old are surprisingly like them in background. The professional element seems to be increasing in both
parties and the new Labour M.P.s have slightly better schooling.
But the changes within each party are small. The contrast in background between the two sides of the House remains. . . . Education and occupation do not by themselves determine a man's
behaviour but they certainly influence it. Even those who saw
little to choose between the party policies might see a distinction
between the partisans'.

Political parties, of course, have other roles to play in the electoral
process besides the selection of candidates. For example, they draw
up policies and programmes and submit them to the electorate;
they select, by one means or another, the leaders between whom
the electorate will choose and thus, to a great extent, decide the
political personnel of government. In addition, they are constantly
engaged in the processes of communication and propaganda, as
well as keeping a watch, through their M.P.s, the constituency
parties, and the activists, on what leaders and governments are
doing. Since in many of these roles, and especially as regards the
contacts between electors and governments *in between* elections,
there are many other channels and organizations besides political
parties, we shall next turn our attention to the inter-election period
in general and return later specifically to political parties.

3

Pressure Groups, Advisory Committees, Consultation

Rousseau declared that the English people thought they were
free but in fact were free only every few years to choose their
masters. Since Rousseau was opposed to any groups or organizations between the individual and the State it is not surprising that
he ignored all the means of democratic influence and pressure

which operated between elections. Today such means may be as important as elections. Before examining them, however, it is useful to look briefly at the notion of the 'mandate'. 'Why don't they keep their promises?' 'What right do they think they have to do that?' These oft-heard popular queries are in fact related to the general notion of the mandate.

The development of the idea of the mandate was due to the extension of the suffrage and the practice of putting programmes before the electorate. It includes two ideas: firstly, the acceptance of the programme by the electorate implies a mandate to implement it (2) failure to seek a mandate is an argument against doing certain things. Conservatives have been particularly concerned with the second of these, though in a limited way. As long ago as 1886 Lord Hartington (a Liberal Unionist) asserted that 'although no principle of the mandate may exist there are certain limits which Parliament is morally bound to observe. The House of Commons has no right to initiate legislation, especially immediately after its first meeting, of which the constituencies were not informed and of which they might have been informed'. He was, of course, concerned with Gladstone's Home Rule Bill for Ireland. The Liberals, and later the Labour Party, used the positive argument of the mandate to justify legislation but did not admit that a mandate was always necessary. In 1907 Sir Henry Campbell-Bannerman argued against the Conservatives, on the Liberal Education Bill, that 'the Constitution knows nothing of the doctrine of the special mandate, nothing whatever'. Yet in 1923 Mr Baldwin declared that he wanted 'a mandate' for Protection. The general idea may be summed up by saying that a party will not, as a Government, submit measures to Parliament without announcing beforehand that it proposes to carry them if it can; conversely, if it has announced such measures it has a mandate for them. Issues at election time are normally raised by the Government, though the Opposition may force issues to the forefront (as Labour did with the balance of payments problem in 1964) and, it is argued, ought to state their views clearly on subjects which have been before Parliament and left undecided. Outside bodies may also raise issues which have become important. The rank and file (in Party

Conferences, for example) may insist on the inclusion of certain issues.

It has been argued that some issues ought clearly to be submitted to the electorate, especially those affecting the liberty of the subject or the structure of politics. But the extensions of the franchise in 1918 and 1928 were not so submitted, nor was the Parliament Act of 1949. It is doubtful whether the Conservatives would have asked for a mandate to enter the Common Market in 1962–63 though this clearly had far-reaching constitutional as well as economic consequences. A party may ask for a 'doctor's mandate' i.e. 'let us prescribe the cure for the disease of the body politic' as in 1931. But the need for urgency in a declaration of war, or for secrecy in certain financial measures, may make the seeking of a mandate impossible. It is also argued that the people as a whole can decide only on broad issues, not details. Alternatively, as Australian experience suggests they will respond to questions of detail on the advice of the party which they support. Yet in 1950 Lord Simon criticized the doctrine that a Government had absolute and unquestioned authority in all circumstances to carry out legislation in a listed programme however casually it appeared in a party manifesto—'items shoved into an election manifesto' as Mr Churchill put it. There have, of course, been many vital changes without a mandate: the abandonment of the Gold Standard in 1931 (by a 'National Government' formed precisely to prevent such action!); devaluation at various times; the Hoare-Laval Agreement on Abyssinia in 1935, though it was ultimately rejected. Could Mr Wilson have asked for a mandate for some precise policy to deal with the complicated Rhodesia problem in 1965?

There are also persistent problems of interpretation of a mandate. Elections are conducted so as to make the mandate confused and debatable. They are not confined to one issue (an argument against holding a general election to decide a specific issue). Issues may be formed very broadly and personalities, or party loyalty, rather than policies may predominate. Attempts may be made to concentrate on the *past* record of a Government. Further, doubt is cast on the continuing validity of a mandate when some of the items in it are left to a period shortly before the next election is due; both circumstances and public opinion change. Expediency is a frequent factor in a decision whether to include a particular item in a programme (as Mr Baldwin refused to include rearmament in 1935) or whether to accept or reject a claim that something was included (even if only by implication) in a mandate. Parties in power, sometimes with scant grounds, claim that they have a popular mandate for proposed legislation. Parties in opposition profess themselves shocked at the absence of a specific mandate. Both sides will find 'good reason' not to believe public opinion polls on the matter if it suits them! On the other hand, the people's influence cannot make itself felt unless issues are submitted. Nor if a Prime Minister decides upon an election purely to suit party purposes. In general, it has been argued that there is 'little value in the idea that the Government is entitled to do nothing for which it has not got specific approval—the test being whether the Opposition recognizes such approval. The Government will make the maximum claim and the Opposition seek to reduce it to a mimimum. What the Government's mandate finally becomes is what the Government and the Opposition between them succeed in convincing the public it is'. Realistically, what the public believe the mandate to be is unlikely to be tested until the next election, when the issues, as usual, will by no means be crystal clear, and when, indeed, arguments over earlier 'mandates' may well have been forgotten. Another writer has said that 'it is politically wise and constitutionally sound not to over-emphasize lawyers' arguments about mandates'. As Sir Austen Chamberlain remarked ' "unconstitutional" is a term applied to the fellow who does something you don't like'.

The argument may be further complicated as in 1950 over the Iron and Steel Bill. The Labour Party certainly 'asked for a mandate' for this in general terms and, technically at least, this was confirmed by its winning a slender majority of seats in 1950. As The Times said, 'although the doctrine of the mandate is highly dubious, the Government's claim may be justifiable in a narrowly legalistic sense'. But the article went on to say that the power to impose decisions must be used 'with discretion' (an argument discussed further below) although in this case the Act was already on the Statute Book. *The Guardian* introduced a further refinement by calculating *votes* not seats as a test of the mandate and asked for another election. But this was clearly to bolster up a moral argument; the Constitution knows nothing of votes, only seats in the House of Commons. It may, of course, be deemed *politically* wise not to press a controversial measure when the country is evenly divided. Some politicians argued it out in similar terms. Lord Salisbury emphasized the matter of votes—assuming that it was correct to add Conservative and Liberal votes together to constitute an 'anti-Labour' majority. On this argument, as we have seen, a Government seldom has fifty per cent of the votes cast and thus would rarely have a mandate to govern. Lord Samuel said that to continue with steel nationalization would 'infringe' the spirit of our Constitution (again discussed below). Lord Jowett retorted that the Conservatives would have carried out their mandate to repeal the Act if they had a majority in the Commons 'without nice calculations about proportional representation'.

Reference above to 'discretion' and 'The spirit of our Constitution' reminds us that there have been looser interpretations of the mandate than that described in detail above. No Government, it has been said, should introduce fundamental changes without a substantial majority. But what is the meaning of 'fundamental' and 'substantial'. Or that, as with *The Times*, a Government should use its majority with 'wisdom and discretion'. An obvious retort is that we tend to think that a Government acts with wisdom and discretion when we approve its policy. In fact, so long as it is able to maintain its majority in the Commons there is no constitutional test of the validity of a Government's acts except the judgment of the voters at the next general election. In view of arguments in 1965 it should, perhaps, be added that 'keeping its majority' should refer to the possibility of *deliberate* abstention or voting against it by the Government's supporters and *not* to a chance defeat resulting from sickness or delay in travelling, or to successful 'ambushes' manipulated by the Opposition. Finally, it has been suggested that the Government must not 'outrage the feelings of the minority'. This, of course, is not a constitutional argument at all. It simply indicates that perhaps at some point a minority will not submit to the power of the majority. There is no objective test of 'outrageous' legislation. The Government cannot refrain from carrying out its programme because the Opposition claims that 'mutual confidence' is being destroyed. This would mean that one party would be entitled to permanent tenure of office—or that the other could exist only on sufferance.

The doctine of the mandate, then, is of little value in any attempt to estimate either what governments *can* or *should* do. Orders may be orders but will they always be carried out? Between elections, individuals and groups are, as Richard Rose puts it, able 'to vote with their feet'. Governments and Parliaments are not always, if ever, faced with problems which they can solve by their own actions. They need active co-operation from industrialists, trade unionists, professional organizations, social administrators, consumers, people in need like pensioners, and many other segments of society (including, in some cases, local authorities). Some of these groups are unorganized, some only involved intermittently in the political process. But there is a vast array of organized interest groups which provide continuous information about their sectional interests to the Government and which may help or hinder the latter in securing compliance with its public policies. Almost half the electorate belongs to at least one pressure group which from time to time speaks for its members on issues of common concern to them (apart from 'political groups' to which we refer later). The trade unions, for example, are the chief means through which millions of manual workers and their wives, mostly people of limited education and leisure, can hope to influence the Government. 'They are an effective reminder that middle class intellectuals cannot speak for everyone'. It is true, of course, that groups do not always express the views of their total membership any more than political parties do; officers or small cliques of leaders may dominate decisions within the pressure groups. Nevertheless, in many fields, public policy is made by a process of bargaining between leaders of semi-autonomous groups and between them and the Government; these groups may not serve to equalize influence over the decision-making process but they prevent dictation.

Pressure groups have to operate within limits imposed by the political culture and the political system. Rose has suggested six possible relationships between pressure group activity and the political culture in Britain. Groups may be in complete harmony with the political culture e.g. the R.S.P.C.A. (Is it part of the political culture that it is a *Royal* society for animals but only a *National* society for children?) Or there may be a gradual increase in acceptance of norms which support certain demands like the demand for colonial independence or for the abolition of capital punishment. Or groups may have to bargain in situations of fluctuating support for their demands as at different times there are different attitudes to employer or trade union groups who may have to modify their tactics accordingly. Or groups may carry on their activities in the face of general cultural indifference e.g. those concerned with non-smoking. Groups may carry on in the face of long-term cultural change as does the Lord's Day Observance Society. Or, finally, there may be conflict between predominant cultural values and pressure groups e.g. the pacifists or the unilateral nuclear disarmers.

Whatever the relationship may be the political culture limits and guides what the groups will demand of the Government and provides commonly accepted standards by which the demands of groups and the methods they use to promote them can be judged. It is important that in democratic societies pressure groups find it necessary to argue that their demands are in the 'public interest' as well as to their own sectional advantage. 'The steel industry serves *you* well!' If profits are made it is in *your* interest that this should be so. The doctors are concerned with the welfare of the patient, not with their own conditions of work and level of re-muneration—except, of course, that the latter can affect the former. Teachers are a professional body concerned with the interests of education; if they demand higher salaries this is in the community's interest. (Political parties, of course, are also concerned to protect the 'national interest'. 'Don't let the Socialists ruin it!') It is not suggested that there is anything wrong with this double approach; indeed, having to put on a show of 'public interest' may help to ensure that the public interest is, in fact, not overlooked. Moreover the results of pressure group and party activity and the extent to which their further demands ought to be met may ultimately be judged by the extent to which the claim 'in the public interest' turns out to have been justified.

As we have said, groups must also adjust their activities to the political system. They can exert influence only within the well-established network of political institutions and must use acceptable techniques and practices. In the U.S., for example, Congress and its committees may be as powerful as executive and administrative organs. In Britain groups must bargain with ministers and civil servants, often through established advisory and consultative organs. If the Cabinet makes a decision M.P.s will normally vote with their party and not in accordance with interest group pressures. It is not always easy for pressure groups to transfer their influence from one party to another since each party's pattern of policy restricts the scope of group activities and influence. Business interests would clearly not pressure the Labour Party in favour of anti-nationalization policies, nor trade unions the Conservative Party for a reversal of legal decisions unfavourable to their position. On the other hand, both groups must maintain some connections with any Government; trade unions consult with Conservative Ministers and business-men do not ignore Labour's National Plan or such bodies as the National Economic Development Council because there is a change of government. But these are contacts with governments. Contacts with individual M.P.s are much less important. Finally, contacts with the 'peripheral public'—grass-roots campaigns—are probably even less important; they may, in fact, be a sign of weakness. Governments need information from and co-operation with interest groups but they can often hold the balance between them. Restraints operate both ways in any political system.

Before looking more closely at interest groups in Britain, we briefly develop this last point a little further by asking what prevents such groups from getting their own way. Five limitations may be suggested. Firstly, there is a good deal of overlapping of membership between groups, and individuals may, in fact, be divided in their allegiance and therefore less than whole-hearted in their support for any particular group. Secondly, there are what have been called 'countervailing influences'; for almost every group pursuing one particular interest there is likely to be another with opposed views, though they are, of course, not always of equal strength. Consumers' groups are usually weaker than producers' groups. Thirdly, even if no such opposing groups exist there are many 'potential groups' whose efforts may be called out if another group appears to be threatening certain values or interests. Such potential groups are frequently what are called in the U.S. 'good government' or 'civic' groups. Fourthly, as we have emphasized already, there is a certain 'ethos' in society which may ensure that certain demands and practices will or will not be followed. Finally, in so far as there is a 'public interest' it may be sustained by political parties (who must 'aggregate' the various interests and cannot afford to appear as 'interest dominated'), by the civil service, and by the Government, as well as by 'disinterested' publicists and journals. These five factors do not, of course, always ensure that pressure groups will be 'kept in their proper place' but they are an extremely powerful counterpoise to the influence of such groups. How powerful, especially in the last case, will depend on such factors as the extent to which the decision-making process takes place 'in a gold-fish bowl' i.e. is open to public appraisal, and how far civil servants are prepared to take a positive attitude towards interest groups and not merely to seek the best possible compromise between them. Some recent studies in the field of economic planning have suggested that in these two respects the 'public interest' is not as surely safeguarded as in some other countries.

So far we have used the terms 'pressure group' and 'interest group' without distinguishing between them. It has been suggested that the former may be misleading because groups are not always in a position to apply a sanction in order to achieve their ends, nor are they always in continuous opposition either to other groups or to the Government. The latter may give the impression of something 'sinister' and, moreover, it is too narrow since many groups seek to foster a cause rather than promote an interest. There are also 'attitude' groups which are less formal and continuous and also less well-integrated with the decision-making process. A distinction has been made between Protective (sectional) Groups and Promotional (national) Groups but, again, the classification is not always clear, although the former indicates that groups may be as concerned to *prevent* something as to get something done. Professor S. E. Finer[1] prefers the American term 'lobby' for all three groups. He defines 'the lobby' as 'the sum of organizations in so far as they are occupied at any point of time in trying to influence the policy of public bodies in their own chosen direction; though (unlike political parties) never themselves prepared to undertake the direct government of the country'. We need not pursue the argument over words further except to note that 'lobby' generally refers to the activities of pressure groups in the American Congress where its members are open to such influences; in Britain such groups are more likely to frequent the Whitehall corridors of power than the Westminster lobbies.

From a practical point of view we are concerned with organized groups which seek to influence political officers without seeking formal control of government and which have limited objectives. Individuals in groups either seek economic favours or advocate causes which are beyond them as individuals. Informal lobbying becomes formal pressure group activity with agents, and organization and public relations activities, though many interests can exert pressure without such formal organization. They may use various techniques, including the provision of 'information', recruiting campaigns, publishing, giving financial support to political parties, (openly or otherwise), and other methods. As we have seen, they may be as much or more concerned with negative policies, with preventing rather than promoting governmental activity. As with other organizations there is a distinction between members, active members, and leaders, and varying degrees of oligarchical control, though they are neither unrepresentative nor monopolistic. Within them there is a certain degree of bureaucratic control and

[1] *Anonymous Empire*, Pall Mall, 1958.

influence especially since in Britain they may have contacts with the Civil Service and these are often conducted through 'opposite numbers' i.e. pressure group counterparts of civil servants in the relevant departments.

In the last forty years or so there has been a tremendous increase in the involvement of individuals in groups of this kind. Existing organizations have expanded to include a vastly increased number of members; there has come into existence an increasing number of specialized organizations; their scope and influence have been enhanced by many amalgamations and federations. All this is due to the fact that social and economic life has become more complex, with increased social division of labour, specialization, and the growth of new professions; that better communications have made national organizations more possible; and that the scope of public reponsibilities and control has continued to increase. Today, at the very least, we may discern business groups, labour groups, the co-operative movement, professional groups (including students!), civic groups, specialized sections of the population such as old age pensioners, the churches and evangelical groups, educational, recreative, and cultural groups. We examine briefly how these groups may influence government legislation, administration, and general policy.

We have already seen that the mandate theory does not go far to explain the content of government policies. Parties and governments do not make their policies in a vacuum. The various lobbies may exercise considerable influence provided their demands fit into the general ideology of the party or government concerned. At a later stage when a Bill is to be framed and even more after its publication there will be consultation either through informal contacts or existing consultative and advisory committees with the interests likely to be affected. Sir Ivor Jennings has said that such consultation is now virtually a convention of the Constitution. We may note here a possible danger: such consultation frequently means that Parliament is presented with a *fait accompli* (over which M.P.s may have had little or no influence in the absence of those specialized committees which we discuss later); Ministers urge M.P.s not to press amendments because these might upset agreements already reached with the interests concerned. Such interests are rarely consulted through M.P.s; trade union M.P.s are frequently by-passed in favour of contact with the T.U.C. or the trade unions concerned, even with a Labour Government.

These contacts between interests and departments will continue during the stages of the Bill. But they may also be extended to Parliament during the committee and report stages. Groups may, as we have seen, be affiliated to a party, or be more indirectly connected with it by the provision of funds; groups may have sponsored candidates, sometimes of more than one party, like the National Union of Teachers; they may have looked for representation among M.P.s *after* election—their officials may have become M.P.s or M.P.s may have become Presidents etc. as with the Association of Municipal Corporations; finally, the groups may simply make approaches to M.P.s likely to listen. They will then use the various 'ventilating procedures'—petitions, questions, motions etc.; they may be in constant attendance providing briefs for M.P.s and seeking to influence the various clauses of the Bill in Standing Committee. They may eventually attempt to appeal to the electorate, but, as we have seen, this 'grass-roots lobbying' is often a confession of defeat. Once issue is joined in public, M.P.s are extremely unlikely to vote against the party line. However, there is yet another stage: groups also watch carefully the administration of Statutes and the regulations made under them (about which, indeed, groups may be consulted, sometimes on statutory authority, sometimes informally) as well as proposed amendments (which, again, they often help to elaborate in consultation with the Civil Service).

All these activities within the political system and crossing the boundary between that system and others in society are clearly with us to stay. They are as important as the relations between governed and governors which are institutionalized in elections. There are, of course, as we have observed, dangers. Sectionalism may become a threat to consensus. Rich organizations may be more influential though no more worthy than poor ones. Strongly mobilized interests are more powerful than those more weakly mobilized and this may be an advantage for sectional rather than 'general public' interests. The leadership of groups may be un-representative; how far, for example, does the British Medical Association really represent the doctors as a whole? Finally, it has even been suggested that there is always the possibility of corruption, blackmail, or sabotage, operating in a sort of 'twilight zone' which it is very difficult for outside observers to penetrate. (Certain investigations, like those of the Committee on Inter-mediaries in 1948 have, however, not unearthed such behaviour). Whether the safeguards against these dangers referred to earlier are adequate is a matter of opinion. We return to this point in our examination of the role of Parliament.

Meanwhile, we conclude this section with a further analysis of the more formal opportunities given to interests and groups through consultative and advisory committees, through membership of boards, committees and other bodies, through the provision of information and 'expertise', especially by giving evidence to Royal Commissions and other committees of inquiry, and through various kinds of involvement in other parts of the decision-making machinery. First we examine some of the most important parts of this machinery.[1]

For example, sixteen Royal Commissions have reported in the last twenty years. They are a traditional means of inquiry into matters of great social importance as in the nineteenth century but now appear to be confined largely to areas in which the parties have not taken up clear positions as on divorce, gambling, capital punishment, and 'moral issues' in general; they are often given limited terms of reference. Some matters entrusted to them have been relatively trivial like rewards to inventors, the pay structure of the Civil Service; in these cases either the demands of powerful interests were in conflict with departmental view or else govern-ment departments were interested parties. The Royal Commission on the Remuneration of Doctors and Dentists followed on dead-lock in negotiations between the Government and the B.M.A. Only the Royal Commission on Population was empowered to conduct a free-ranging investigation aimed to provide essential

[1] *Commissions, Committees, and Competence*, Alan Beattie in *New Society*, 29 July 1965.

factual information. Legislative or administrative action may follow a Commission's report as with doctors' pay, mental health, London Government. But its influence may spread in more subtle ways as happened with the Royal Commission on Capital Punishment and especially the announcement of its Chairman that he had been converted to abolition during the course of hearing evidence. Sometimes, however, the work done is wasted. For example the Willink Commission on the Police was given narrow terms of reference, conducted no real research and heard little real evidence. The most recent Royal Commission on Trade Unions and Employers' Associations seems designed to delay the need for a government decision, though the Conservative Party in 1965 seemed to be prepared to prejudge the issue by making proposals to the Party Conference to 'regulate' the activities of trade unions.

Departmental Committees are nowadays more significant than Royal Commissions. Looking first at Advisory Committees, these are normally on a standing basis and are either consultative or expert or, like the Central Housing Advisory Committee, a combination of the two. Consultative committees provide a regular means whereby departments can get to know the reactions of interest groups to particular legislative or administrative acts e.g. those affecting agricultural or industrial policy. Members are usually appointed through nominations by the relevant interest groups and their advice is almost always private and oral. This puts them almost in the category of 'temporary civil servants' called in to advise the Government; Lord Hinton's report on transport in 1965 was in this category and could only be discussed on the basis of a Government White Paper which could not be compared with the advice given. Expert committees operate, for example, in the fields of technology and science; the communication process is usually one-way, from expert to department; advice is written and not usually published. There are over five hundred Advisory Committees, and they cover every department except the Foreign Office, the Stationery Office, Defence, Inland Revenue, and Customs.

Committees of Inquiry, often misleadingly called Advisory

Councils, may be either permanent or *ad hoc*. The former usually operate in the field of the social services and are often statutory. They may include experts, individuals in the relevant vocations, and interested laymen. They are rarely dominated by interest groups, as are the Consultative Committees, though the members may be nominated by such groups as well as being appointed because of service as individuals, and often through informal contacts. It would be interesting to investigate how members are chosen, how frequently the same names appear and *what* sources of information and recommendation are open to Ministers and their civil servants through whom advice is so often channelled. Is there an 'Establishment' of 'advisers' and 'consultants'? The Central Advisory Councils on Education are a good example of this category. There were more than forty *ad hoc* committees which reported in the period 1958 to 1962 alone. They generally comprised three to five members and were required to investigate specific problems. It is a matter of interest why particular types of committees or commissions were chosen for particular purposes. The Press has been investigated by two Royal Commissions since 1945. Broadcasting was investigated by an *ad hoc* committee. The Robbins Committee on Higher Education was accorded virtually the status and reception of a Royal Commission. There is, however, a tendency for the Departmental Committee to be preferred because of its flexibility, relative informality and— it has been suggested—its greater amenability to departmental influence.

There has been some discussion recently of the advantages and disadvantages of this proliferation of commissions and committees. Clearly, the business of government today has a scope and complexity with which the Civil Service—even if reformed so as to give greater weight in both numbers and seniority to professional, scientific, and technological recruits—would find it difficult to deal in the absence of outside assistance. It is not only that technical knowledge is required but that the co-operation of organized groups is essential. The National Plan could not have been drawn up without the assistance of industry and commerce; the significance of this help is emphasized by the suggestion of people like Mr Enoch Powell that 'non-co-operation' would be an effective way of stopping government intervention. The 'generalist' tradition of the Civil Service (discussed later) limits its technical 'know-how'. The whole machinery is 'an organized and regular means by which an over-centralized administration can acquire the information, expertise, and sectional co-operation it needs'.

But all this, it is argued, must be combined with overall *political* judgment. Ministers and civil servants are professionals in respect of 'political brokerage and effective government'. Some would argue that there is too much 'brokerage' and not enough 'positive policy'. We would add here the importance of M.P.s, but this is discussed later. 'The number of crucial political decisions in which information and expertise, as opposed to political judgment, are the vital factors is very few and where such factors are of importance they must be closely linked with political considerations'. This fits in with our analysis in Part I of the *need* for politics. In other words, an important question is whether consultative committees do, in fact, 'demonstrate the health of a democratic political system'.

The consultation of sectional interests is clearly of great importance in government but it is not a substitute for it. Nor are departmental committees the only institutions in which the public interest may be determined. Parliament, the electorate, the Cabinet are all involved and, indeed, should have pride of place. The view that committees are not a vehicle of political sectionalism since they operate subject to general controls may be dangerous: it may be precisely the emphasis on sectional bargaining in such committees that helps to explain the lack of public concern about the health of the more traditional and general political institutions. There is a danger, so this argument runs, that departmental committees may destroy effective government without being strong enough to replace it with anything else. This is largely a question of how governments use such committees; it appears that ability to co-ordinate, let alone effectively guide and influence, their activities is not what it might be, and that governments do not even use committees always in such a way as to facilitate *effective* reports.

What, then, should be the role of such committees on this argument? They can report on the specific means whereby a policy already decided upon by governments may best be implemented e.g. the introduction of a decimal coinage. They can give expert advice within a clearly defined policy, as Lord Beeching did. In other cases, however, as with the Buchanan Report on Traffic Management, they may be given neither the time nor the facilities to conduct extensive research nor a clear government lead as to which of a number of crucial *political* alternatives were to be chosen. Committees may also make an important contribution to public debate, provided they are able to conduct research, as with the Crowther and Milner Holland Committees and the Robbins Committee which, however, was also asked to give specific advice. How *not* to do it, it has been suggested, is shown by the Pilkington Committee on Broadcasting, which, on a subject-matter of heated public debate, produced a report which was neither a lucid account of the state of informed opinion nor an impartial inquiry and research operation.

In general, the consultation of sectional interests is important, but it should not be regarded as the central process whereby the public interest is determined. Members of committees should be chosen not for their 'representative' character but for their competence to direct research and organize evidence. The Government must have a clear sense of *political priorities* and the ability to choose firmly between them. 'Committees of advice are not a substitute for public policies, nor committees of inquiry for effective government'.

4

Political Parties

In Britain, effective government is generally seen as resting, among other things, on effective political parties and, indeed, on an effective two-party system. For this reason we consider political

I

parties at this stage although we have already looked at them to some extent in relation to elections, candidates, issues, and pressure groups and shall look at them again in relation to the machinery of government, the 'conversion processes'. In one way the most important role of political parties is, in the broadcast sense, in 'organization'. As regards the electorate, Professor Herman Finer has written that 'without parties an electorate would be either impotent or destructive by embarking on impossible policies that would only wreck the political machine'. They formulate issues, get out the vote, aggregate and compromise interests, and mobilize support for leaders. In very similar terms Lord Campion has said that 'for centuries party has been the dynamic and also the organizing agency in Parliament and without Party Parliament would fall into impotence and anarchy'. In this connection parties are concerned with both input and output functions. Parties may be examined from many points of view; their policies; their social composition; their internal organization; their general place in the political system. We shall be concerned primarily with the last of these, though this is clearly affected by some aspects of the other three.

It is interesting to begin with a number of definitions of party. Edmund Burke described party as 'a body of men united for promoting the national interest upon some particular principle upon which they are agreed'. Disraeli did not 'understand that party is anything but public opinion embodied. We protest against the doctrine that there is a distinction between political party and public opinion. We maintain that party is public opinion embodied whether it represent the opinion of a majority or minority; it, at all events, represents the opinion of a great section of the community'. Disraeli was arguing against Peel's desertion of his party on the issue of the Repeal of the Corn Laws in response to 'public opinion'. though, in fact, Peel was more convinced by Cobden's argument. More realistically, A. L. Lowell, an acute American writer on British politics at the beginning of the twentieth century, suggested that 'a party in modern parliamentary government would be more accurately defined as a body of men united by their interest of sustaining a common ministry'. Finally, and still more realistically, the sociologist, Max Weber, has described a political party as a voluntary society of propaganda and agitation, seeking to acquire power in order to procure chances for its active militant adherents to realize objective aims, or personal advantage, or both.

As we mentioned in our discussion of the 'necessity of politics' there have from time to time been demands for a 'National Government', for a 'Ministry of all the talents'. In the seventeenth century the Earl of Halifax thought that the 'best kind of party is but a sort of conspiracy against the nation'. In the twentieth century, Ramsay Macdonald, leading a minority government, suggested that the House of Commons regard itself as a 'Council of State', a demand repeated by Mr Christopher Hollis in *Can Parliament Survive?* and coupled with a suggestion for more loosely organized parties, a relaxation of the control of the Whips, and more free votes in the House. But governments not based on party seldom last long, or, if they do, become immune to effective criticism. They are capable of dealing with only one specific issue e.g. winning a war or dealing with an immediate crisis, but not with continuous policy. Without party, as Harold Laski put it, there is no one to 'drive a stream of tendency through the affairs of state'. Sir Ivor Jennings has emphasized the democratic assumption that there are differing views as to the correct policy in any situation; no honest man is entitled to assert that one policy is better than another—he can only *think* it is so. The critic who asserts that party is unnecessary usually believes in the rightness of his own views so profoundly that he does not realize that he is partisan. Finally, there is the pragmatic argument that the majority, which can be organized effectively only through party, is more likely to determine what is good for the majority than is the minority; they 'know where the shoe pinches'.

Parties, we have stated, operate not only at various points in the political system; they flow over into other systems in society. As an historical fact, some parties have begun in the legislature and only later 'spilled over' into the constituencies and the electorate; this is true of the Conservative and Liberal parties in Britain. Others, like the Labour Party, began as 'outside parties', and then thrust themselves into the machinery of government; they found that being virtually no more than a pressure group was insufficient to achieve, first, their limited ends and, later, their more general programme. All parties today, however, must operate at all levels and in all spheres. In one sense a party always begins in society rather than the State. In Sir Ernest Barker's analysis, for example, it begins as a set of coherent and connected political ideas, formed and enunciated in the process of social discussion. It becomes a body of persons permanently united in entertaining such a set of ideas; they then formulate a policy and programme. Finally, party becomes an organization with its own recognized leaders, for the purpose of carrying a programme into effect, firstly by securing a majority of votes of the electorate (more accurately, enough to make it the majority in the legislature), then by turning its leaders into the political government. It is 'a mediator between the process of social discussion and the practice of political action. . . . It is a social formation which has two distinct but complementary functions—first that of serving as a social reservoir for the collection of a set of connected political ideas from the area of society; and secondly that of serving as a political conduit by which the ideas so collected flow from their social reservoir into the system of the State and turn the wheels of political machinery in that system'. Parties reach their full form only with the growth of the Cabinet system.

Richard Rose sees a party as a group of office seekers, a body of men agreed on principles, an electoral machine, and a social group—all these things in part and simultaneously. Within both the Conservative and Labour Parties, broad-based though they are, there are small groups whose principles are sufficiently different from those of most Englishmen as to constitute a sub-culture. But for a much larger number of individuals their cultural attitudes reflect to some extent their party ties. Parties may develop youth sections, women's sections, and other adult social and political activities; they seek to 'socialize' their potential supporters into life-long adherence, accepting party policy and the party's distinctive interpretation of basic cultural norms. They stimulate political participation and encourage both voluntary labour and a pool of potential candidates, local and national. They confer status (a sense of position in society) on their most active supporters and those in national roles, but they also welcome support from those whose status derives from spheres outside politics. Every party delights to boast, for example, when it has the support of academic circles or the largest membership in university political clubs! Parties, as we have seen, may be linked with pressure groups, or act, for example, for 'the middle class', or for 'the underprivileged'. They are also an important part of the communications network, sending 'political messages' from national leaders to the rank and file and to the voters—and, perhaps, conveying messages in the other direction. They also have administrative tasks whether outside or inside Parliament; their committees, cliques, and conferences deliberate on policy and attempt to 'legitimate' it by linking it to principles. ('This is modern socialism' or 'This is a return to true Conservatism').

We refer only briefly to the internal organization of parties, which, indeed, has been mentioned in connection with the selection of candidates. The Conservative Party is based upon constituency associations with individual membership (grouped into Areas); these are linked federally in the National Union of Conservative and Unionist Associations. There is a Conservative Central Office, whose chairman is appointed by the party leader in Parliament; it controls national publicity and a number of other national services and works through Central Office Area Agents. There is a Conservative Research Department whose chairman is also appointed by the leader. There may be other unofficial research and propaganda groups like the Bow Group.

The Leader, who until 1965, that is, including the selection of Sir Alec Douglas Home, was 'evolved' by processes of consultation of a somewhat mysterious nature despite the fact that in 1964 some of them appeared in the open because of the coincidence of an Annual Conference, but is now, as with Mr Heath, virtually elected by the Parliamentary Party. He enunciates party policy, listens to and anticipates the views of back-benchers, colleagues, party committees, the rank and file (Mr Heath was the first leader, in 1965, to sit in throughout the Annual Conference instead of addressing it *ex cathedra* after its close), and the electorate. There is a great deal of informality in these processes, which are intended to discover 'the sense of the party'; but most power is exercised at the top. The Conservatives have an intense concern with winning elections and holding office and the party's commitment to a particular set of policies is not deep. There are many, many more Conservatives who consider that they have a prescriptive right to rule than who argue that a period out of office might be good for the soul if not for the country, and even this small minority does not argue the case with the intensity of some Labour 'purists'. Nevertheless after its defeat in 1945 and again in 1964 considerable attention was given to recognizable policies and programmes as an alternative to those of Labour. The whole organization is calculated to foster unity against the Labour Party (and far more Labour supporters are prepared to admit that a Conservative Government might not be 'too bad' than there are Conservatives to say the same thing about Labour). The party is well disciplined and although differences of opinion emerge as over Suez, the abolition of resale price maintenance, the Common Market, Rhodesia, for the most part 'dirty linen' is washed in private. This kind of public unity in the face of sometimes intense differences in private—a great asset so far as the 'public image' is concerned—is in part due to the homogeneous social nature of the party leadership. The Profumo scandal dealt something of a blow at this image of 'old boy behaviour'; it remains to be seen whether a new kind of leadership will, in fact, emerge with Mr Heath.

The Labour Party is federal in both theory and practice. It includes Trade Unions, Co-operatives, constituency associations and one or two Socialist Societies. The majority of the membership is indirect. Trade Unions have considerable influence in the party; six Trade Unions, in fact, control a majority of the over six million votes at the Annual Conference. On the other hand, it has been shown that Conference seldom splits between Trade Union and constituency party delegates; there is almost always cross-voting between the groups and *generally* a majority in both for any given decision. The Parliamentary Party elects the Leaders (annually when in Opposition) and makes and applies policy in the House of Commons. In 1960 it refused to be bound by a Conference decision in favour of unilateral nuclear disarmament but it aimed none-the-less (successfully) to legitimate its position by obtaining a reversal of the vote in 1961. Long-term programmes are drafted by sub-committees of the National Executive Council, with the help of the 'civil service' in Transport House and unofficial groups like the Fabian Society, but the Parliamentary Leader and Deputy-Leader sit *ex officio* on the N.E.C. The Annual Conference meets for five days each year and is nominally the highest authority in the Party. But it is unusual for the N.E.C. which is normally guided by the Parliamentary Party to be defeated. When the Leader is Prime Minister he naturally exercises considerably more influence. It is a myth that a Labour Government, or even the Parliamentary Party in Opposition, is the 'tool' of 'faceless' and irresponsible members of an 'outside' party. On the other hand, many members have a deep concern with ideological questions and disputes are often only contained by the prospects of office—and still more by obtaining it, as evidenced by Mr Wilson's management of 'the left' after the 1964 Election.

There would be little point in examining the organization of the Liberal Party in detail. Its claim to be midway between 'conservative' and 'socialist reactionaries' symbolized in 1965 by the removal of headquarters to Smith Square between the other two Head Offices, is difficult to sustain. There was considerable argument at the 1965 Annual Conference as to whether to give general support to Labour, to cry 'a plague on both your houses' and to use whatever balance of power the party possessed in the national interest (as defined, of course, by the Liberal Party), or to go all out to defeat the Government in the unlikely hope of being able still more clearly to hold the balance of power after another general election—though risking the return of a Conservative Government. In October 1965 it appeared likely that, whether by deliberate design or through conviction on particular issues, the Liberal Party would, in fact, help to sustain Mr Wilson's Government. The party is more or less a cross-section of the community, though less supported in the working-class and in the older industrial areas. It is not concentrated either socially or geographically, though the taunt is sometimes made that it really represents only the 'Celtic fringe'. Perhaps the most disconcerting thing for the Liberals is that one survey revealed that half the electorate did not know what attributes to ascribe to the Liberal Party.

We turn now to some aspects of the internal relationships within political parties and, following Professor Blondel,[1] examine the characteristics of the ordinary members, the local leaders, the regional leaders, and the national leaders. In general, the social structure of the membership of each of the two major parties seems to correspond broadly to the structure of the electorate which supports them. There is one important and not unexpected exception with regard to the Conservatives, whose members come from 'non-manuals' more than they 'should' if they are to reflect the distribution of Conservative votes among the different occupational class groups. Non-manuals, however, do not normally show a high degree of political involvement even at the level of joining a party—and doing no more. With respect to political views, Conservative members do not appear to be notably more right-wing than the electors who support the party; there are, perhaps, proportionately more 'left-wingers' among Labour Party members. It must be recalled, of course, that most members are not active, though the proportion seems to be higher in the Labour Party. Some interesting facts about 'activists' were revealed in a study of the Exeter constituency, during the 1964 election by Dr R. A. Dowse and Mr J. Stanyer. 'Active' men appeared to be divided about equally between the three parties, but the vast majority of 'active' women were Conservative; as a result this party had twice as many members who were expected to work at election time as the other two parties together. The women, especially the Conservatives, were relatively uninterested in policy but they were more intolerant of other parties, in contrast to members of the general public. Activists as a whole appear to be more intolerant of their opponents than voters; extreme attitudes are normally reinforced through association with others who have such attitudes. Neither in their work situation, nor in their family and social life are activists likely to meet

[1] Op. cit.

with contrary opinions. In Exeter, activists expectedly revealed strong party attachments; there was 'good government' only when their own party was in power. The Conservatives were strongly anti-trade union, the Labour activists spoke of big business, Old Etonians, and the upper class, the Liberals were against both big business and trade unions. Activists also have their attitudes reinforced at public meetings—designed mostly these days to enthuse the converted rather than to persuade the inconvertible!—and were more ready to electioneer. It is just worth remembering that fewer of these attitudes are revealed by the paid professionals—agents etc.—who are frequently almost a-political and on friendly terms with their opposite numbers.

The activists are largely responsible for choosing the local leaders, who may become local councillors and exercise considerable influence over the selection of parliamentary candidates. There is, of course, a hierarchy of local leaders, moving upwards from the larger committees to the smaller executives, but both subject to some extent to outside influences e.g. from the agents. Local leadership appears to be more middle class than the membership; leaders come from especially high levels in the Conservative Party whose associations are primarily 'social' and from somewhat lower levels in the Labour Party e.g. from white collar workers who are not too far removed from the 'manuals', a few shopkeepers, managers, teachers, professional men and, of course, trade union organizers. Much uninformed nonsense is talked about the 'militant' attitudes of local leaders and activists. An analysis of resolutions sent to Party Conference shows that the proportion of 'extremist' resolutions is much smaller than is generally thought. Fifty per cent of such resolutions are non-partisan and the partisan ones are not all extremist. The latter are usually concentrated on two or three topics each year and, are, of course, singled out by the Press. Many local parties do not send in any resolutions. In general, the views of the local leaders appear to be pretty representative of the views of the rank and file members if not of the electorate.

There is not much to say of regional leaders. In the Conservative Party, as we saw in our discussion of the selection of candidates, the Chairmen are usually prominent leaders at regional as well as at local levels; they come from the top social groups and include many M.P.s. In the Labour Party regional leaders are relatively unimportant, indeed, their activities are largely concerned with organization.

Much will be said of the national leadership when we discuss Parliament and the Cabinet. For the moment all that we need say is that the national leaders in the parties themselves obviously include the parliamentary group and especially its most prominent members; some leaders of pressure groups, whether or not affiliated to the party; the top-ranking members of the party organization and its bureaucracy, though they have limited influence only except where leadership is weak or divided—as when Morgan Phillips, Secretary of the Labour Party, played a prominent role in public discussion and at Party Conferences. M.P.s play a larger part than may appear on the surface, both behind the scenes and as elected delegates and members of executive bodies. But many of them are frequently in disagreement with parliamentary leaders, especially when in opposition. How, in fact, decisions are made within parties is to a large extent one of the mysteries of the political process. Books on the subject are usually more revealing about the formal machinery than about the informal processes, while memoirs not only suffer from a natural tendency for authors to exaggerate their own influence but often refer to a period long since past and not necessarily similar to contemporary conditions. General principles like Michel's 'iron law of oligarchy' or the various *élite* theories mentioned in another context tell us as little about actual parties as about other organizations. We can only guess at how effective the two-way traffic of ideas and influences is and to what degree 'democratic centralism' prevails even in parties which shudder at the thought of the source of this particular theory and practice.

Political parties usually have some broad guiding theme, some preponderant motivation shared by at least the active members. They may be nationalist; attached to certain political or moral principles—the latter sometimes ideological or utopian; based on a socio-economic class; attached to charismatic or personal leadership; representing certain religious attitudes; representing regional interests; or, a mixture of any of these. Some parties are mainly concerned with broad issues—a constitutional party with a preference for a particular form of government—though presumably it intends to use that form for certain secondary purposes. Some are more concerned with specific issues as was the Liberal Party in its heyday with Free Trade. Or there may be a two-party system divided mainly into 'ins' and 'outs', the parties being what have been called secular, pragmatic and bargaining parties.

With the last, which is broadly the situation in Britain although with certain undertones of principle, we have already seen that the electorate is neither presented with a choice between two mutually exclusive parties nor with one set of policies masquerading under different labels. Parties, even under such a system, do not agree on all major issues nor on particular items of policy. In Britain major issues have emerged one by one over a period of time and have been solved before becoming attached to later issues; so the religious issue was settled before the emergence of the franchise issue and the latter before the serious emergence of economic issues. As a result the practice developed of settling differences peacefully by agreed procedures based on compromise; of self-restraint, and more frequently than is admitted by partisans on either side, of putting national duty before party. Moreover, a positive value is attached to the assimilation of new ideas and a negative one on ideological consistency. The homogeneity of the electorate also leads parties to resemble each other in the process of competition for votes; marginal constituencies and floating voters encourage similar programmes like those which emerged during the currency of the term 'Butskellism'—so little difference was there, it was alleged, between Mr Butler and Mr Gaitskell and their parties. Further, the parties contain certain groups which differ from each other about the programme of their own party; each major party is itself a coalition. The outcome of a particular election influences public policy in only a limited number of policy areas (whether due to circumstances, to the effect of responsibility in office, to new information about the actual state of the country, or to a civil service advice) and does not threaten a total change of policy. It has also been suggested, as we saw, that the single-member constituency places a high premium on the different groups within a party being prepared to sink some of their disagreements in order to have the chance of sharing in the control of government.

At certain periods doubts have been expressed as to whether this general agreement between parties and their policies could continue forever. In the 1930's especially there were gloomy views about the possible emergence of fundamental conflict. At other times the opposite fear has been expressed—that the two major parties might become so close to each other as to eliminate any significant difference between them, so that no fundamental economic and social changes are being sought by either party. This is, of course, the Communist view of the British Labour Party; but it is also the charge, on different grounds, of some Conservatives about their own party's tendency to 'me-tooism'. It is a matter for argument whether today there are still important differences between the parties—a problem which cannot be resolved merely by an examination of election programmes. As we have said, many Conservatives have felt in recent years that their party has too frequently 'caught the Socialists bathing and stolen their clothes', a matter for concern rather than con-gratulation—though for the majority only after an election has been lost. Journalists and commentators looked to the Annual Conference of 1965 to produce new policies under a new leader. Some leading articles offered (somewhat muted) praise in the belief that this had happened, or, at least, that its possibility could be discerned. Contrariwise, many members of the Labour Party have regretted what seems to them to be a 'watering-down of the pure milk of Socialism'; they will probably remain relatively muted while the party is in power; indeed, Mr Wilson's oppo-nents have charged that he, himself, became 'moderate' only because of his small majority. We cannot pursue this theme further here.

We must, however, note Richard Rose's contention that be-tween elections differences within parties are as important as differences between the parties; though the extent to which the former differences will be pressed clearly depends on the political situation; the Labour revolt in 1947–50 over the possibility that, after all, iron and steel might not be nationalized seemed unlikely to be repeated in 1965 over the postponement of re-nationalization. But there are 'factions, tendencies, and non-aligned partisans' within parties. The first at times constitute almost separate parties, like the 'Bevanites' in the Labour Party; the second represent a static set of attitudes to the government's programme; the third emphasize the differences between the parties. Ideological considerations, it has been said, are of special importance in delineating the differences within parties; the acceptance of a common set of values brings politicians together in support of certain policies and programmes. But the quality of leadership is important, especially when differences penetrate the Cabinet or the Shadow Cabinet.

In general, it may be said that the Conservative Party, as an electoral organization, is a party of tendencies. There are differences between *ad hoc* and changing groups of members; some are (if only mildly) reactionary, others defend the *status quo*, others favour gradual reforms. But factionalism as defined above is rarely a threat. In the Labour Party, on the other hand, there is a long history of factionalism; groups have been static in their reactions to such things as German rearmament, the H-bomb, the insistence on nationalization—though not to entry into the Common Market. On some major issues the non-aligned partisans have had the final say; they defeated Gaitskell on his proposal to get rid of Clause IV (nationalization) but supported his defence policy.

These differences, however, concern the internal relations of the party and are most important, or at least most obvious, when the party is in opposition. It remains to add, though this is dealt with more fully later, that such divisions are of no real significance to a Prime Minister. His followers are unlikely to desert him in sufficient numbers to bring defeat on a vote of confidence in the House. Governments fall rather through dissensions in the Cabinet than through adverse votes in the Commons.

It has not been possible, even if it were desirable, entirely to eliminate from our description of political parties the implication that, on the whole and so far as we have gone, the British system works reasonably well. Britain's 'secular, pragmatic, bargaining' parties have played their part in the emergence of a pretty viable political system. On what basic principles does this kind of party system rest? Firstly, it is clear that tolerance is essential. Parties of 'integration' which seek to influence the whole of the members' way of life and attitudes, and to obtain control of the political machine both by means of and aiming at destroying all differences of opinion, cannot work a parliamentary system. Secondly, and this follows from the first point, the majority must never be permanent; there must always be the possibility, and most people not blinded by partisanship would say the actuality, of a change of party government. We have argued this point earlier. Thirdly, and again this stems from the previous argument, parties must be based upon factors of opinion which can change, and not be recruited on the basis of race or religion or even of economic status. We do not normally love M.P.s who cross the floor of the House, though the most eminent of them, Sir Winston Churchill, did so on several occasions. But the possibility of changing one's party and especially one's voting allegiance is a *sine qua non* of democracy. Under these circumstances parties will embrace a wide range of opinion and, in the daily conduct of affairs, will distinguish between opposition and obstruction. Finally, as we have argued at length, the system depends upon fundamental agreement on certain values, but especially upon procedures for resolving differences, upon democratic principles and practices. As has been said, 'the division between parties should never be so trivial that it makes politics a game for the prize of office, nor so fundamental that the one desires to destroy the other'.

Perhaps one further implication has made at least a ghostly appearance in this argument: that, generally, a two-party system is preferable to a multi-party system. We referred to this in our analysis of the possible consequences of proportional representation for stable and effective government. It will appear again in our analysis of the machinery of government. There seems to be some evidence in history and in contemporary events that neither a one-party system nor a multi-party system is likely to provide the kind of government which the political culture seems to approve. But more must be said of this later.

5

Political Communication and Public Opinion

Although, as we have seen, political communication has been described as an input function of the political system, in fact it is a process which must go on throughout the system itself and is also an output function. There is vertical communication as between leaders and followers, holders of government offices and citizens. There is also horizontal communication between leaders, ministers and civil servants. We shall look first at the general notion of 'public opinion', then at the channels of communication between government and governed, and finally at the communication processes in general within the political system.

Although there may be such a thing as 'world-opinion', which is certainly cited, for example, in the United Nations, by Americans concerned with their 'image' over such things as treatment of Negroes, by Africans and others in relation to the behaviour of White Rhodesians, we are primarily concerned with opinion within a particular community. A community has been described as a group of people with many habitual relations or communications with each other; the 'public' is then the political part or aspect of the community, people looked at with respect to their political relations and communications, as 'engaged in a political division of labour'. Consensus we have already defined broadly as basic agreement on the part of the public on the general method of organizing and conducting the political process. It should be distinguished from 'public opinion' which is a belief held by a number of people on a more or less specific political issue. When we speak of 'majority-consensus' we mean majority belief in a number of inter-related basic issues.

We need not spend much time on the fact that a State may include more than one community since our concern is with the United Kingdom, except to note the existence of communities in Scotland, Wales, and Northern Ireland which have characteristics distinct from the community which is coterminous with the political kingdom of the U.K. It is important to note, however, that States must normally be (more-or-less) communities if they are to remain viable, although within them there may be intense social groups which constitute sub-communities as well as local communities. Every community enforces various degrees of conformity merely by existing and without formal procedures of enforcement; custom, habit, fear of isolation or frustration are powerful influences. John Stuart Mill feared that public opinion might be as tyrannous as a despotic government and David Riesman has drawn attention to the preponderance of 'other-directed' persons in the U.S.—those who conform to outside pressures rather than to internal values. Both these writers appear to have been concerned with the influence of 'community' or of living in a community rather than with public opinion as we understand it, at least in a political context, today; though there is a connection between the two since Mill's 'tyranny' and Riesman's 'other-directedness' may affect political as well as other attitudes.

But there is a variety of 'publics', as of communities, in the sense of groups possessing 'attitudes to politics', despite the fact that politics operate within a framework of community custom and under the influence of a dominant political culture. Even in war-time there are dissident groups. These attitudes, moreover, change and in changing may affect political processes. In every State there is the problem of conflicting loyalties between, for example, the national community and such other influences as social class, locality, occupation. Such conflicts may produce anxiety, apathy, alienation, intermittent anomy (strikes, riots, demonstrations etc.) or actual open conflict. Such tendencies may today be enchanced by the existence of problems caused by complex technologies, apparently unmanageable foreign affairs and so on. 'What can *I* do about it'? Rulers may respond to such tendencies by propaganda or by the cultivation of charismatic leadership as much as

by information and national persuasion. Nor, of course, are rulers
the only persuaders, hidden or otherwise. Whatever these problems
and the reactions to them may be, in order to understand the
political system it is clearly essential to study the separation as well
as the community of interests.

In this context it is vital to emphasize again the distinction
between *consensus*, or agreement upon basic principles of politics
and government, and which is likely to be more procedural than
substantive, and *public opinion*, a belief which arises over any
controversy and which is held by a number of people—especially
the 'politically-relevant' people—about a political issue. We
cannot discuss in detail the problem of how to ascertain 'public
opinion' on any particular issue, except to note the suggestion
that at least six factors are involved: the number of alternative
opinions held; the distribution of these opinions among the various
social groups; the intensity with which the various opinions are
held; the number of people holding such opinions; how opinions
may be organized (even 'manufactured') by different groups and
interests; and the rate of change of opinions over a period of
time. Our task must be confined to the simpler one of examining
some of the influences which help to mould public opinion (or
opinions).[1] In doing this we shall not reopen the question
of basic attitudes or the means of socialization, nor the more
specialized mechanisms of pressure groups etc., but merely look
at some of the more general channels of communication and their
effects.

As part of the background to this examination, however, it is
essential to bear in mind the changed conditions of politics. In
the nineteenth century in Britain politicians were concerned
mainly with small electorates consisting for the most part of fairly
well educated people some of whom, at least, were traditionally
interested and informed about politics. The modern electorate is
so vast that it can be reached only through the mass media of
communication. Moreover, as our analysis of voting habits revealed, the electorate must to a very large extent be addressed in
simplified and over-simplified terms which are not calculated to

[1] *The Governors and the Governed*, William A. Robson, Allen & Unwin, 1964.

K

encourage intelligent discussion of complex issues. Slogans are hardly relevant to such problems as the balance of payments, nuclear weapons, disarmament, foreign policy, the Common Market, economic and fiscal policy.

This problem is particularly severe where economic issues are concerned. 'Political problems tend to concentrate electoral interest, economic problems tend to disperse it'. How many people read, let alone understood, even the popular version of the National Plan published in 1965? Equally important, to what extent did the mass media assist the electorate to understand it and evaluate it in an objective manner. (It must be admitted that many politicians contributed little to such objective appraisal). Economic problems can, perhaps, be understood to some extent if they are seen by the citizen to have a direct bearing on his own immediate concerns— which may, however, not be the best criteria of judgment. A refusal by the Prices and Incomes Board to accept a wage increase has an immediate impact, but may not the long-term interests of those affected be better served by a decision which helps to stabilize the cost of living? Farmers, however, are little interested in the problems of the miners or other industrial workers while well-to-do members of the middle class may not even *understand* the problems of the 'under-privileged'. Doctors in search of a pay rise may condemn dockers doing precisely the same thing. As for more general economic problems, few citizens understand that their solution may have a direct bearing upon their own lives and they are not greatly interested in others. This, of course, is the weakness in the 'know where the shoe pinches' theory of democracy; such knowledge is not necessarily followed by an appreciation of the best remedy.

Professor Robson has asserted that such factors as these help to account for the fact that 'a semi-literate populace is provided with a semi-literate press to supply its needs'. Politics is seldom news. Politics must be 'dramatized, personalized, or sensationalized' in order to obtain space in the popular press. Editorials in such newspapers seldom rise above the level indicated by a description of the first popular newspaper as 'written by office boys for office boys'. Serious items like the Budget are presented under such headings as 'a penny more on beer and baccy', though one must except the television documentaries of recent years. Only the 'quality newspapers' carry serious and reasonably full accounts of political speeches, parliamentary debates or important reports and White Papers.

Clearly the enlarged electorate of today knows less about politics than the smaller electorate of yesteryear, though millions can provide exact descriptions of the lives of film stars and 'pop-idols' or statistics of cricket and football feats. Indeed, if stars of stage, screen, or sportsfield can be induced to express public opinions on politics they are more likely to be influential than statesmen or dons. Even their known association with a party, though they make no political pronouncements at all, may help their party—at least in the minds of television authorities who, for example, withdrew an episode of 'The Avengers' because Miss Honor Blackman was a self-confessed Liberal. On the other hand, the defeat of England captain Ted Dexter in Cardiff in 1964 suggests that Welshmen at least take a more sophisticated view of politics! More seriously, more may be known of and more interest taken in the doings of even an obscure member of the Royal Family than those of influential politicians, despite the fact that the monarch is of little consequence in the decision-making process. Whether the opinions of His Royal Highness the Duke of Edinburgh are on the same level as his oft-quoted jokes is a moot point; but the fact that when he makes a statement of political significance there is an uproar seems to suggest that some people at least believe that such remarks may be influential. It would be interesting to know how many people realized that when the Queen wrote to Mr Ian Smith in 1965 she could only have done so on the Prime Minister's advice. However that may be, we may laugh or despair with Professor Robson when we recall that in one survey seventy per cent of the schoolchildren questioned knew who Elvis Presley was, but only twenty-five per cent had heard of General Eisenhower.

Equally important is the fact that the dissemination of news, opinion and information is now a highly organized industry with strong monopolistic tendencies and considerable dependence on advertising revenue. Young readers of today may scarcely recall the existence of the *News Chronicle* and the *Daily Herald*, while the *Sun* struggles to maintain itself and the Labour Party is only now experimenting with its own newspaper—the last of the social democratic parties in Europe to do so. In 1961 three great newspaper trusts controlled sixty-seven per cent of the total daily circulation in Britain. One after another local dailies have disappeared, as have competing evening newspapers. Large circulations are, in fact, economic necessities to a modern newspaper. Even a million readers cannot guarantee survival. To obtain increased sales, it is not just a question of amalgamations; controversial items of news are watered down and intermixed with expressions of opinion; features which might give offence to a substantial group of readers are eliminated; political views or news are slanted to avoid contravening 'accepted convention'. Entertainment is more important than education and trivial human interest stories than serious discussion. Even the *Daily Worker* attempts to cash in on the success of its racing tipster. 'What Mr Khruschev had for lunch when he met President Kennedy' is almost as newsworthy as what he said.

Headlines give the impression that there is not much more than *one* important event that has happened each day and, of course, the editors decide what it was. It has been argued that the function of a newspaper is 'to tell the sovereign people what it wants to hear'. But the sovereign people may equally be lulled into believing that it only wants to hear what it is told. In view of all this it is perhaps of some comfort that newspapers do not appear to exercise an important influence at least on voting during an election campaign —though the atmosphere encouraged or created by them between elections may influence the criteria by which parties and policies are judged. Certainly no Democrat would be elected as President in the U.S. if he had to rely upon even balanced newspaper support. In Britain, Labour voters are three times as likely to be found reading Conservative newspapers than Conservatives to be found reading Labour newspapers. (There aren't nearly so many, of course!) The late Lord Beaverbrook, however, may have exercised some influence behind the scenes but he could rarely exercise even a marginal effect on election results. Perhaps this is just as well in view of Mr Baldwin's famous description of newspaper proprietors as seekers after power without responsibility, 'the prerogative of the harlot through the ages'.

Nor is the situation entirely different with radio and television. The B.B.C. may perhaps comfort itself with the thought that it has from time to time been accused of both an anti-Labour and an anti-Conservative bias. However that may be, there is some evidence that it does tend, not necessarily in its news or documentaries but in its general programmes, to encourage an 'establishment' or orthodox picture of life, a tendency which is not weakened by the constant pressure to modify or even to abandon its more adventurous satirical programmes. It is, of course, possible that these programmes in particular 'cock a snook' at 'the powers that be', whatever government is in power. But this is only to emphasize the relative lack of balanced comment. Perhaps as serious is the allegation that television interviewers, politically responsible to no one, appear at times to assume the role of public critics of politicians and exercise more influence than Parliament itself. Or, alternatively, M.P.s who appear on television are selected more for their photogenic and dialectical qualities than for their standing in party and government. Opinions differ about commercial television. Leaving aside the advertisements which, like the glossy magazines, clearly encourage a cosy way of thinking and an addiction to affluence (which one can argue helps one party more than another), independent television has, perhaps in some ways shown more courage in defying conventions than the B.B.C. On the other hand, its political programmes at election time tend to emphasize sloganized political in-fighting rather more than serious discussion.

It may be, of course, that television, as has been suggested by some, is not a medium for serious prolonged discussion. But this attitude, again, may be based rather on the assumption that the viewers must be given what they are supposed to want as measured by TAM ratings than what they might be educated to prefer. Is television a medium of education or entertainment? The same question has been asked of the theatre but television has yet to show the same social conscience and uninhibited social criticism as, for example, the plays of Shaw and Galsworthy in an age when such criticism was less acceptable. Of one thing there can be no doubt: audiences for serious programmes fall far short in numbers of those for light entertainment and a large number of people probably listen to party political broadcasts only because they cannot switch over and are too lazy, or conditioned, to switch off. Are we, as the late Ed Murrow, one of America's ablest, most controversial and courageous broadcasters once asked, reaching the stage where—as in totalitarian States—'the role of television is not to teach or facilitate self-government . . . but to make the governed content not to govern themselves?' Are we the 'proles' of George Orwell's '1984'? Surely Murrow was right in urging that 'we must rid ourselves of our allergy to unpleasant and disturbing information'.

Again, however, it is necessary to attempt a balanced judgment about the effect of television. An investigation during the British General Election of 1959 revealed that television was the only medium which significantly increased the voters' understanding of the campaign issues. On the other hand, while most viewers disliked crude attacks by one party on another and preferred a more constructive approach, television did not appear to affect voters' preferences. Rather did it harden those preferences and provide a means, by judicious selection, of justifying them. Most viewers thought their own party's programmes were the best. It is perhaps somewhat alarming that it now seems necessary for politicians to acquire a 'television personality'. Sir Alec Douglas Home was clearly a liability to his party on television in 1964 and Mr Wilson an asset. But what possible connection is there between being an effective 'telephoney' and an effective statesman?

This problem, of course, is not confined to election periods. It has been argued that television ought to explain the background to the great issues of the day throughout the whole period of political argument. If it be true that election campaigns influence only a small proportion of voters, and most of them to vote as they would have done anyway rather than to abstain, it is doubly important to consider the influences to which they are subjected between elections. Doubly important because of the growing influence of professional practitioners of publicity techniques; political policies and politicians *can* be sold by the same processes as those which sell cigarettes, patent medicines, soap, perfumes and pop stars. The late Mr Adlai Stevenson (how many people recall who he was, apart, perhaps, from the fact that he dropped dead in a London street) once denounced the idea that 'candidates for high office can be merchandised like a breakfast cereal as the ultimate indignity to the democratic process'. Yet, in the view of many, techniques have become little less important that the selection and design of the programme. Images are deliberately created, and we have seen how important they may be during elections. The image is not necessarily a true reflection of the party but merely an attempt to portray what the political public is most likely to 'buy'. We need not exaggerate the possible influence of the 'hidden persuaders' to point the danger of this kind of development. The same may be said of the 'cult of personality' which is replacing the validity of an argument as a persuasive influence. The ultimate result of this may be not so much the practice of 'I am their leader, therefore I must follow them', as the more insidious thought that 'what they want can be manipulated by me'.

So far we have concentrated largely upon the means whereby the electors may be influenced by the mass media. But what of the equally important problems of the information available to governments and of direct communication between government and governed? So far as the government is concerned it is no longer a question simply of promulgating a new law or of publishing regulations. Knowledge of and participation in 'elaborate measures affecting agriculture, industry and trade, research programmes, health campaigns, town and country planning schemes, educational programmes, highway and traffic developments, and many other governmental activities' are necessary. Knowledge about government policies by the public and about popular reactions to such policies is more than ever essential, as we indicated in the general analysis of Part I.

'Intelligence' has always been recognized as an important factor in defence policies, but it is no less important to civil departments. This is not just a question of obvious information but also of research—recognized as important in science and technology but not, until recently, in public administration and the social sciences, witness the belated establishment of a Council for Research in the latter fields. Even now it is doubtful whether this Council will control, even proportionately, the amount of money available for the physical and natural sciences. And we must at least raise the question whether expenditure on space research is really as important as research into social and economic problems. Apart from fundamental research, however, politicians and civil servants need to be continuously informed about developments in every field. Since they cannot be expected to study, still less understand all the technical information available, it must be 'digested, simplified, interpreted and served out to them in every small and carefully selected doses'. An *internal* information service is equally important to enable everyone to understand the policies and objectives of any particular organization. This is an essential basis of effective co-ordination and of consistency in policy and in its application. We consider this further in our examination of the administrative machine. Since, in the last resort, Government is itself 'a particular organization', it is also important that there should be a constant flow of information between different departments and administrative agencies.

This last is 'horizontal' information-flow. But if a democracy is to be effective the vertical flow between governors and governed on a two-way basis is at least of equal importance. Information officers are an essential part of every government organization since, as we have seen, the mass media cannot be relied upon for purposes of government. But information officers must supply absolutely reliable and objective information. Public relations constitute a somewhat different problem. Policies and programmes must be explained to citizens both as a means of ensuring their co-operation and of their deriving their just and due benefits from such policies and programmes. This is partly a question of psychology; for example, how many people know that they are entitled to National Assistance benefits but will not claim them because of misunderstanding as to 'the atmosphere' in which they are provided? These techniques are an essential feature of effective government. 'Those who oppose in principle the use by governments of the aids of publicity and public relations will usually be found, on close examination, to favour weak government.' On On the other hand, the danger of undermining effective criticism of government and of biasing public opinion must be avoided, especially if these techniques are to encourage a two-way traffic of communication.

Let us try to summarize the effect of all this and the problems which remain, largely following an analysis by Richard Rose, who, revealingly, heads his inquiry, 'Communication and Non-communication'! Readers will recognize this approach as similar to our own analysis of the political process in Part I, with the concepts of inputs, outputs and feedback. A steady flow of information *from* the peripheral public is essential if the Government is to respond to mass concerns and preferences. This will flow along informal channels, parties, pressure groups, elections, and will be regulated by various 'gatekeepers'. Conversely, there must be a flow of information to the public from the Government if its directions are to be understood and obeyed. This communications network is vertical as from governors and governed and vice versa. We noted in Part I that the greater the number of levels and channels of information the greater the risk of distortion. Politicians may be unable to verify the accuracy of incoming messages.

Yet 'feedback' is essential if both governors and governed are to take into account each other's behaviour and adjust their future actions accordingly. There is need for both deference and leadership, within the framework of public opinion. We have, again, noted that the majority of people are 'socialized' for passive political roles; they accept the norms of political *representation* and of the rights both of majorities and minorities. Parties may perform this representative function; in so far as they represent a class they may, indeed, do this without much feedback. On specific problems groups rather than parties may perform the representative function. But conventions may reduce the flow of information; we shall see how this operates later with respect to individual and collective ministerial responsibility. The civil service, of course, normally advises in private and does not necessarily understand or represent public opinion. M.P.s are handicapped in obtaining information as, again, we shall see in our discussion of the House of Commons —although they are *par excellence* 'the people's representatives'. Even the Press may suffer various constraints; its representatives are not always in close contact or, if they are, what they are told may be off the record or confidential. This is quite apart from the Official Secrets Acts and the laws of libel. In other words there *is* a problem of non-communication as well as of communication.

How do the channels of information affect the people's reaction and attitudes? Rose suggests that only a minority of Englishmen have sufficient interest or information to maintain a meaningful conversation with a party official or an M.P. about politics. Many people feel pyschologically inhibited from talking politics. The proportion of people seeking personal contact with M.P.s is small and usually such people are concerned with minor matters and personal problems. An individual, for the most part, chooses between agents; though, as we have seen, people speak through their actions, especially at a general election. An election, how-ever, merely gives an 'on balance' judgment for or against a party, with nothing made very clear about particular policies. We have already noted how useless, in general, is the doctrine of the mandate. Public opinion polls may be a means whereby citizens can influence governments but apart from problems of their reliability, leaders are notoriously unwilling to believe anything which they do not wish to believe. Psephologists (students of voting behaviour) may know little more than politicians but it is difficult to accept a politician's 'I just don't believe it' in the face, for example, of a recent poll finding that his party is ten points behind its rival. In any case, it may be asked whether governments should 'follow my leader' by acting entirely according to the whims of the public at any given time.

The Press, radio and television give diffuse accounts of the working of Government. These media may also attempt to transmit messages from the political public. But they have only a very limited knowledge of a cross-section of the community and anyone who has watched an interviewer gathering opinions through a microphone on the street corner must feel that the camera is often more candid than convincing. As we have seen, the popular Press certainly does not inform adequately. Pressure groups often manufacture rather than transmit news. Political parties may both inform and represent only a minority of their small membership rather than the general voters, though, as we have seen, this minority is very largely a cross-section of the community. We need not repeat our comments on the use by government departments of committees, enquiries, consultative processes etc. but merely recall that they ought not to be regarded as providing an infallible expression of public opinion.

There are clearly many weaknesses in the process of political communication which need attention if democracy is to flourish. 'That is not law which public opinion hath not made'. But if we cannot ascertain public opinion, if the public cannot be assured of sound information on which to form an opinion about government activities, it is slight comfort to remind ourselves that 'eternal vigilance is the price of freedom'. To be aware is one thing; to be aware of what to look for, another; to know how to act, something else again.

SECTION II

Government Institutions

I

Commons, Lords, and Crown

Our study of what are mainly input functions, from voting patterns through pressure groups to political parties, and with political communications pervading all of these institutions and processes, is complete. We now move to the 'conversion processes' whereby these inputs become outputs and first to the major governmental institutions involved in these processes. We have reversed the usual constitutional order of the three elements of the sovereign body, the Queen-in-Parliament, because this is a more realistic order in respect of actualities of political power. Indeed, these actualities might even seem to suggest that the Cabinet ought to take precedence of the other three—and perhaps even the Prime Minister of the Cabinet; but neither could exist without the authority of Parliament and to take the latter first is in many ways more convenient.

The term 'legislature' is generally used because the formal embodiment of policies and proposals in statute law is the ultimate exercise of sovereign power, at least in a unitary state like Britain where the courts have no power to declare such law unconstitutional. In fact, legislation is one function only of the representative assembly and, indeed, may be only formally in its control. Laski's analysis of the functions of the House of Commons is as good a starting point as any. First, the House has 'to make and sustain a Government with the initiative in legislation and policy'. Seventy years earlier, at a time when in theory at least the Commons really controlled the Executive, Bagehot wrote in very similar terms that 'the legislature, chosen, in name, to make laws, in fact finds its principal business is making and keeping an executive'. This, as we saw, is largely achieved by the existence of parties and the influence of party loyalty and discipline. Laski's other five functions are the ventilation of grievances, the extraction of information, debate to inform and sustain public interest, the selection of the personnel of government on the basis of reputation in the House, and the provision of various opportunities for private members to contribute to the processes of government.

Sir Gilbert Campion, Clerk to the House, in a memorandum to the Select Committee on Procedure in 1946, offered a somewhat different analysis and attempted to relate the various activities of the House to each head. First, the House represents public opinion; it is, in fact, doing this throughout the whole of its activities and we need not attempt to allocate any particular procedures to this function. Secondly, there is legislation. Thirdly, there is control of finance. Fourthly, there is 'formulation and control of policy'. We examine each in turn.

In view of our comments on the use of the term 'legislature' it is interesting to note that the House of Commons normally spends only one half of its time on legislation. Almost the whole of this legislation is presented to the House by the Government, though some Private Members' Bills do succeed in finding their way to the Statute book, usually on relatively non-controversial subjects and frequently with Government assistance in the later stages. This does not mean, of course, that the idea for every legislative proposal originates with the Government. Some are imposed by force of circumstances. Much is derived from party policy which is accepted by the Government. Much derives from departmental proposals which have been pigeon-holed by civil servants to await a favourable opportunity. A great deal is the result of pressure group activity and some the result of public opinion. (We shall not discuss Private Bills which are concerned mostly with particular institutions like local authorities or public corporations and which go through a different, partly 'quasi-judicial' procedure).

When a Bill, thrashed out in the Cabinet or its Legislation Committee and drawn up by the parliamentary counsel in due legal form (if it is a Government Bill, but all Public Bills go through the following stages), is presented to the Commons (or in some cases first to the Lords) its First Reading is generally formal. Second Reading Debate, normally in the full House (though in 1965 it was agreed that certain Second Readings of 'uncontroversial Bills' might go to Committee) provides an opportunity for the discussion of general principles but it also lays down the basic framework of the Bill which cannot be altered at the Committee stage. This stage is concerned with the details of the Bill and amendments are confined within the afore-mentioned principles, unlike the practice in U.S. Congressional and most continental committees. It is usually taken 'upstairs' in one of the Standing Committees of about fifty members unless the Bill is of great constitutional significance, is likely to go through quickly, or a Government with a small majority (and, therefore, probably with a majority of only one in Standing Committee) fears too frequent defeat. There follows the Report Stage, usually brief, and a final Third Reading at which the major parties once more deploy their general arguments of principle, though the result, with the Whips on, is normally a foregone conclusion. Governments, of course, during all this process, may accept amendments which do not go to the heart of the Bill (occasionally they have even withdrawn Bills). Any other proposed change is discussed as a matter of 'confidence' and defeat would normally lead to the Government's resignation or, more usually now, to a dissolution and a General Election.

The Standing Committees are not specialist, although one takes Private Members' Bills and Scottish Bills go to the Scottish Committee, and take Bills as they come; in most cases, however, M.P.s who have a special interest in or knowledge of the subject can obtain nomination by the Committee of Selection, subject always to the maintenance of at least a minimum Government majority of one. When the Bill has passed through all its stages in the Commons it goes through similar stages in the Lords. Lords' Amendments are considered by the Commons: if accepted, as many are since they may have been made on the Government's suggestion or merely 'tidying-up' amendments, there is no problem. If they are rejected the Lords may then 'concur'. If, however, the Lords insist on their amendments and the Commons will not give way the Parliament Act may be invoked and after one year the Bill becomes law despite the Lords (Money Bills can be delayed only for one month). In 1964–65 the Lords amended several Labour Government Bills but up to the end of the first session had not insisted on any amendment after its rejection by the Commons. The Queen's assent is today a pure formality.

Acts of Parliament have increasingly to be filled out in detail with a large number of regulations or 'statutory instruments' usually made in the departments concerned. It has been argued that 'delegated legislation gives the Administration too much power by authorizing the making of laws without, in many cases, the opportunity for parliamentary scrutiny before they are made'. Griffiths and Street, in their authoritative study of 'Administrative Law', have replied that 'today, most critics of delegated legislation admit its inevitability and concern themselves with keeping it within the closest practicable bounds. . . . Parliament has not the time to examine the full details of every proposal, nor can the details of extensive changes be so accurately foreseen that they can be provided for in the principal statutes. Statutory provisions must be adaptable; discretionary powers must be entrusted to the Administration'. They go on to suggest that Bills contain certain principles of policy and execution for the House of Commons to consider; matters of detail should be left to subordinate legislation. The latter would be considered in conjunction with the various interests concerned. 'The control of policy is primarily a matter of political responsibility and the control of detail and techniques primarily the responsibility of the specialist'.

In fact, the House does have an opportunity of considering most, although not all, of these statutory instruments which are 'laid on the Table of the House', either by passing an affirmative resolution to accept them or, more usually, within a period of forty days by 'praying to annul' them. It must be said that in most of the debates arising out of such 'prayers' the discussion has raised political rather than technical issues and, indeed, the 'prayers' have often been withdrawn, an indication that there was no serious intention of trying to alter the regulation by defeating it. The House cannot amend regulations but may persuade the Government to do so. There is also a Select Committee on Statutory Instruments, the 'Scrutiny' Committee, which is not allowed to discuss the 'merits' of the instrument but can report to the House if it offends against any one of a number of technical or legal requirements; few instruments are thus reported. It may very well be that the way in which legislation, 'parent' or 'child', is *applied* is of considerably greater importance to the ordinary citizen than the manner in which it is made in Parliament.

The financial activities, which occupy about ten per cent of its time, of the House are very complicated. But first we must note that the consideration of Estimates in Committee of Supply has virtually ceased to have financial significance and, like Campion, we shall consider this primarily under the heading of 'formulation and control of policy'. We now attempt to summarize briefly financial procedure and then to inquire to what extent the House really controls finance today. The granting of public monies and the imposition of taxation is the function of Parliament and there is a general principle that 'redress of grievances' or, at least, their full and public representation must precede such grant. Hence the debates in Committee of Supply. The process must begin in and be finally determined by the House of Commons—a result of the struggle with the Lords which culminated in the argument over Mr Lloyd George's 'People's Budget' of 1910 and the Parliament Act of 1911 which virtually destroyed all the Lords' power over 'Money Bills' (as strictly defined by the Speaker). But all grants and taxes must be proposed by the Crown i.e. a Minister; M.P.s may decrease but not increase grants, though they may *argue* for such increase. This is why debates may seem unreal to outsiders; in order to discuss a particular item of expenditure there must be a motion to *reduce* it, though in the ensuing debate an increase is urged!

We shall not discuss the technical details of excess votes (for a year already completed), supplementary estimates (for the current year) or votes on account (to provide money before the final authorization of the Estimates), but concentrate upon the main financial procedures in one year which runs from 1 April to 31 March. Both the Committee of Supply and the Committee of Ways and Means are Committees of the whole House; the Speaker is not in the Chair and there is greater freedom of debate than in the House as such. The former sanctions expenditure by considering and approving the Estimates, but as we shall see, the debates are seldom devoted to financial matters as such; they are rather general policy debates and the Opposition chooses most of the subjects. The latter Committee authorizes the 'actual payment' to cover the Estimates through the Appropriation Bill(s) but also the raising of money through the Budget Debates and the Finance Bill.

Estimates are drawn up in the departments and the Treasury and presented to Parliament about February. Twenty-six days are allotted to debates in the Committee of Supply but a 'guillotine' to stop further debate for the time being must fall before March 31 so that the Government may be voted funds for the next financial year; the Committee of Ways and Means completes this stage by passing a Consolidated Fund Bill (the Fund being that into which all Government monies are paid and from which they are drawn on the appropriate authority). But taxation must also be authorized and in early April, usually, the Chancellor of the Exchequer introduces his Budget. Debates on the 'Budget Resolutions' and on the Finance Bill in which they are subsequently embodied are not subject to the '10 o'clock rule'—hence the all-night sittings such as those in 1965 which were particularly prolonged owing to the controversial nature of certain new tax proposals like the Corporation Tax. Yet not one change can be made in the tax proposals without the agreement of the Government, so long as its party majority holds, though some alterations have been accepted and some proposals withdrawn. The House is often thinly attended, only a few members being interested in any particular item, but so far all proposals to send even parts of the Finance Bill 'upstairs' to a committee have been rejected. Meanwhile the Committee of Supply continues to debate the Estimates

L

and some time in July or August, the Appropriation Bill, the final authorization of expenditure on the basis of the Estimates, is passed. Outsiders may find it difficult to understand why there should be two differently named Committees when, in fact both consist of the whole House but history is not easily rejected even to accommodate contemporary needs.

Further financial control—indeed, some would say the only real control—is provided by the Public Accounts Committee of fifteen members, usually under the chairmanship of a prominent Opposition member. With the assistance of the Comptroller and Auditor-General, an officer of the House, it examines the completed accounts in weekly meetings from February until the summer recess; it is said that officials are 'often in an acute and obvious state of nervousness.' The P.A.C. conducts a post-mortem on past expenditure, but its reports frequently suggest new procedures and practices which, if also backed by the Treasury, will subsequently be adopted by the departments. The Select Committee on Estimates is supposed to examine current expenditure, but apart from such exercises as seeking to discover reasons for variations between previous and current year's Estimates, it looks rather at certain aspects of administration and certain selected topics. It has, for example, examined the nature of 'Treasury Control', Recruitment to the Civil Service; the working of the University Grants Committee, the Ferranti contract, and many other topics in recent years. We refer to it again in our section on specialist committees.

How much does this 'control' amount to in practice? On the evidence of a large number of observers, not much! Many would echo Ramsay Muir's complaint of years ago that 'the power of the purse is supposed to be the main source of the authority of the House of Commons. It has become wholly unreal. There is no parliamentary country in the world in which Parliament has less power over finance than in Britain'. Sir Austen Chamberlain regarded the House as 'not an efficient body for checking expenditure. . . . It is quite true that one section of members calls for economy here and another section calls for economy there, and so on over the whole sphere, but at any given point there is always a majority for spending more, not less'. And this was before the days of the 'spendthrift Socialists'! Many years later, Sir Frank Tribe, a Comptroller and Auditor-General, opined that the number of back-benchers who consistently pressed economy in government had got smaller and smaller over the last twenty-five years. Every M.P. felt free to press for more expenditure and the 'financial conscience of the nation', shared in Gladstone's day by the whole House, was now left to the Government. This is partly due to the 'climate of opinion', partly due to the fact that social welfare schemes as well as defence requirements make inevitable long-term commitments such that expenditure cannot be controlled on an annual basis, while even three-year 'forward looks' cannot bring economies unless *policy* is changed. In addition, there is an organizational reason for lack of control: 'members must realize', as a civil servant wrote, 'that even 630 of them cannot hope to follow in detail the path of every penny of public money, and should therefore trust their 690,000 public servants to see to this, while they oversee policy. . . . There is no better safeguard for economy than an honest executive. . . . The integrity and carefulness of civil servants is beyond praise'. Though perhaps not always their skill in view of such examples as the negotiation of the Ferranti contract. We discuss Treasury Control in our section on the administration.

What of Campion's last function, the control and formulation of policy? In practice policy is formulated by the Government, subject to whatever circumstances and centres of power and influence must be taken into consideration. Nor is 'control' a realistic term to use for the role of the House of Commons, which acts rather as a critic, watchdog, and seeker of information than as a controller. As Professor Crick has said, 'control means influence, not direct power; advice, not command; criticism, not obstruction; scrutiny, not initiative; publicity, not secrecy'. There are ample procedures, up to a point, for this kind of 'control'. In the last resort, however, not only is the battle between executive and legislature fought out on unequal terms, with the dice loaded in favour of the former; even if this were not the case, party discipline would normally hold and the Government agree only to such modifications and remedies as were acceptable to it. However, something like forty per cent of a normal session is devoted to 'control'.

As mentioned, debates in Committee of Supply are devoted to criticisms of policy items, mostly raised by the Opposition. Particular votes may be put down so that the policy of the department concerned may be criticized, or the business of Supply may be taken formally and an Opposition Motion discussed. Then, each Session commences with the Queen's Speech outlining the Government's proposed legislation and policies; six days are devoted to a debate on the Address in Reply to the Queen's Speech, providing further opportunities for criticism and hostile amendments leading to a vote. There are also a considerable number of Adjournment Debates in which M.P.s may raise matters of interest and during which Ministers are expected to reply. These include the 'Half-hour adjournment' debates which take place at the end of each sitting even when the '10 o'clock rule' is suspended and the previous business continues for many hours longer and even into the next day. There are also 'holiday' adjournment debates when any number of topics may be raised, as well as adjournment debates held in place of 'substantive motions' in order to allow the House to range widely over a subject without being tied to the specific wording of a motion and without necessarily coming to a vote. The famous debate which led to the downfall of the Chamberlain Government in 1940 and brought Mr Churchill to power, took place on the innocuous motion 'that this House do now adjourn'; that so many Conservatives voted against the motion, while far more abstained, was taken as revealing a lack of confidence in the Government. Then there are 'urgency debates' under Standing Order No. 9, intended to allow the House to debate 'a definite matter of urgent public importance' even at the expense of the regular 'orders of the day'. This procedure, however, has become hedged about by so many restrictions that it is extremely difficult to persuade Mr Speaker to accept such a motion. The few which are allowed, however, can be extremely embarrassing to the Government and sometimes lead it to change its mind.

Finally, of course, there is Question Time, 'the grand inquest of the nation'. Undoubtedly the opportunity to ask forty or fifty questions a day from Monday to Thursday, together with a number of awkward supplementary questions, is an important weapon in the hands of M.P.s and a source of concern both to the Government and to the civil servants who prepare the answers and try to anticipate supplementaries. But no vote follows Questions (unless S.O. No. 9 is successfully cited) and giving notice of an attempt to 'raise the matter on the adjournment' depends on finding an opportunity to do so. The Government can ride the storm, provide evasive answers, or prolix and uninformative answers, or even plead that it is 'not in the public interest' to reply—though no Minister tries to get away with this too often. Moreover, Questions are often sent in well in advance and by the time they are answered have become stale; meanwhile more topical ones are kept off the order paper. Not all questions are reached in the forty-five minutes allowed and a written answer gets no publicity and, of course, no supplementaries can be asked. There are so many departments that a rota is arranged, which means that each has a turn only periodically. Not even all the Prime Minister's Questions are always reached. Questions may set in motion machinery for the remedy of minor grievances, although frequently to ask a Question indicates that the M.P. has failed to obtain satisfaction in private and is unlikely to do so in public. But they seldom alter matters of policy to which the Government is committed. Question Time in the British House of Commons is unparalleled anywhere else in the world; but, as we shall see, other legislatures may have more effective ways of 'getting at the Government'.

Some other points about the House of Commons at work are worth mentioning. The procedures we have outlined, whatever their limitations, are scrupulously adhered to by the House. Mr Speaker safeguards the interests of individuals and minorities and is strictly non-party. Although the first Labour Speaker was not elected until 1965 (there was, unusually, a contest in 1951) there have seldom been any but minor criticisms of Mr Speaker and these not in any way of a party nature. He sees to it that all views are expressed, preserves dignity and order, and the Opposition can rely on him for scrupulously fair treatment. Moreover, the customs, conventions and standing orders of the House are respected in such a way as to give ample opportunity for M.P.s, including the Opposition. In a normal session the Government will take not much more than forty-five per cent of the time of the House, while over thirty per cent is allocated to 'Opposition business'. Of the rest, perhaps fifteen per cent is 'indeterminate', being taken up with business which derives neither from Government or Opposition; the rest, except for certain periods, is given up to Private Members' business.

It is true that Governments can and do take Private Members' time but they would never interfere with Opposition time. Apart from Supply Days and other regular opportunities, it is understood that time will always be found for a formal censure debate, though the Government may seek compensation in the form of agreed time for its own business. All these arrangements are made 'though the usual channels' i.e. the Chief Whips on either side. There are, it is true various ways in which debate may be curtailed apart from Mr Speaker's right to prevent irrelevance and 'tedious repetition'. The number of amendments to a Bill to be discussed may be reduced by the 'Kangaroo', but it is Mr Speaker or his Deputy who 'jumps over' certain amendments *not* to suit the Government's convenience but so that all the important points may be discussed without unnecessary repetition. The calling of an amendment may have unforseen results: during the debate on the Beveridge Report during the war, a critical amendment to the Government's motion of welcome was, after some pressure, called; the subsequent debate appeared to reveal the Conservatives as lukewarm about implementing the Report while Labour members under Mr Aneurin Bevan led the attack. Some have argued that this helped to define an important issue and may have influenced the results of the 1945 Election. The closure may be moved by a Minister during a debate but it will not be granted by Mr Speaker unless he is satisfied that the debate has continued long enough for all important views to be aired. Finally, there is the guillotine or 'closure by compartment', by which a time-table is laid down for discussions on each stage of the Bill and for the taking of votes. The guillotine is normally used only if an agreed Time Table cannot be drawn up. There is inevitably an outcry from the Opposition, but it has not been unknown for M.P.s to spend overmuch time on earlier sections in order to claim that insufficient time was left for the rest. It is part of the normal parliamentary game for the Government to accuse the Opposition of 'obstruction' and for the Opposition to cry 'gag;' Independent students of Parliament have broadly come to the conclusion that most guillotine arrangements provide reasonable time for discussion if M.P.s use the time reasonably, and that there is little difference between the two major parties in the extent to which they use the procedure.

Some account must be given of the most widely canvassed suggestion in recent years for enabling M.P.s to exercise more effective scrutiny and supervision over government activities. This is the suggestion for specialist committees. We have referred to the Public Accounts Committee, the Estimates Committee and the Scrutiny Committee and deal later with the Select Committee on the Nationalized Industries. The Standing Committees on Bills, as we have seen, are not specialized, and there is no comprehensive system of permanent committees specializing in the different branches of the public service with statutory or conventional rights to question, criticize, and be consulted by ministers and officials and to have their opinions considered by the legislature. Campion records that the House has generally concluded 'that such bodies cannot be really important unless they are given control of policy, that to control policy they require to be able to initiate expenditure, and that if they are given control of policy and the initiative in expenditure, they cannot fail more or less to duplicate the functions of ministerial departments, and thus produce an undesirable division of government responsibility'. But no one has ever seriously suggested that committees should 'control' policy or 'initiate' expenditure. Campion himself, as an experienced Clerk to the House, has said that 'it does not seem beyond the wit of man to devise a committee system which, while retaining the essentially subordinate and advisory character of committees, might make the House of Commons more generally capable of informed criticism'.

We cannot deal in detail with the prolonged arguments which have ranged over this problem for many years nor with the constitutional objections which have been raised to the proposed reform. We state only that for the first time in the history of Parliament a Select Committee on Procedure in 1965 did at last make some recommendations which tended in the direction of specialist committees. The most important of these, however, that the terms of reference of the Estimates Committee should be slightly extended to read 'to examine how the Departments of State carry out their responsibilities and to consider their Estimates of Expenditure and Report', was not accepted by the Government, although the proverbial 'open mind' was kept. The Estimates Committee was, however, empowered, if it wished, to 'function through Sub-Committees specializing in the various spheres of governmental activity' with its existing terms of reference. It was also encouraged to believe that it might have the services of more Clerks and some specialist assistance. Some M.P.s fear that the role of the House might be diminished and its debates become less significant if committees were given real powers, although the purpose of such committees is to bring more knowledge to such debates. Others fear that the responsibility of Ministers might be undermined, although this would surely depend on the Minister and, in any case, the Government would always have a majority on each committee; moreover, it is well known that existing committees have little influence unless they are unanimous. However, in the Procedure Debate in October 1965, there did seem to be more support than ever before for at least a 'controlled experiment', as one M.P. put it, along the lines of specialist committees. Most important, perhaps, was the general feeling that by whatever method, the influence of the House vis-à-vis the Executive must be 'restored' lest Parliament, like the monarchy before it, become a 'dignified' rather than an 'efficient' part of the Constitution.

We conclude this section with a brief account of the essential role of the House of Commons. 'The function of Parliament is not to govern but to criticize, not to control the Government, but to act as a forum for criticism and a focus of outside opinion'. Thus, Sir Ivor Jennings. Moreover, its criticism is directed not so much towards a fundamental modification of the Government's policy, though it may achieve some changes of detail, as towards the education of public opinion. 'The Government governs and the Opposition criticizes', though back-benchers on the Government side may also criticize. As we noted earlier, both Laski and Bagehot, though widely separated in time and political outlook, postulated as the first function of the House of Commons the making and sustaining of a Government with the initiative in legislation and policy.

The Government exists because it has a majority in the House of Commons; it is a party Government whose strength derives from the maximum vote it can obtain when the Whips are on. In theory, the House of Commons controls the Government, the latter is responsible to the former; the House could refuse supplies or refuse to pass essential annual legislation like the Army and Air Force Act. In practice, through the party system the Government controls the House. An M.P. is returned to support a party; if the Government suffers a chance defeat it can compel the House to reverse the decision, as Mr Churchill did in 1943 over an unexpected vote in favour of equal pay for women teachers which the Government opposed. In the last resort the Government has the weapon of dissolution, though loyalty is a more important factor than fear of threats. Support, indeed, is not so much due to strict party discipline; even in the Labour Party the appearance of strictness is greater than the reality. The main point is that an M.P. does not wish to see his party defeated and this applies also to the electors who supported him.

There is, however, no Government dictatorship. The majority must be treated with respect and given reasonably full information in response to questions. The Government must keep its majority not only in the House but at the next election. M.P.s are the link with constituency opinion and must be listened to with respect— despite the cynical comment that an M.P. 'sits on the fence with both ears to the ground'! Even the strongest Governments have been known to bow to 'the sense of the House', especially when it is clear that this expresses a strong public opinion. 'Management', Sir Ivor Jennings has said, 'is often nothing more than an ability to make concessions gracefully'.

Ultimately, however, the Government governs. The House of Commons is a deliberative and not a governing body. Two statements which emphasize this viewpoint are worth quoting. Gladstone told the House when it was considering Roebuck's Motion to set up a committee of inquiry into the conduct of the Crimean War, 'your business is not to govern the country, but it is, if you think fit, to call to account those who do govern it'. At greater length and with typical Cockney emphasis, Mr Herbert Morrison told the Select Committee on Procedure in 1946, 'I say it is the Government that is responsible (for executive current administration). It is responsible to Parliament. . . . Parliament's business is to check the Government, throw it out if it wants to, go for it, attack it, criticize it, by all means, but Parliament is not a body organized for current administration, not in this country'.

Sir Ivor Jennings has again developed this point. 'If Parliament's main function is to criticize, the Opposition is its most important part. . . . Democratic government demands not only a Parliamentary majority but also a Parliamentary minority. . . . If there be no Opposition, there is no democracy'. The House must attack the Government in general and individual Ministers, it must act as a check on corrupt or inefficient administration, it must attempt to prevent individual injustices. There must be a recognition by both sides that the Government governs openly and honestly and that it is prepared to meet criticism not by secret police and concentration camps but by rational argument. All these features can be seen in the organization of Parliament. There is a Shadow Cabinet, and Her Majesty's Opposition is Her Majesty's Alternative Government. The Leader of the Opposition has a salary and a recognized status. The Parliamentary game is played according to certain rules and most people would agree that it is bad to have snap votes, to refuse requests for 'pairs' (to enable M.P.'s of each side to be absent) and, as it was argued in 1965, to refuse some relief to the sick from the necessity to attend merely to vote when their vote is a foregone conclusion. Nevertheless, there has been a great increase in the power of the Executive and a relative diminution in the authority of the House. To this we return later.

The *House of Lords* in action is a very different body from its usual text-book description. It has some nine hundred hereditary members, two archbishops, twenty-four bishops, nineteen Law Lords (who together with the Lord Chancellor and any ex-Lord Chancellors constitute the House of Lords as the highest Court of Appeal) and, since 1958, some fifty Life Peers. It is possible, however, for an hereditary peer under certain conditions to renounce his title, as Mr Wedgwood Benn, Sir Alec Douglas Home, Mr Quintin Hogg and others have done. Even of the hereditary peerages more than half have been created since 1880 and about two hundred and fifty of the peers as a whole are either first holders i.e. made hereditary peers fairly recently or appointed for life. The average number voting in a division is about eighty, though even this exaggerates the normal attendance since it is swollen by a few large divisions on such matters as the Parliament Bill, commercial television, capital punishment and the Rents Bills. Of these eighty about one-third are first holders or appointed and the peers in this category do about half of the work of the House. The eighty are not always the same but less than three hundred and fifty peers ever attend at all. It is possible to obtain 'leave of absence' (normally indicating an intention not to participate in the work of the House); but no reform proposals involving the complete exclusion of the hereditary element have come near to acceptance.

Bagehot once remarked that the cure for admiration for the House of Lords was to go and see it. What are the functions of the Lords? They conduct general debates which are often good; they are short, few peers normally participate and these usually with relevant experience, they are less partisan. The best debates are educative, or would be if they were effectively publicized. Yet it has been said with some truth that there is as much nonsense and boredom in the Lords as in the Commons! Non-controversial Bills can be introduced first into the Lords and may have an easier passage in the Commons if they have been fully discussed. The members of the Lords may introduce their own Bills but this is comparatively rare and the Bills are sometimes silly and sometimes destructive if deliberately designed to go against declared Government policy. Even *The Economist* has disapproved attempts to introduce major controversial legislation. On the other hand, the passage of Lord Arran's Bill to legalize homosexual practices in private between consenting male adults may suggest that the Lords can be more progressive than the Commons. Moreover, the Lords in 1965 at last passed the Bill to abolish capital punishment which it had for so long resisted. The Lords also get through a great deal of committee work; they deal with Private Bills, Provisional Orders, special orders, statutory instruments, and relieve the Commons of much work. It has been suggested, however, that this might be done as well by a House of Commons Committee or even by the General Council of the Bar.

The most controversial function of the Lords is its consideration of major Bills and the possibility of amending or rejecting them after receipt from the Commons. Many amendments, as we saw, are made at the Government's suggestion to fulfil undertakings given in the Commons or to tidy up legislation which is sometimes hurried through in the Commons. The real problem arises when the Lords seek to make amendments of substance which go contrary to Government policy. They may even seek to force an election 'so that public opinion may be consulted', though it is difficult to see on what grounds an hereditary and appointed Chamber can claim to force the elected representatives of the people to appeal to the people! In the period 1868–1945 the Lords rejected twenty-seven Bills and 'mutilated' twenty-six others; only two of these were Conservative Bills. From 1945–1951 the Lords attempted serious amendments to the Gas, Electricity, Transport, and Town and Country Planning Bills and insisted that the Iron and Steel Bill should not come into operation until after another election. Until 1911 there was no remedy against this kind of action save the creation of peers—or a threat of this, which sufficed in 1911 to persuade the Lords to pass the Parliament Bill. This removed the control of the Lords over Money Bills and reduced its powers over other Bills to a delay of two years. In 1949 this was reduced further to one year.

The House of Lords as at present constituted inevitably has a large Conservative majority, even when the 'backwoodsmen' do not turn up to defeat a—to them—particularly obnoxious proposal. A Liberal or Labour Government between 1911 and 1949 could get no major Bills through against the opposition of the Lords in the last two sessions of a Parliament. Since 1949 no major Bill similarly opposed can, because of the Lords' delaying power, get through in the last session. It has been argued that a good political machine needs a brake as well as an accelerator. But the brake has normally been applied only with a 'radical' driver. The Lords frequently claim that it may be desirable to ensure second thoughts or 'further consultation of the people' but the point again arises as to what authority the Lords have to decide when this is necessary. The Conservative Rents Bill of 1958 caused at least as much outcry in the country as many Labour proposals but no effort was made to secure 'further consideration'. Perhaps the Lords might reply that a group of Conservative back-benchers in the Commons were doing just this. This is true but does not explain why the matter cannot be left to the Commons even with a Labour Government—except on the argument that the country needs protection only from possible Labour excesses and not from Conservative. This, of course, is a valid *political* argument, albeit clearly partisan; it can have no *constitutional* validity.

We cannot discuss in detail the various proposals which have been made for reform except to say that they have foundered mainly on the question of powers; even proposals to improve the composition of the Lords have in some quarters raised the fear that this enhanced prestige might cause too frequent a use of existing powers. Unicameralism has never received wide support in Britain despite the aphorism of the Abbé Sièyes that 'if the Second Chamber agrees with the first it is superfluous, if it disagrees it is obnoxious'. Since October 1964, the Lords have carried several amendments against Government wishes but throughout the first session of the current Parliament, when the Commons have 'insisted' upon their version, the Lords have withdrawn. Those who seem to encourage the Lords to harry a Labour Government are likely to be faced either with abolition or a serious curtailment of existing powers. Should such issue not be joined it is probable that the policy of the Labour party will continue to be one of 'let sleeping dogs lie'. This, however, does not suit those who, like Lord Salisbury, believe in the necessity of a strong Second Chamber, since if dogs sleep for too long they may never awaken again!

The Monarchy has diminished in power and political influence even more than the Lords since the days when Bagehot thought it a wonderful thing that people should be so interested in a retired widow and an elderly man-about-town. It still remains true, as Laski said, that 'the metaphysics of limited monarchy do not easily lend themselves to critical discussion'. But, however briefly, we must attempt the task.

Most of the monarch's functions are formal. She is present at Privy Council Meetings (themselves little but a formality) when the most important kinds of delegated legislation are passed. She appoints the Prime Minister and other ministers, ambassadors, judges, military, naval, and air force officers and senior civil servants. She creates peers and confers honours (very few, of which the Order of the Garter is an outstanding example, on her own responsibility). The judges are Her Majesty's Judges and she exercises the prerogative of mercy. She summons, prorogues, and dissolves Parliament. Her assent is needed to legislation. But in nearly every case these functions are performed on the advice of a minister (or are dictated by political circumstances) though where a formal act is required she can ask for explanations and give advice and may even record her misgivings and reluctance. As Sir Ivor Jennings has said, 'while the Queen's personal prerogative is maintained in theory it can hardly be exercised in practice'.

The Royal Assent to legislation has not been refused since 1707; it is as dead as Queen Anne. The summoning, proroguing, and dissolution of Parliament are normally done on the advice of the Prime Minister. When in October 1965, it was decided to *adjourn* rather than prorogue Parliament in case a hurried recall was necessitated by the Rhodesian crisis, it was the Prime Minister who made the decision. The circumstances in which it has been speculated that a dissolution might be refused are too remote to deserve discussion here. As the standard work on constitutional law by Wade and Philips states, 'it has for some time been a convention of the constitution that the Queen will dissolve Parliament at the request of the Prime Minister of the day'. As to the suggestion by a constitutional historian that no one 'can doubt that, in the very last resort and *in extremis*, it is to Her Majesty alone that the people can look for the ultimate guardianship of the Constitution', such a situation postulates the breakdown of constitutional government, and, possibly, the end of the monarchy. The choice of Prime Minister is usually obvious; it must be the leader of the majority party, though we still do not know whether, if a Conservative Prime Minister were to retire or die when in office, the party would elect a leader before anyone would accept a summons to form a Government, as the Labour Party have stated would be their procedure. In any event, royal influence over the choice would be negligible and would have to conform to political realities. In the appointment of other Ministers the Prime Minister has a free hand; Mr Attlee firmly scotched the rumour that the King had any influence over the last minute switch of Mr Dalton from the Foreign Office to the Exchequer and of Mr Ernest Bevin the other way.

In so far as royal prerogative powers exist independently of Parliament, this is because Parliament has not seen fit to regulate them. Any Act of Parliament may destroy, modify or impliedly supersede the prerogative; new powers are always created by statute and prerogative powers cannot be restored or added to. Where they continue to exist they are, in fact, a weapon in the hands of the Government, not of the monarch. Such powers include the declaration of war and peace, the signing of treaties, the recognition of other States and Governments (e.g. the recognition of the Pekin Government of China), the appointment of diplomatic representatives.

We are left, then with Bagehot's 'right to be consulted, right to encourage, right to warn'. Sir Ivor Jennings considers that informal advice is more effective than writing a memorandum, but the effect of the advice will depend upon the length of period on the throne, interest in and capacity for work, and similar imponderable factors. Moreover, as Bagehot emphasized, it is unreasonable to expect the monarch to be more than an ordinary man—and A. J. P. Taylor has suggested that a woman on the throne probably has less influence. We cannot discuss in detail the occasions on which it has been surmised that various monarchs may have exercised an influence over decisions. In general, it is firmly established that in any case the Prime Minister has the last word; if he accepts advice he does so because he wishes and not because he is compelled.

To return to the 'metaphysics', far more important today than the power and influence of the monarch in political affairs, are the 'dignified and ceremonial' functions. The monarchy is a focus for patriotism and an example of voluntary service. The Queen is the personification of 'the State', a term relatively unfamiliar in British political science; we prefer 'the Crown', 'the impersonal, immortal, symbol of ultimate unity and continuity of purpose'. (Whereas in the U.S. trials are designated as 'The State' or 'The People' against 'X', in Britain it is 'Regina'). This applies also to the 'Headship of the Commonwealth' which in the Republics has no constitutional significance at all and in the 'realms' no more significance than in Britain. Mr Wilson's advice to the Queen to write direct to Mr Smith during the Rhodesian crisis in 1965— for even if we speculate that it *may* have been her idea it could not have been carried out except 'on advice'—simply called into play the tradition of loyalty to 'the Crown' as an element in the argument. That the message was written in the Queen's own hand was simply part of 'the metaphysics' of an appeal to a leader who persisted in proclaiming a desire to remain loyal to the throne even though he considered that circumstances might necessitate a unilateral declaration of independence which, however glossed over, must constitute treason—to 'the Crown'.

Some years ago the *Observer* carried an article which is most apposite as the conclusion of this section. Monarchy can represent, express and affect the aspirations of 'the collective sub-conscious'. The existence of a constitutional monarch, by satisfying profound emotional needs, leaves the business of government to proceed in a quieter, more sober and more rational atmosphere. The Government can be criticized and dismissed; it is protected by no aura of sanctity. The monarch is an archetypal figure, she can 'do no wrong' not merely legally but psychologically (except on rare occasions like that of the Abdication Crisis in 1936, in which case it was even easier to change the incumbent of the throne than on the earlier occasions when Charles I and James II had to be dealt with more forcibly). The monarchy is a safeguard both against uncontrolled empiricism guided by no principles at all—and dictatorship.

2

Cabinet Government

The people may be the 'political sovereign' and Parliament the 'legal sovereign' in Britain but to the simple question 'who runs this show?' the most accurate answer would be 'the Cabinet and the administration'. From 6 August to 25 October 1965, Parliament did not meet. But the 'Queen's Government' continued to deal with a series of important problems as well as to manage the day-to-day affairs of the country. Mr Wilson negotiated about independence for Rhodesia and Mr Brown published the National Plan to the accompaniment of press and television comment but with no parliamentary probing. There is no Parliament between dissolution and the meeting of the newly elected House, but the Cabinet continues in existence. We begin to see why Sir Ivor Jennings described the Cabinet as 'the core of the British con-stitutional system'.

There is, of course, no separation of powers between the legis-lature and the executive. Indeed, in Bagehot's words the Cabinet is an instrument for linking the executive to the legislative branch of government. When Mr Patrick Gordon Walker was defeated in Smethwick he was nonetheless appointed as Foreign Secretary but his defeat at Leyton made his resignation inevitable unless he was made a peer, since by convention all Ministers must normally

M

be Members of Parliament. Mr Wilson's Cabinet included only two members of the House of Lords, the Lord Chancellor and the Lord Privy Seal, who was leader of the Lords; five other Ministers were in the Lords as were eight Parliamentary Secretaries. Laski described the Cabinet as essentially a group drawn from that party or coalition of parties which can command a majority in the House of Commons in whose name it governs.

The normal size of the Cabinet in the twentieth century is between sixteen and twenty-three, the last being the size of Mr Wilson's Cabinet, larger than Sir Alec Douglas Home's which Mr Wilson had described as too large. As we shall see, however, there is always some sort of 'inner cabinet', though not necessarily including the same persons all the time. Many important departments are left out of the Cabinet: in 1965 the Ministries of Health, Pensions and National Insurance, Public Buildings and Works, Aviation, Land and Natural Resources, and the Postmaster-General were thus excluded, as well as the Chief Secretary to the Treasury and two Ministers without Portfolio i.e. without departments. This was apart from three Service Ministers (one a Deputy-Secretary) who were represented in the Cabinet by the Defence Secretary, fourteen Ministers of State who were assigned to various departments for particular purposes or to give general assistance to the Ministers in charge, and the four Law Officers, thirty-one Ministers in all. There are, of course, a number of Parliamentary Secretaries.

The size of the Cabinet depends to some extent on the personal preference of the Prime Minister, but he is guided by the need to include as many of the leading members of his party as possible and to represent the various groups and shades of opinion; by the convenience of having a reasonable number of reliable friends and close supporters; by the need to achieve adequate co-ordination between departments; and by the desirability of avoiding friction and jealousy between the 'ins' and the 'outs' as well as to silence potential critics. It has been suggested that the last factor may have influenced Mr Wilson to include such members as Mr Frank Cousins, Mr Anthony Greenwood and Mrs Barbara Castle. The separate 'communities' expect to be represented, hence the inclusion of the Secretary of State for Scotland and a new Secretary of State for Wales. Certain high officers of State are almost invariably included, for example the Foreign Secretary, the Chancellor of the Exchequer (excluded for a time during World War II), the Lord Chancellor, the Defence Secretary, the Commonwealth Secretary. Others may be in or out according to their general ability or the importance of their department at any given time. When Mr. Churchill at first excluded the Ministry of Education in 1951 it was felt that this demoted education as a subject of importance and pressure changed this decision. Ministers not in the Cabinet may, of course, be brought into Cabinet or Cabinet Committee discussions as required.

Finally, there are always a number of Ministers in the Cabinet who are not in charge of departments; they may have seniority or possess special qualities and are used as general advisers to the Prime Minister, Chairmen of Cabinet Committees, or to oversee certain important spheres of government. There are some traditional sinecure offices for this purpose such as that of Lord President of the Council (in 1965 also the Leader of the House of Commons), the Chancellor of the Duchy of Lancaster (in 1965 charged with long-term planning for the whole of the social services), the Lord Privy Seal (in 1965 Leader of the House of Lords), as well as Ministers without Portfolio and the Paymaster-General (making three in 1965 but not in the Cabinet). In recent years it has been customary to designate a Deputy Prime Minister; in 1965 this was Mr George Brown, First Secretary of State and Secretary of State for Economic Affairs.

So far as the actual personnel of the Cabinet is concerned, the Prime Minister as we stated, has an absolutely free hand. Whatever influence the monarch may have is entirely due to the willingness of the Prime Minister to listen to advice; the time has long since passed when Queen Victoria could keep Sir Charles Dilke out of the Cabinet because of his divorce, or refer scathingly to such 'unhistoric names' as Bryce and Morley; George V is said to have had some misgivings about his first Labour Ministers in 1924 but appears to have become easily reconciled—even to the extent of being amused (in very un-Victorian fashion) at Mr J. H.

(Jimmy) Thomas's description of a colleague as 'a bloody 'ell 'ound, Sire'!

The burden on Cabinet Ministers has increased tremendously in recent years. To deal with numerous departmental matters, committee work, the demands of Parliament, party organizations and the constituencies, with a wide variety of important Cabinet decisions involving immense magnitude of choice and responsibility, involves not only work but worry—the latter, according to Sir Ivor Jennings, being what 'ages Cabinet Ministers—though some are an unconscionable time a-dying'. As long ago as 1950 the *Economist* referred to 'the very great growth in the volume and complexity of the business arising before the higher ranks of government. The most urgent need in the further development of British administrative methods is to find some way in which the intolerable burden on a man who combines the role of policy-maker, executive, parliamentarian and constituency representative can be reduced. Personal fatigue may atrophy power of decision'. Some parliamentary relief might be provided by making it unnecessary for Ministers to be on call in the House to spend time tramping through the division lobbies yet in 1965 it still seemed uncertain whether the simple remedy of proxy voting would be accepted. It is true that the Cabinet normally meets only two or three times a week for a total of six to eight hours but this takes no account of special meetings, committees and other commitments which are probably as burdensome and more time-consuming. Above all, there is little time for forward thinking and planning, a problem which has led to suggestions for a smaller Cabinet and a better division of labour.

During various periods in World Wars I and II a smaller Cabinet was, in fact, appointed; in 1916 a body of five in which only one member had a department and from 1939–45 a body of eight. Partly as a result of these precedents Mr Amery has argued for a similar Cabinet in peace-time. A Cabinet of twenty over-worked Ministers, he believed, is incapable of thinking out definite policy or of securing its effective and consistent application. General policy is hardly discussed and the Cabinet 'is little more than a standing conference of departmental chiefs'. Nor does an elaborate

Committee system meet the need; the framing of policy should be separated from routine day-to-day administration. There should be a Cabinet of six, free from ordinary departmental duties, which would deal with current administration by bringing departmental Ministers directly concerned into Committees chaired by a Cabinet Minister. There would also be a group of standing committees for the study of policy in the main fields of government, each with its own research and planning staff. The Prime Minister would be chairman but each would have a Deputy Chairman. This Cabinet Minister would be more than a mere co-ordinator; he would be 'the recognized policy Minister for his group of departments, with the knowledge and authority derived from his regular handling of his subject matter both on current affairs committees and standing policy committees and would have his own staff behind him'.

Despite the frequent emergence of an informal 'inner cabinet' and the occasional use of 'overlords', the formal arrangements suggested by Amery have found no more support than the less drastic proposals of the Haldane Committee on the Machinery of Government which in 1918 suggested grouping departments into ten major units and keeping the size of the Cabinet down to this number. As to Amery's scheme it is doubtful if policy and administration can be separated so easily. 'He who has in his hands the execution of measures is in very truth the master of them', wrote Sir Henry Taylor in a little nineteenth century handbook, *The Statesman*. 'The distinction . . . between policy and administration, though attractive in theory is illusive in practice', wrote Mr D. N. Chester from both practical experience and academic study, an opinion shared by Sir John Anderson based on experience both as a civil servant and as Lord President of the Council in World War II. Nor is it feasible that policy Ministers should control a group of departments whose Ministers have the mastery of their daily work. Anderson, as a man of quite exceptional abilities and background, a 'pastmaster of the art of the Whitehall game', independent of party, and working in a coalition government in war-time, managed it. But this is exceptional. Moreover, if the Cabinet Minister were given his own staff there would be a strain on the departmental loyalties of officials, and Ministers with such staffs would 'generate friction everywhere'. There is also the question of responsibility. When Mr Churchill appointed certain 'overlords' in 1951 Mr Gaitskell questioned him closely about this; eventually, though not for this reason alone, he abandoned the system. Indeed, he stated the personal case against such 'supervising Ministers' in his preference for 'a definite task to that exalted brooding over the work of others which may well be the lot of a Minister, however influential, who has no department'. Finally, the smaller the Cabinet the greater the political problem of deciding who to exclude.

How the Cabinet actually works is, of course, not easy to discover. We shall attempt to estimate the role of the Prime Minister, the place of Cabinet Committees, and the functions of the Secretariat and conclude with some general observations. As Laski has put it, 'the keystone of the Cabinet arch is the *Prime Minister*'. Many developments in recent years have tended to increase his authority. A General Election is really a choice of Prime Minister. He chooses his Ministers, determines who shall be in his Cabinet, reshuffles his Ministers and forces resignations: in 1962 Mr Macmillan sacked one-third of his Cabinet overnight, having earlier described even the resignation of Mr Thorneycroft as Chancellor of the Exchequer, as well as of Mr Enoch Powell and Mr Nigel Birch, as 'a little local difficulty'. We refer later to the power of dissolution. The Prime Minister's power depends on the status of the office, the nature of his party, and his own personality; the first of these is most important. The change from being a Cabinet Minister to being Prime Minister is not merely a change of place but of climate. In Mr Churchill's words 'he enters the stratosphere'; he becomes telescopically distinct from his colleagues and microscopically near to the public. There is a tremendous latent power in the Prime Minister's appearance on television when he normally speaks as head of the nation not of a party—a point made in respect of Mr Wilson's television appearances over the Rhodesia crisis in 1965. This also applies to his publicized relations with the Queen when he is clearly seen to be 'the national leader'.

In addition to ministerial appointments the Prime Minister is consulted as to the filling of the most important official posts such as Permanent Secretaries; he is, of course, First Lord of the Treasury. He arbitrates between departments and decides the pattern of committees. Though he has a small personal staff, the Cabinet Office really works for him and he decides on the Agenda for Cabinet meetings. It is in these meetings that the office really makes the man, though, of course, in the context of his personality. Mr Attlee appeared to the general public as mild and diffident, but as *The Economist* commented in 1950, 'in Whitehall the Prime Minister is a figure almost unrecognizably different from the Mr Attlee whom the public and even Parliament know'. This is almost as certainly true of Mr Macmillan, far from the 'Edwardian dandy' behind the scenes, and of Sir Alec Douglas Home whose public image revealed him as more fitted to be the chairman of a very rural County Council—just as someone said that Neville Chamberlain would have made a good Lord Mayor of Birmingham in a lean year!—but who undoubtedly 'ran' his team.

With perhaps some deliberate exaggeration, the Prime Minister has been described as 'an elected monarch', the real ruler of the country. With a majority in the House of Commons he can make laws without fear of defeat in Parliament—except in the unusual circumstances of 1964 and perhaps only then through ill-luck rather than revolt. He can exercise the 'royal' prerogative by declaring war, conducting diplomacy, or even authorizing the Home Office to 'tap telephones'. We have seen that the Queen is bound to accept advice. Any limits to his power are 'prudential' not 'constitutional'. He need normally fear little revolt in the Cabinet, witness Mr Eden over Suez where he was defeated by outside circumstances and illness not by the opposition of his colleagues despite misgivings on the part of some. This is true even if he attempts to control other departments as both Macmillan and Home did in foreign affairs and the former also in Treasury matters, and as Mr Wilson is said to do in respect of both the Treasury and the Department of Economic Affairs. He has a wide and imprecise mandate from the people, perhaps broadly just 'to govern' and the only alternative is another Prime Minister.

In this connection we should look especially at the significance of the power to advise a dissolution of Parliament. To Mr Attlee this power was 'essential' even though not wielded, since 'some of the most effective weapons are among the least used'. Yet it seems that dissolution has never been used to assert 'intra-party' discipline. Moreover, as such, it would be a weapon that cut both ways since the Prime Minister's office is put in jeopardy. In thirty-two dissolutions since 1833 the Prime Minister has lost office eighteen times; seven out of eleven since 1918. Even when he has not lost his majority he has been weakened since on only four occasions since 1833 has he increased his party strength. This makes the Conservative record of increasing its majority at each election in 1951, 1955 and 1959, the more noteworthy. On the other hand, on average, four-fifths of the M.P.s in the Prime Minister's party have retained their seats, nor has it always been the 'rebels' who have lost theirs. The real weapon in the Prime Minister's hands is his power to insist upon the withdrawal of the party whip if appeals to loyalty utterly fail. As we saw, party discipline is fundamentally due to the acceptance of popular sovereignty within a framework of parliamentary representative government; parties not individuals are voted for by the electorate. The important aspect of dissolution is the Prime Minister's ability, within limits, to choose a time for dissolution which he considers most favourable to his own and his party's fortune. Sir Alec Douglas Home hung on in 1964 in the face of unfavourable polls and a widespread feeling that the country needed an end of uncertainty, and nearly won in 1964. On the other hand, seven dissolutions of the last nine have taken place when Parliament was near the end of its five-year term.

The Cabinet could not get through its work without some division of labour. This is the reason for the growth during and since World War I of a system of *Cabinet Committees* to reduce 'the apoplexy at the centre and the anaemia at the extremities which normally affect Leviathan ... by a committee diet', as Professor Smellie has put it. Up to 1939 there appeared to be up to twenty Cabinet Committees in any one year. Most of them were for particular and limited subjects, though some became

Standing Committees and 'vital parts of the permanent though hidden mechanisms of our working constitution'. Hidden, because the structure and working of the Cabinet remains one of the hidden places of the Constitution and, for obvious constitutional reasons, the pattern has never been actually described. As Mr Herbert Morrison wrote, 'the Cabinet as a whole must be responsible for everything that happens. . . . How the Cabinet does its business and to what extent it delegates certain things to Cabinet Committees is . . . the Cabinet's business because it accepts responsibility'. Sir John Anderson echoed these sentiments by asserting that 'the unity of the Cabinet on which sane government depends is only possible if it can resolve its differences in secret'.

We have, however, some general knowledge of the system, which usually involves organization in two layers, ministerial and official, though the two are not always kept separate in actual practice. Before World War II, for example, there were the Committee of Imperial Defence and a Home Affairs Committee which became a sort of Legislative Committee concerned with planning the session, looking at draft Bills and at parliamentary business in general. The War Cabinets worked through a system of committees, one of which, under Churchill, the Lord President's Committee, was 'almost a parallel Cabinet concerned with home affairs.' Mr Morrison provided a great deal of information about the Labour Governments of 1945 to 1951 in his 'Government and Parliament'. High powered committees included Defence; the Lord President's Committee; a Social Services Committee; a Committee on Manpower; two Committees on Legislation, one to oversee the general progress of the legislative programme during the session and the other on Future Legislation; and, from 1947, an Economic Policy Committee and a Production Committee. At various times there were at least seventeen other committees. Doubtless there have been changes between 1951 and 1965 but there is equally no doubt that more and more use has and will be made of committees.

The greater the division of labour in the Cabinet, the greater the use made of committees, the more need is there for effective co-ordination. This cannot be done merely at the political level.

Accordingly we examine briefly the expanding role of the *Secretariat* or *Cabinet Office*. It is fascinating to recall that in the latter part of the nineteenth century Lord Salisbury could still speak of the absence of records as 'a fundamental requirement of the Cabinet system'. This was because the flow of suggestions in Cabinet meetings must attain 'the freedom and fullness which belong to private conversations; members must feel themselves untrammelled by any consideration of consistency in the past or self-justification in the future.' But there have been many examples of the consequences of this attitude; on one occasion two Ministers apparently asked Lord Hartington's Private Secretary what decision had been taken in the Cabinet. Lord Hartington had to get his secretary to inquire of Mr Gladstone 'what the devil was decided for he be damned if he knows'! And this on a matter which caused John Bright's resignation! Up to 1916 there was no agenda and no order of business and no record of proceedings save the Prime Minister's confidential letter to the monarch. Ministers went away frequently thinking decisions had been taken but which, in fact, had not, or which were repudiated by their colleagues; sometimes they were unaware that a particular decision affected their departments and civil servants, as a result, were in a similar state of ignorance.

In 1916, however, the secretariat of the Committee of Imperial Defence was taken over by the Cabinet and despite attempts to revert to the old lack of system it has remained and developed. At one time it had both a Statistical Office and an Economic Section, though the latter was transferred to the Treasury. Agenda papers are now circulated in advance, minutes are kept, decisions are recorded and notified to Ministers and departments concerned. There is a Secretary to the Cabinet and it is at this level that there is the most effective fusion between ministers and civil service. This growing role of the Cabinet Secretariat, together with the growth of patronage available to the Prime Minister within a greatly expanded administrative system, is a large part of the explanation of the Prime Minister's enhanced power.

Descriptions of the machinery of government such as we have attempted do not tell the whole story, but anything further must be based largely on speculation. With this caveat, however, the reader may be interested in such speculation on the working of the Cabinet. From the start it would seem likely that in a Cabinet selected on the basis described there must be many occasions when Ministers are not of one mind on important issues in private. In policy making there must be disagreements in the Cabinet, especially when there is dispute between the spending departments and the Treasury, though not all other inter-departmental disputes by any means are settled without Cabinet intervention. Sometimes the results if not the precise nature of these disputes are revealed by ministerial resignations, usually of the spending Ministers as with Mr Aneurin Bevan, though of the Chancellor of the Exchequer in Mr Thorneycroft's case.

Matters on which the political parties feel strongly will be decided at Cabinet level or by a few senior Ministers. But many measures derive in large part from the civil service and involve various interested groups. Decisions may be made at a lower level and in Committees to which powers have been delegated. The Prime Minister himself may decide between different points of view, perhaps in consultation with a few Ministers. Even if the Cabinet ultimately decides, it is faced with proposals which have been thrashed out through many complicated processes. It does, however, remain the final court of appeal between departments or if a Minister is getting out of step. So far as the management of Parliament is concerned this is second to administration and is left as far as possible to the Leader of the House of Commons and the Whips. As we saw, party policies are worked out in the departments and the Cabinet Committees, in private talks between the Prime Minister and the Ministers concerned, though differences may be settled in the Cabinet. The Prime Minister may take the initiative in many cases but will normally give an outline of his proposals to the Cabinet. The Foreign Secretary makes a weekly statement to the Cabinet but clearly he must take a large number of decisions on his own initiative, possibly consulting the Prime Minister and one or two other relevant colleagues. The Chancellor of the Exchequer discloses his Budget proposals to the Cabinet only at the last minute but clearly many of them will have been discussed earlier and, in any case, the financial proposals are part of general economic policy and must be generally approved, especially where there is a separate Department of Economic Affairs, possibly ready to argue a different case in the Cabinet. After October 1964 it was sometimes relatively easy to discern who had the better of the argument between Mr Callaghan and Mr Brown, presumably as a result of having persuaded the Cabinet. In all this, however, it is clear that Treasury officials and outside advisers like the Governor of the Bank of England must have participated. The specially imported adviser, Mr T. Balogh, may have had his say also but it is relatively easy to deduce that it was not particularly persuasive. It has been argued that the case is otherwise with Dr Kaldor whose hand has been seen in certain tax reforms. But, to repeat, this is largely speculation, however, 'intelligent'. In Commonwealth and Colonial affairs also Ministers must clearly take the initiative, but with particularly difficult problems like Rhodesia, Aden, Cyprus, Malaysia and so on, Cabinet decisions are needed. The Prime Minister may take a firm hand as Mr Attlee did with India and Mr Wilson with Rhodesia.

It has been deduced from all this by Professor J. P. Mackintosh[1] that 'while British Government in the latter half of the nineteenth century can be described simply as Cabinet government, such a description would be misleading today. Now the country is governed by the Prime Minister who leads, co-ordinates and maintains a series of ministers all of whom are advised and backed by the civil service. Some decisions are taken by the Premier alone, some in consultation between him and the senior ministers, while others are left to heads of departments, the Cabinet, Cabinet Committees, or the permanent officials. Of these bodies the Cabinet holds the central position because, though it does not often initiate policy or govern in that sense, most decisions pass through it or are reported to it and Cabinet Ministers can complain that they have not been informed or consulted. The precise amount of power held by each agency and the use made of the Cabinet depends on the ideas of the Premier and the personnel and situation with which he has to deal'. It is, of course, permissible to ask, as Mr D. N.

[1] *The British Cabinet*, Stevens, 1962.

Chester has done, in what sense the Cabinet has ever really governed the country; at no time could it have taken all the decisions, initiated all the policies, been aware of all the actions of the departments. 'In any complex system or organization it is most unlikely that any one body or person will be able to make all the decisions, whatever meaning is attached to the word "make".' When we talk of the growing power of the Prime Minister and conversely, of the inevitable delegation of the power to make decisions, as well as of the ever more complex machinery of decision-making this does not mean that the Cabinet is *merely* an advisory body nor that the Prime Minister is like an American President. The doctrine of collective responsibility, to which we now turn, is an important reason why the latter, at least, is unlikely.

3

Collective and Individual Ministerial Responsibility

'The peculiar contribution of the British Constitution to political science is not so much representative . . . as responsible government', writes Sir Ivor Jennings. But what precisely does this mean? Politically, Ministers are responsible to the House of Commons (not to the House of Lords). Administration is controlled by politicians who are either members of the House of Commons or are represented by political subordinates there. All decisions of any consequence are *ultimately* taken by Ministers as such or by the Cabinet. Even if decisions are left to civil servants a Minister must take the political consequences of defects, injustices and bad policies—with consequences which we discuss later.

The Cabinet is *collectively responsible* for the whole policy of the Government whether it is brought before the Cabinet as a whole or not. This collective responsibility of the Cabinet is central to the whole structure of our parliamentary system. Lord Salisbury expressed the idea neatly in 1878. 'For all that passes in Cabinet each member of it who does not resign is absolutely and irretrievably responsible and has no right afterwards to say he agreed in one case to a compromise, while in another he was persuaded by his colleagues'. A vote is seldom taken in the Cabinet but the Prime Minister's summing up, including any decision, must be accepted by all. Ministers must vote in the House for the decision; they must not make speeches contrary to Cabinet policy. It seems that today this extends to Junior Ministers (Sir Edward Boyle, Financial Secretary to the Treasury and Mr Anthony Nutting, Minister of State at the Foreign Office, resigned over Suez in 1956) and even, on occasion, to Parliamentary Private Secretaries who are not in the Ministry at all and receive no remuneration over and above their salaries as M.P.s. In recent years Mr Eden, Mr Duff Cooper, Mr Bevan, Mr Wilson, Mr Head, Mr Thorneycroft, Mr Enoch Powell, Lord Salisbury, among others, have resigned because they felt unable to share collective responsibility for certain Cabinet policies.

The danger of seeking to circumvent the principle of collective responsibility was clearly revealed in 1931–32 when the National Government wished to consider the introduction of tariffs as a means of meeting the economic crisis. Certain Ministers committed to Free Trade were permitted by an agreement to differ to express contrary views but remain in the Cabinet. This arrangement was rightly criticized; most significantly it did not last long since within a few months the Ministers resigned in protest against an extension of protection. During 1965 there was some amusement —and, perhaps, some justifiable criticism—because of Mr Cousins's apparent unwillingness to speak openly in favour of the Prices and Income Policy which was opposed by his own union, the Transport and General Workers Union, from which he was 'on leave of absence' while Minister of Technology. What was described as his 'ostentatious' sitting with union delegates at the Annual Conference rather than with his colleagues on the platform and his 'marked reluctance' to join in the ovation given to Mr Brown,. were regarded in some quarters as at least a 'silent breach' of collective responsibility.

The converse side of this practice of collective responsibility is that the whole Government will normally back an individual

Minister, although in practice it rests with the Cabinet whether they accept or disown a ministerial decision if it has not been previously agreed. If the Minister is not thus backed he alone resigns as Sir Samuel Hoare did in 1935 over his discussions with M. Laval concerning Abyssinia—though it was strongly argued that the Cabinet was responsible and that Sir Samual Hoare was sacrificed to save its face. He was soon back as First Lord of the Admiralty! If the Minister is backed the matter becomes one of 'confidence'; if there is a debate in the House the Whips are on and M.P.s either support their Government or run the risk of resignation or dissolution. No majority Government in recent years has had cause to fear parliamentary defeat, except by sheer accident of illness or unavoidable absence without a 'pair', as in 1950–51 and again since October 1964. A Cabinet decision whether or not to support a Minister is in large degree based not on possible parliamentary consequences but on public opinion. Although technically every vote—except a free vote—is a vote of confidence, what the Government will *treat* as a matter of confidence is, primarily, a question for the Government. It will normally consider such matters as possible loss of prestige if it too frequently accepts defeat, the nature of the issue, the importance of the item on which it has been defeated, and the effect on the continuity and progress of its business in the House. On this issue the *Observer* commented in 1964, when the Labour Party had been returned with a majority of only four, that

'There is no constitutional obligation on the Prime Minister of the day to resign if he is defeated in the House. But if he is repeatedly defeated, it will be a sign that he has lost command of the House—and, therefore, ultimately, the capacity to govern. In theory, he will finally be compelled to resign when he can no longer get Parliament to vote him the money to carry on the nation's business. In practice he will resign long before that point is reached for fear of annoying the electorate, thus damaging his chances at the next election. A Prime Minister with a small majority is, obviously, in danger of getting into this situation if he loses the loyalty of even a handful of his supporters. But it is only if *that* happens that the Opposition can bring down the Government within the five-year period. The idea that a Government would lose its ability or right to govern because of one accidental defeat is, therefore, incorrect; but it can afford almost no defections.'

The Economist took the same line.

'If the Government lost its majority in a single division through fog or some other accident, it would not be improper for it to put the matter to another vote to reverse the House's decision next day. The Government should resign after some single division (or withdraw a particular Bill) only if it is beaten because of genuine abstentions; although if it was beaten by accident so often that resort to second votes held up the whole parliamentary programme, this would provide another genuine constitutional signal that the Government had lost its full effectiveness and should depart.'

These extracts refer to 'resignation'; in fact the Government would almost certainly not resign but would appeal to the Country.

The doctrine of collective responsibility is reasonably clear and essential to the working of parliamentary government. There are more doubts, however, about the working of the doctrine of *individual ministerial responsibility* in practice. We have seen that most senior Ministers are responsible for a department or, more accurately, for the duties allocated to them. This means that a Minister is answerable to the House of Commons and must explain and defend his exercise of powers and duties, and that no one else can. It is also held to imply that if he loses the confidence of the House he must resign. Resignations of individual Ministers may occur, as we saw, in response to the doctrine of collective responsibility. They may also occur because Ministers quit rather than be dropped or are, in fact, dropped; this is answerability to the Prime Minister and to colleagues, not to the House. Finally, there are resignations in deference to the convention of individual ministerial responsibility.

Professor S. E. Finer has analysed the cases in the last ten years. They fall into three broad categories according to the reasons for resignation: the general qualities and the capacities of the man; the personal actions or policies of the Minister; and 'vicarious' acts or policies i.e. departmental deficiencies. Most significant, however, is that certain factors seem to operate so as to *prevent* the full operation of the convention. The Minister may be removed only temporarily and be re-appointed to another post, as with Sir Samuel Hoare; or there may simply be a reshuffle in the

Cabinet so as to retain the Minister in a different capacity as when Mr Shinwell was moved from Fuel and Power to the War Office or Mr Strachey from Food to the War Office. Mr Shinwell then went to Defence. Or everything may depend on whether the Prime Minister is firm about either dismissing or retaining the Minister and whether the Minister is reluctant or willing to go; Mr Dalton resigned for a slip of the tongue in 1947 but two years later Mr Strachey was determined not to go over the 'groundnuts affair'. Finally, 'collective solidarity' may protect a Minister, however serious his mistakes, as with Mr Shinwell and Mr Strachey or with Mr Lennox Boyd in 1958 despite the revelations of the Devlin Report about conditions in the Hola Camp. Two factors may inhibit the invocation of collective solidarity: no party may have an overall majority, which was true of five of the twenty resignations considered by Professor Finer; or the Minister may have alienated his *own* party or a substantial element in it, which was the case with ten of the twenty examples and notably with Sir Thomas Dugdale's resignation over the Crichel Down affair. The other five cases were due to 'exceptional circumstances'. It is clear that many Ministers have not resigned although they were as blameworthy as many of those who did. Everything seems to depend on the Minister (how compliant he is), the Prime Minister (how firm he is) and the Party (how clamorous it is)! Is there, then, really a rule at all?

We have seen that the Minister must answer for his civil servants, who cannot speak for themselves. Is this always fair to the Minister and are there any limitations to this part of the convention? The notorious Crichel Down case throws light on this. It revealed 'a number of officials, some obviously not well-informed, acting like ordinary human beings, sometimes differing among themselves'. It was one of a large number of cases, inevitably settled without reference to the Minister or at least without adequate and sufficiently early reference to him to alert him to the fact that the case might be 'politically charged'; a possibility which civil servants themselves should foresee since as Lord Bridges has said, 'a civil servant, while being the least political of all animals must be constantly aware of the political content of his work'.

N

Sir Thomas Dugdale's resignation as Minister of Agriculture 'was a brave and welcome reinforcement of the doctrine of ministerial responsibility' but it has been asked how such resignation can be a solution to every-day cases of official error?

Sir David Maxwell Fyfe, Home Secretary, attempted to define the actual position. Ministers are responsible where a civil servant acts properly in accordance with the Minister's policy and, even more, where he carries out an explicit order from the Minister. The latter is also responsible where the civil servant makes a mistake or causes delay (except on an important issue of policy or where a claim to an individual right is seriously involved), in which case the Minister acknowledges the mistake and accepts responsibility and states that he will take corrective action in the department. But where an action has been taken by a civil servant of which the Minister disapproves and of which he has no prior knowledge, and the conduct of the official is reprehensible, the Minister is not bound to defend the action. As an addendum to this, however, it was stated that the Minister remains constitutionally responsible to Parliament in the sense that 'he alone can tell Parliament what has occurred and render an account of his stewardship'. The irreverent might ask, 'so what?'.

Is there much more to hope for from parliamentary action? In the same debate and in his book Mr Herbert Morrison took virtually the same line as the Home Secretary. 'Publicly the Minister must accept responsibility as if the act were his own. It is, however, legitimate for him to explain that something went wrong in the department, that he accepts responsibility and apologizes for it, and that he has taken steps to see such a thing will not happen again'. Action in the department is, of course, important: 'the civil servant should at all times know that the lawful orders of Ministers must be carried out'. It is true that since Ministers get the credit for the good actions of anonymous officials they ought to accept blame for bad acts. But two questions remain: should the hammer of resignation be wielded in order to crack the nut of bad administration which the Minister could not possibly have prevented; and does such resignation provide a remedy for the aggrieved citizen or even ensure against a repetition of similar maladministration? We pursue the second question in a later section.

4

The Civil Service and Administration

It is not our purpose in this section to describe in detail the organization of the civil service or of the administrative machine. These can be found in any descriptive text-book and, in any case, change so frequently that no book is ever completely up-to-date. Rather are we concerned with the relations between the political executive and the permanent administration and the impact of both on the individual citizen and his daily life. Accordingly, we shall begin with an account of ministerial-civil service relations which were touched upon in our discussion of ministerial responsibility and then proceed to examine certain aspects of the decision-making process. This will lead us naturally to an examination of the 'control of administration' for the protection of the citizen.

A. L. Lowell, an American expert on British Government, wrote as long ago as 1904 that 'of all the existing political traditions in England, the least known to the public, and yet one of those most deserving attention, is that which governs the relation between the expert and the layman'. Political power and responsibility are vested in the non-expert layman but he is supported and guided by the expert. An apt reply to the statement that the job of the Minister is to tell the civil servant what the public won't stand is that the job of the civil servant is to tell the Minister what won't work. The expert or specialist group fills all the positions in a department below the level of the Minister and two or three parliamentary colleagues whose position in relation to civil servants is not always clear. The Minister has a closely organized hierarchy of permanent officials culminating in the Permanent Secretary. (Permanent Under-Secretary when the political head is a 'Secretary of State' not a 'Minister'.) Both political and permanent elements are necessary; the officials might get on alone for a time but, as Sir William Harcourt said, 'a government of civil servants would be very efficient and very able, but they would all be hanged from the lamp-posts before the end of six months'.

We should note in Britain the important place of the 'generalist'. The chief permanent officials are frequently no more expert in the department's substantive work than the Minister; their forte is 'general management'. As Sir Warren Fisher, one-time Head of the Civil Service, said, the Administrative Class civil servant is 'not (except by accident) a specialist in anything, but rather the general adviser of the Minister, the general manager and controller under the Minister, with ultimate responsibility to the Minister for all activities of the department'. The British civil service is rightly described as 'one of the world's best administrative organizations'. The lines of authority are generally clear and direct; civil servants are obedient, competent, and honest. Once policy is decided, its implementation is rarely vitiated by administrative confusion or official sabotage.

Nevertheless, there have been increasing doubts as to the suitability of the system for meeting modern needs. It has been suggested that the machine is more apt for running existing affairs than for planning to meet emerging problems, better at routine than at experimental tasks. There is insufficient professional, scientific, and technological knowledge and too little acquaintance with new ideas in the social sciences. Civil servants, at least in the higher ranks, often regard themselves as the possessors of a 'conventional wisdom' which is impervious to criticism. Remedies canvassed include the recruitment of more specialists and more opportunities for them to reach the highest positions; entry at a later age after gaining other relevant experience; greater interchange between civil servants and other administrators in different fields; greater use of temporary civil servants with special expertise, not only in the departments but in the Cabinet Office and, possibly, in a separate Prime Minister's Office. These problems are too complicated to discuss further here; we turn to some more traditional questions.

In discussing ministerial-official relations we are primarily concerned with the 3,500 members of the Administrative Class and
especially the two hundred or so at the top. It is true that the
general public more often comes into contact with clerical and
executive officers at a much lower level—behind the counter of
the local Ministry of Labour or Pensions and National Insurance
Offices, at the Income Tax Offices, in the Post Office or the Tele-
phone Exchange, rather than in the corridors of Whitehall. But
there is considerable evidence to suggest that the attitude of these
lower level civil servants is in large part governed not only by
ministerial attitudes but also by the framework laid down by top
civil servants and within which the rest work. Some reference,
however, will be made to the lower levels in our discussion of the
administration and the citizen.

The Tomlin Commission on the Civil Service defined the
tasks of the Administrative Class as (1) the formulation of policy;
(2) the co-ordination and improvement of government machinery;
and (3) the general administration and control of the departments.
At once we notice the concern with 'policy' which, traditionally,
is supposed to be the concern of Ministers. In fact, of course, as
we saw when discussing proposals for Cabinet reform, the line
between making and administering policy is thin. Senior administrators must exercise discretion in policy; they must know when
fixed rules have policy implications. They are bound to be involved in discussions about changes in both policy and administrative patterns. The desirability and effectiveness of policy may
depend on its administrative implications, for example, in relation
to economic growth. The real distinction between politicians
and civil servants is that the first are partisan, the second non-
partisan. Moreover, in the day-to-day relations between Ministers
and civil servants both may identify with a wide variety of interested parties. The Minister may accept departmental practices
and values, the civil servant may closely identify himself with a
given policy whether it is a matter of partisan controversy or an
issue between pressure groups. Both Minister and civil servant
may identify themselves with their pressure group clients (e.g.
the Ministry of Agriculture and the farmers) or the civil servant may

identify himself with certain professional experts outside the Government. All these possible factors affect both day-to-day relations and even long-term decisions.

The constitutional doctrine of ministerial responsibility clearly means that the Minister has the last word. A civil servant has written that 'the civil service is in the last resort a profession of subordinates to politicians'. The loyalty and impartiality of civil servants are rarely open to question and have been attested to by Ministers of different views. Any charges of deliberate attempts to obtain bureaucratic power or of disloyalty and political bias can be rejected. It is, however, sometimes suggested that the civil servant *knows* so much that the Minister—an amateur and a passing bird—is at his mercy. Ministers, of course, differ in ability, knowledge and strength of character while the civil service includes some of the most brilliant brains in the country. But there is a great deal of evidence to suggest that the Minister *can*, if he wishes, make a difference. Mr D. N. Chester has asserted that 'a change of Minister may almost overnight effect considerable changes in the attitudes and effectiveness of a department, and this even without a change of government'. Mr Harold Nicholson considered that 'a Minister of strong personality immediately alters the whole atmosphere of his department, and in the shaping of events, atmosphere is a far more important element than the written word'. Sir Oliver Franks, with experience in the civil service, suggested that even where officials make decisions for the Minister

'it is important to know his mind and conduct business in that knowledge. The speed with which the wishes and views of an incoming Minister become known reflects the desire of the good official to construct the necessary concept of the Minister's mind on his business'. Sir Ivor Jennings has concluded that 'the tradition is firm that when the Government changes the policy, the departmental policy must change'.

Even these generalizations, however, cannot provide a complete and detailed picture in any particular case; so much depends on circumstances and personalities. Harold Laski has said that 'everyone with the least acquaintance with government cannot but be aware that there is a give and take between every Minister and his chief officials which makes the latter unseen partners, as it were, in the purposes he seeks to implement'. But who gives and who takes, and how much? The role of the civil servant has been described as one of 'healthy assistance,' of 'reasonable and deferential opposition'; but it has also been said that the Permanent Secretary is a 'selective filter which allows to pass only those things of which it approves'. But we return again to the tradition. A civil servant's 'most heinous crime is to enable an M.P. to score a point against his political chief'. If things go wrong, the Minister is blamed; every reason exists for the civil servant to think hard and long before reaching a decision that somebody else may have to defend against hostile criticism. We repeat, the last word rests with the Minister. If the Minister insists, the official 'will shrug his shoulders and remark, "well, sir, it's your responsibility," and go off to lunch at the club and tell his intimate friends in the service that he can do nothing with the Minister who is resolved to make a fool of himself'. The civil servant is entitled to make no written protest; he has no access to either Cabinet or Prime Minister.

A few examples may illustrate these points, though in the nature of things they cannot be contemporary. On one occasion Sir Austen Chamberlain as Postmaster-General insisted upon certain action, against prolonged opposition from his officials; when he finally put his foot down, the official's reaction was, 'well, sir, need you do this stupid thing in this stupid way'; the official then proceeded to suggest the best way of doing what he had opposed so strenuously. When Mr H. B. Lees-Smith became Postmaster-General he took with him a number of ideas for administrative reform; within a short time he was telling his colleagues at the London School of Economics that his officials had persuaded him of their impracticability. Sir Kingsley Wood produced virtually the same ideas, insisted that they should be tried, and made a reputation which took him via the Ministry of Health to the Chancellorship of the Exchequer! George Lansbury became First Commissioner of Works when his left-wing and unthought-out ideas scared his permanent officials; his first response to their attitude of *non-possumus* was, 'well, brother, you've told me what can't be done, now tell me what can.' We owe to him, among other things, bathing in the Serpentine. His officials were soon proclaiming him the best First Commissioner ever and his Permanent Secretary became a life-long friend and companion. There is the story that when Addison went to the Ministry of Agriculture his Permanent Secretary was opposed to some of his projects; Sir Arthur Street was eventually so enthusiastic about at least one of these that as Mr Attlee, with unwonted humour, declared, 'you could have obtained an affiliation order against the Permanent Secretary', so enthusiastic did he become about 'the new baby'. It has been suggested that when Mr Attlee took over responsibility for policy towards independence for India he compelled acceptance from the officials at the India Office, in contrast to Mr Bevin who, it is alleged, imbibed the pro-Arab prejudices of the Foreign Office to such an extent that he became less than enthusiastic about Labour's official policy towards an independent State of Israel. When Arthur Henderson went to the Foreign Office in 1929 he told Hugh Dalton that the first forty-eight hours mattered. Although the technique of circulating copies of *Labour and the Nation* was an ineffective means of persuading officials to a new point of view, Henderson adopted a more subtle approach and made it clear to his officials that there could be 'too much continuity of policy'. There are doubtless many examples in the post-1945 period which are not yet sufficiently known for comment.

It is not easy, of course, to get rid of unsympathetic officials, though Neville Chamberlain managed to 'kick Sir Robert Vanisttart upstairs' to the post of Chief Diplomatic Adviser and relied on Sir Horace Wilson, more amenable to the policy of appeasement of Hitler. Chamberlain was, of course, Prime Minister. His success is not altogether an argument for enabling Ministers to get rid of unsympathetic advisers; subsequent policy was not a noticeable success and some still recall Mr Harold Nicholson's scathing description of Chamberlain and Sir Horace Wilson at Munich: they were like two curates going for the first time into a pub, and were unable to distinguish between a social gathering and a rough-house! Not everyone, anyhow, can get rid of an adviser whom he cannot persuade. When Sir Reginald Dorman-Smith became Minister of Agriculture he was told by his Permanent Secretary, 'whatever you may think of me or any other civil servant here you cannot sack us'. When George Strauss as Minister of Supply tried to retire an officer he 'raised against myself all the cameraderie of the civil service', and found every obstacle placed in his way and had to accept a compromise. In one way this is a good thing; at least it avoids any suggestion of a 'spoils system'. But it may lead to the position apparently taken up by Strauss's predecessor, Mr Wilmot, who was described as 'run by his civil servants'.

However, it is unusual for ministerial-official relations to reach the stage where the civil servant ought to go. The system works well enough without such sanctions. Many Ministers, including, for example, Sir David Maxwell Fyfe and Sir Herbert Samuel, have firmly stated that provided a Minister is content to decide general policy and not get immersed in detail, he can, in fact, run his department. There is no doubt, for example, that Mr Aneurin Bevan ran the Ministry of Health during the long drawn out struggle with the B.M.A. over the Health Service, that Mr Hugh Dalton ran the Treasury during the era of low rates of interest and 'cheap money', and that Mr George Brown is master of the Department of Economic Affairs so far as his officials are concerned. If we quote Labour Ministers in particular it is because it is often assumed that civil servants are more likely to be in tune with Conservative Ministers. It was, however, Mr Attlee, who declared that 'we always demand from our civil servants a loyalty to the State and that they should serve the Government of the day whatever its political colour. That understanding is carried out with exemplary loyalty'.

As stated earlier, it is not our intention to provide a detailed description of the administrative machinery of Britain. The following is an account of some matters of historical interest and a brief summary of the major departments and their functions. The basic unit of administration is the ministerial department with a political head. There are a number of sub-departments and semi-independent administrative organs of which today the most significant are the public corporations which run the nationalized industries and also some independent organizations with 'recognized administrative functions'. We have already referred to the array of advisory and consultative bodies, and shall consider the decentralized agencies such as the local authorities and the new regional machinery in a later section.

The expansion of the functions of the State can be traced in the founding and development of departments. In Britain there has been no 'once-for-all' administrative reorganization. Blue-prints like those produced by the Haldane Committee on the Machinery of Government in 1918 have been generally ignored; history, tradition and empiricism have all left their mark in the administrative machine. As Professor Smellie has put it, 'every Minister presides not only over part of the machinery of government of the modern state, but also over a legal museum which illustrates the continuity of our constitutional development'. The King's Council was the starting point of our judicial institutions, our administrative arrangements, our Parliament, and our Privy Council, parent to the Cabinet. The older departments cover the basic activities of governments—defence, finance, law and order, the newer departments the more recent social and economic functions.

The Treasury existed even before the mediaeval office of the Exchequer. Since the days of Queen Anne it has always been 'in commission' with no Lord High Treasurer. The First Lord of the Treasury, the Prime Minister today, continued as the principal Minister of the Crown, but the management and direction of the Treasury fell to the Chancellor of the Exchequer. The Junior Lords of the Treasury today are the Government Whips and the Parliamentary Secretary the 'Patronage Secretary'. The First Lord remained by nature of his position able to control the Civil Service, including appointments to top places in all Government Departments. The Permanent Secretary (now two Joint Secretaries) became the Head of the Civil Service. Today the Treasury is responsible for the collection of revenue (the Inland Revenue and Customs and Excise Departments are separate departments but are both the final responsibility of the Chancellor of the Exchequer); for the presentation of the Civil Estimates to Parliament and the control of spending by government departments; for the civil service establishments; for financial problems connected with the preparation of the Budget, the control of the National Debt; and for such problems as those connected with Bank Rate and the Balance of Payments. In 1964 the Labour Government established a Department of Economic Affairs under a First Secretary of State (Mr George Brown, also Deputy Prime Minister) to be responsible for a plan of economic development and 'all economic policy related to industrial expansion, allocation of physical resources and regional implications of the expansion programme'. The Department was responsible for the National Plan in 1965, the Prices and Incomes Board, the National Economic Development Council and the 'little Neddies'. Despite the establishment of this Department, this is not the first time that the problem of the relations between a Ministry of Economic Affairs (or Production) and the Treasury has emerged and no-one really knows yet what their relative position may be. The Treasury loomed large in 1964–65 because of the general economic situation. It continues to exercise 'Treasury control' over estimates, staff, salaries, establishment, and the machinery of government. As stated, it has two Joint Permanent Secretaries, one in charge of the financial and economic work of the Treasury and the other, the Head of the Civil Service, in charge of the Establishments section, management, and efficiency.

The office of Secretary of State goes back to the reign of Henry III. Originally a clerical officer in the palace, he became one of the most important royal ministers. Foreign Affairs were separated from Home Affairs in 1782, the beginning of the Foreign Office and the Home Office; the former now has also four Ministers of State, the latter one. A Secretary of State for War (including Colonies) was appointed in 1794 and Colonies were separated sixty years later. A separate Secretary of State for the Dominions came into existence in 1925; he became Secretary of State for Commonwealth Relations in 1948. There is also a Minister of State. In 1964 a new Ministry of Overseas Development took over some functions from Colonies and Commonwealth and also from some other departments. There was a Secretary of State for

India from 1858 to 1947. Meanwhile a separate Secretary of State for Air was appointed in 1917. The Secretary for Scotland, appointed in 1885, became a Secretary of State in 1926 and now there is a Minister of State also. A Secretary of State for Wales, with one Minister of State, appeared in 1964. Mr Churchill was considered by some to have 'degraded' the ancient office by appointing a Secretary of State (rather than a Minister) for the co-ordination of Fuel, Power and Transport in 1951 but this 'overlord' did not last long. A fairly recent innovation has been the appointment of a 'First Secretary of State'—Mr Butler when placed in charge of the controversial Central African problems and, in 1964, Mr Brown as Minister for Economic Affairs. He also has a Minister of State. Meanwhile, however, the Secretaries of State for War and Air have disappeared and are now, like the First Lord of the Admiralty, subordinate to the Secretary of State for Defence. There is a Deputy-Secretary of State for Defence who is Minister of Defence for the Army, and two Ministers of Defence for Navy and Air. There is, finally, a Secretary of State for Education and Science, with a Minister of State. Each Secretary of State is responsible for a major department of government; all are constitutionally occupants of the same office and statutory powers are sometimes conferred on *a* Secretary of State; but each is too busy to encroach upon the work of the others and there is a convention that he does not.

We have mentioned the First Lord of the Admiralty. The office of Lord High Admiral was put into commission by Henry VIII. Since the early eighteenth century there has been a Board of Admiralty and the First Lord was virtually Minister for the Navy. As stated, he is now a Minister under the Secretary of State for Defence.

The Lord Chancellor was the most important royal servant in the mediaeval monarchy. He was originally a chaplain, secretary of the sovereign, and Keeper of the Royal Seal. He attended Parliament and became 'Speaker' of the House of Lords. As 'Keeper of the King's conscience' he received petitions for the 'royal grace and favour', but this function eventually went to the Chancery Courts and thence to 'Equity'. The Lord Chancellor, however, remained Head of the Judiciary. This latter role, his membership of the legislature, and of the Cabinet, are an interesting commentary on the extent to which Britain enjoys a 'separation of powers'.

So far we have traced the emergence of departments from individual offices. We now turn to offshoots of ancient institutions. The Privy Council, also descended from the King's Council and in Tudor times a functioning group of royal advisers, is now a purely formal body. The Lord President of the Council, as we saw, is now a 'Minister without Portfolio'. The most important Committee of the Privy Council, is, of course, the Cabinet, and members of the latter still take their oath of secrecy as Privy Councillors (though there are Privy Councillors who are not members of the Cabinet).

But the Privy Council has also spawned many modern departments. A Committee on Trade and Plantations became the Board of Trade whose 'President' is, in fact, a Minister; he is now assisted by three Ministers of State. A Committee on Education became the Department of Education, the Board of Education, the Ministry of Education and now the Department of Education and Science. In 1964 when the Ministry of Technology was created pure research was left to the Department while the new Ministry took responsibility for the Atomic Energy Authority, the National Research Development Corporation, and the industrial side of the Department of Scientific and Industrial Research. Another offshoot of the Privy Council became the Ministry of Agriculture and Fisheries.

The Board of Trade itself has fathered many departments, the most notable of which are the Ministry of Labour (1917), the Ministry of Transport (1919) from which the Ministry of Aviation was separated (1951), and the Ministry of Fuel and Power, now the Ministry of Power.

Many older administrative bodies became Ministries, expanded, and then hived off some of their functions. The Poor Law Commission became the Poor Law Board. In 1871 it became the Local Government Board and absorbed some health functions previously performed at times by a Board of Health, at times by the Privy

Council. This became the Ministry of Health in 1919, but as a result of reorganization in 1951, involving this Ministry and the newer Ministry of Town and Country Planning, there emerged a Ministry of Housing and Local Government and a (reduced) Ministry of Health. In 1964 a separate Ministry of Land and National Resources was added. Meanwhile various social insurance functions had been hived off from various bodies and given to a Ministry of National Insurance which in 1953 became the Ministry of Pensions and National Insurance. Certain functions were given to a quasi-government body, the National Assistance Board.

Other departments have been established by statute at various times, like the Ministry of Works in 1942 (preceded by the Commission of Works). We do not describe wartime Ministries such as Shipping, Food, Production. Some, like the Ministry of Supply, have been abolished and their functions transferred elsewhere. This process continues: in 1965 there was a possibility, for example, that the Ministry of Aviation might disappear. Such changes are rendered somewhat easier by the Ministers of the Crown (Transfer of Functions) Act, 1946, which enables the Prime Minister to transfer functions from one Minister to another by Order-in-Council though no department of state can be dissolved without reference to the House of Commons.

The Law Offices, of course, are of ancient lineage. They now include the Attorney-General, the Solicitor General, the Lord Advocate (Scotland) and the Solicitor-General for Scotland. Finally, the Post Office traces its origin to the old prerogative powers of the Postmaster-General but it is now a vast department administering a service in some respects similar to those provided by the Public Corporations.

Brief mention only can be made of these Public Corporations and other 'quasi-government bodies'. They include a wide variety of agencies such as the B.B.C., the Independent Television Authority, various Marketing Boards, the Regional Hospital Boards, the Port of London Authority, Development Corporations of certain New Towns, as well as the British Railways Board, the Electricity and Gas Councils (with their Area organizations), the National Coal Board and the British Overseas and British European Airways

Corporations. The Public Corporations as such were established in order to recruit top-level personnel from outside the ranks of the civil service, to relieve the Minister of the burden of excessive routine work, and to try to obtain a balance between efficient commercial enterprise and necessary public control. The Minister's powers are regulated by statute and he usually has power to 'hire' and 'fire' members of the Boards and to lay down general policy; he exercises much influence by consultations on what has been described as 'an old boy basis' and of which Parliament may not learn.

Parliament is, in any case, limited in its control since Questions may not be asked on any matter which does not lie within the Minister's responsibilities. Debates on the Annual Reports and Accounts and on private bills sponsored by the corporations are too frequently used either for airing local grievances or (though less now than in earlier years) for raising political arguments rather than for appraising impartially the whole range of the corporation's work. Perhaps the most effective means of parliamentary investigations is through the Select Committee on the Nationalized Industries. There are also a number of Consumer Councils but, generally speaking, they have not been as successful as was hoped, because they do not appear sufficiently well-known to the public, are sometimes regarded as insufficiently independent, and are inadequately equipped to deal with the problems arising.

5

Control of the Administration

Mention of Consumer Councils reminds us that one of the most difficult and urgent problems of the modern state is to ensure adequate response to public opinion and a cheap, flexible, and impartial way of remedying public grievances arising out of administrative decisions and practices. What can the citizen do and where can he go to obtain that 'redress of grievances' which, traditionally, is the function of Parliament? We saw that the doctrine of ministerial responsibility provides no guarantee that grievances will be remedied, and that the weapons in the hands of M.P.s are inadequate, although no one would wish to minimize, still less weaken the role of M.P.s as raisers of 'constituency grievances'. There is little argument that parliamentary processes are in need of supplementation even if they could be made more effective e.g. by the establishment of specialist committees. The 'Scrutiny Committee' on delegated legislation has, as we saw, only limited functions. First, however, we must attempt to define the precise nature of the problem.

A constant series of administrative decisions from the top level downwards may affect the citizen at any number of points in his daily life, though in many cases he is unaware that he is within range until 'something hits him'—when he realizes that ignorance of the law is no excuse. Rules, regulations and orders, the statutory instruments to which we referred earlier, involve administrative decisions within the framework of Acts of Parliament, and Parliament may have examined neither the 'parent' act nor its offspring with a view to consequences for individual citizens, which, in any case, may not be obvious to the layman until they emerge in an individual case. Some of these regulations affect only civil servants; others affect the general public. In addition, there are a large number of decisions taken by various bodies such as administrative tribunals (the Minister, in some cases, may himself be a 'one man tribunal'), public corporations, local authorities, and 'domestic tribunals' such as the General Medical Council. We do not attempt to discuss decisions by private bodies like trade unions, individual employers, or large commercial concerns from the consequences of which the individual may equally need protection, except to note that here the State may be a protector rather than an invader of rights. Many of these decisions are purely *administrative* which means, as we shall see, that they may be subject to no form of control other than the political. This point is worth emphasizing. We have already questioned the effectiveness of ministerial responsibility, parliamentary control, the efforts of individual M.P.s. We shall see later that there are many limitations on the extent to which the courts can control the process of decision-making. We shall see also that despite improvements in the procedures of administrative tribunals and public inquiries there is still much to be done both by way of extending the right of appeal and also the range of decisions which are open to 'impartial adjudication'. Even these extensions, however, would not meet the problem of purely administrative and discretionary decisions i.e. the problem not of maladministration but of 'administrative action which John Smith does not like'.

Professor Brian Chapman[1] has suggested that there are four main aspects of control of public administration. First, there must be some way of ensuring that public administration is always carried out within the letter of the law as laid down by Acts of Parliament and regulations made under them. Secondly, with respect to discretionary decisions such as those concerned with pensions, licenses, contracts etc. there should be machinery to guarantee equity, reasonableness, and impartiality. Thirdly, there should be means of obtaining compensation for damages of a general kind resulting from administrative action—not merely damages for special and restricted categories of action as laid down by a multitude of separate and uncoordinated laws. Finally, there should be safeguards against any abuse of power, the use of power for wrong ends under political or corrupt influences. We shall not examine the various problems precisely under these categories, but examine rather the *machinery* for the control of administration, which may be concerned with one or more of the above categories.

The question of *judicial review* is complicated and technical and we can examine it only very generally and in over-simplified terms. The Courts, of course, cannot declare an Act of Parliament 'unconstitutional' as in the U.S. though, in fact, by 'judicial interpretation' they do in many cases 'make law' and, it is argued, may 'make policy' through what has been called their 'inarticulate major premises'. The charge has been made that 'it is difficult to explain a good deal of judicial interpretation of legislation in the field of public law, except upon the assumption that the judges

---

[1] *The Profession of Government*, Allen & Unwin, 1959.

did not like what Parliament was doing and sought to confine Parliament's activities to the narrowest possible area'. The charge has not been satisfactorily met since Harold Laski made it before the Committee on Ministers' Powers in 1931. On the other hand, in recent years it has also been suggested that in some cases excessive 'judicial restraint' has made the Courts appear to lean over backwards to avoid frustrating government policy e.g. by holding that the purpose of an inquiry was 'to inform the Minister's mind' and was therefore not subject to the controls placed on 'quasi-judicial' operations.

However that may be, there are limitations on the extent to which, for example, the courts can control delegated legislation. These relate to the doctrine of *ultra vires*, action 'outside the powers' legally conferred. If certain procedures laid down by the parent act are not followed e.g. statutory consultation is not carried out, this may constitute procedural *ultra vires*. There is also *substantive ultra vires* which, roughly, covers the 'reasonableness' of a regulation. This has been applied rather to local by-laws and would certainly not be applied to the acts of a Minister. Moreover, the Courts will not substitute their own judgment for that of the authority concerned, if the regulation made is an 'honest' use of the power. Despite these limitations, Parliament has seen fit to try various forms of words calculated to exclude the jurisdiction of the Courts altogether; of these the most effective has been to provide in the Act for appeals to be lodged on certain specific grounds within a period of six weeks, after which the decision 'shall not be questioned in any legal proceedings whatsoever'. This has been applied to decisions rather than to rule-making.

So far as administrative acts are concerned the Courts must normally be able to find *some* 'judicial' element—the 'quasi-judicial' category—in any decision before they can intervene. Over the internal management of departments they have no control. Over purely administrative acts like those involved in the Crichel Down case they have no control. Over decisions of 'pure policy' e.g. deportation or naturalization they have no control. In 1965 there was considerable perturbation over a proposal to give the Home Secretary similar uncontrollable jurisdiction over the deportation of certain categories of Commonwealth citizens. There are, however, a number of cases in which the Courts can intervene. If the act is *ultra vires*, as above, this is possible. If a certain 'jurisdictional fact' must exist before a decision is made e.g. is a certain lodging a 'furnished lodging', they may inquire as to its existence. If there are 'procedural defects'—a category deemed to include certain elements of 'natural justice' such as that no man must be judge in his own cause (extended to include the general notion of 'bias'), and that both sides must be heard—they may intervene. If there is a written record of the judgment—more usual since the Franks Committee recommended that *all* decisions should be recorded with reasons for them—the Courts may find 'an error of law' on the face of the record. Finally, there may be an abuse of a discretionary power. The Court may find that it was used for improper purposes, purposes not clearly authorized by law, or that extraneous (irrelevant) considerations have affected the decision. This, like all the categories, is extremely complicated in practice and readers must turn to more detailed work for elucidation.

At least as important as the above technical limitations on the power of the Courts to intervene are the procedures whereby a citizen may invoke judicial intervention. There are a number of 'prerogative' orders, each of which is restricted in scope. *Prohibition* is useful only if it can be invoked before the decision has been made. *Certiorari* (literally, to 'make certain that the decision was made properly') covers most of the possible justifications for review examined above but it can be used only if the Courts can find a 'judicial' element in the procedure; it does not apply to purely administrative acts. *Mandamus* may be used to compel an authority to do its duty and has been extended by the legal fiction that one who exercises jurisdiction on *wrong grounds* may be deemed to have *declined* jurisdiction i.e. has failed to do his duty! This may be used in respect of ministerial acts but *not* against the Crown— which includes 'servants of the Crown', though who falls in this category has been the subject-matter of much judicial discussion! An *injunction* may be obtained to stop illegal acts but again it may be too late. Finally, the *declaration* is increasingly used: the Courts will 'declare' that an action is illegal. Without attempting technical explanations it may be said that the action for a declaration has considerable advantages and that public authorities will almost inevitably obey the law when a Court has thus declared without further need for coercion. It does not apply only to judicial or 'quasi-judicial' acts, but also to administrative acts *provided* that the Minister has not by law been given absolute discretion (which, alas, excludes vast numbers of decisions). As Lord Denning, Master of the Rolls, has declared in his 'Freedom under the Law', 'just as the pick and the shovel are no longer suitable for the winning of coal, so also the procedures of mandamus, certiorari, and actions on the case are not suitable for the winning of freedom in the new age. They must be replaced by new and up-to-date machinery, by declarations, injunctions, and actions for negligence'.

Not surprisingly, however, Lord Denning was not particularly concerned with suggesting new remedies other than those provided through the Courts. Yet, as we have seen, there are many technicalities in the way of the exercise of jurisdiction by the Courts. The latter are also limited by 'judicial restraint', the relatively recent unwillingness to appear to be interfering with the Executive or replacing Parliament (however inadequate parliamentary control may be); by the problem of finding satisfactory remedies since the Courts will not normally hand down a new decision but return the matter for re-hearing; and by the excessive costs often involved. Indeed, the Franks Committee in its 1957 Report remarked that 'reflection on the general social and economic changes of recent decades convinces us that tribunals as a system for adjudication have come to stay'. The tendency for issues arising from legislative schemes to be referred to special tribunals is likely to grow rather than to diminish. The reasons given were cheapness, accessibility, freedom from technicality, expedition, expert knowledge, the danger of grossly over-burdening the judiciary or of 'diluting' the ranks of the judges. It must be made clear, however, that the Franks Committee was able to consider only tribunals and public inquiries—again the 'quasi-judicial' limitation—and not administrative actions like those involved in the Crichel Down case, which ironically, was the cause of the outcry leading to the appointment of the Franks Committee. We summarize the main findings and results of the Franks Report below. They cover a wide range of bodies concerned with land and property, national insurance, national assistance and family allowances, the national health service, military service, transport, taxation and compensation, as well as domestic tribunals and the administrative procedures involved in inquiries or hearings in relation to compulsory acquisition of land, planning, New Towns, clearance and demolition orders. All these clearly affect the citizen in his daily affairs.

The Franks Committee made ninety-five recommendations of which seventy were accepted by the Government. So far as tribunals are concerned, these included the appointment, save in exceptional circumstances, of legally trained chairmen; the right to legal representation; the disclosure by the Minister of full reasons for any decision; the appointment of a Council on Tribunals to supervise the working of tribunals and inquiries and to publish annual reports. It was also recommended that there should normally be a right of appeal to an appellate tribunal and, on points of law only, to the Courts. With regard to inquiries, the authorities should provide full particulars of their case, inspectors should be independent and their reports published, and, again, reasons should be given for the Minister's decision. The Council on Tribunals (with a special Scottish Committee) reviews the activities of *more than two thousand tribunals*, to ensure that their proceedings are conducted with 'openness, fairness, and impartiality'. It reports annually to the Lord Chancellor who presents the Report to Parliament. Some further changes in procedure have been achieved as a result of these efforts but some weaknesses remain. For example, the Council can only review inquiries which the Minister must by statute hold but not the many inquiries held at the Minister's discretion. Moreover, the Council has only advisory powers. Finally, and most significantly, the Franks Committee, despite all this, emphasized that 'over most of the field of public administration no formal procedure is provided for objecting or deciding on objections'.

Even in respect of tribunals the Committee firmly rejected

proposals for a general Administrative Appeals Tribunal which might develop an effective system of public law. There were also gaps in the machinery to deal with abuse of power or maladministration, let alone with discretionary decisions. The Report of the Whyatt Committee, set up not by the Government but by the organization 'Justice', attempted to suggest how these gaps might be filled. To provide for 'impartial adjudication' of the kinds of decisions dealt with by the Franks Committee but not, in fact, covered by appropriate machinery, the Report suggested that the Council on Tribunals should be charged with investigating these gaps and making proposals to fill them. In addition, the Committee recommended the appointment of an Ombudsman or Parliamentary Commissioner to supplement the present means of redress. It must be emphasized that this would still not meet the problem of regulating the exercise of executive discretion in general and that this proposed appointment would still provide no formal, readily available means of challenging vast areas of decision-making. This is borne out by the White Paper on the Parliamentary Commissioner published in October 1965.

It is made clear that 'the commissioner will be concerned with *faults in administration*. It will not be for him to criticize policy, or to examine a decision on the exercise of *discretionary powers*, unless it appears to him that the decision has been affected by a fault in administration' (our italics). As to the scope of his work, the White Paper gives a long list of departments which will be subject to his jurisdiction. But he is excluded from fields where 'there are dominant considerations of national or public interest', where the courts or administrative tribunals operate, where personnel matters in departments are concerned, and where 'purely commercial relationships of departments with customers or suppliers' are concerned. Public corporations and local authorities are excluded from his jurisdiction.

Grievances will come to the Commissioner through M.P.s and he will report, probably, to a Select Committee of the House of Commons, both annually and on *ad hoc* cases. 'It will be for Parliament, with the help of this Committee . . . to consider what action should be taken on the reports of the Commissioner'. The general purpose is 'to give members of Parliament a better instrument which they can use to protect the citizen. . . . This new institution should serve to develop and reinforce our existing constitutional arrangements for the protection of the individual'. But, we repeat, there will still be large areas of decision-making uncontrolled save by political means. Space prevents full discussion of the implications of this and of possible remedies. But it is worthy of note that the Conseil d'Etat, the supreme Administrative Court in France, is excluded from virtually nothing and certainly not from 'discretionary decisions'. In New Zealand the Commissioner is not excluded from 'policy' matters; he can criticize and draw the attention of Parliament to statutory rules or regulations which in his opinion bring about hardship or unexpected consequences. Moreover, it may be difficult to decide whether the exercise of discretionary powers has or has not been due to 'a fault in administration' unless the decision can be examined in detail. The New Zealand cases show that practically none of the Commissioner's findings and recommendations imply any maladministration or bad faith, yet he can make recommendations as to alterations in the decision even though he is not an 'appellate tribunal' with the power to change the decision himself. As Mr Geoffrey Marshall has said, 'if one sets out the facts of any of the celebrated administrative fiascos of the past, it is difficult to decide which aspects of them were proper but unwise, imprudent or unwelcome, and which were improper, unjust, or oppressive'. Clearly nothing must interfere with the effective working of the administrative system, but to argue that the convenience of administration is always and necessarily more important than the rights of the individual is to put in reverse the equally dangerous principle which for long seemed to sway the Courts, that the rights of individuals (and even of powerful corporations regarded as 'legal persons') must be stretched to the utmost even at the expense of the administration and of the policy laid down by Parliament. The decision to appoint an Ombudsman is generally regarded as a step in the right direction. It should not, however, be allowed to obscure the fact that still more is needed if governments are to be generally answerable for their actions. We cannot take the

argument about control of the administration further in an introductory study of this kind.

6

The Courts

Although, as we saw, the 'output' functions of the political system
cannot be realistically studied under the old division into legislative,
executive, and judicial functions, some account of the role of the
Courts in spheres other than the control of administration must be
given. Once more, we shall not present a detailed factual account
of matters dealt with in orthodox textbooks, but merely present
some illustrative points.

Like so many departments of state the highest courts developed
from the King's Council which, incidentally, is one reason why
the House of Lords is the highest court of appeal in the land
(though, as we stated, it is for this purpose made up of the Law
Lords, the Lord Chancellor and perhaps one or two other legally
qualified Lords and is a very different body from the House of
Lords as part of the legislature). For similar historical reasons the
Lord Chancellor is the head of the judicial system. Various courts
have at one time and another hived off from the King's Council,
courts like the King's (now Queen's) Bench, Common Pleas,
Exchequer, Chancery, Probate, Divorce and Admiralty (Sir Alan
Herbert's 'wills, wives and wrecks'!) and the Assizes (the old
itinerant justices). In addition, Petty Sessions and Quarter Sessions
have a long history since the days when the Justices of the Peace
(once described as 'Tudor maids-of-all-work') exercised administrative as well as judicial powers. Yet again, not only have the
ancient courts been reformed by statute but additions, like the
County Courts, have been made.

There is a division in Britain between criminal and civil cases
and courts. In criminal cases Petty Sessions (or Magistrates Courts)
take the less serious offences and also preliminary hearings of more

serious cases; they are manned by Justices of the Peace (though in the Metropolitan Police District and in some large towns there are paid Stipendiary Magistrates, barristers of at least seven years' standing) without a jury. Quarter Sessions are also manned by J.P.s usually with a paid Chairman and Deputy-Chairman, solicitors or barristers of at least ten years standing (though many boroughs have a paid Recorder, a Barrister of at least five years standing); they take more serious offences, with a jury, and also hear appeals from Petty Sessions. The Assizes, manned by judges of the Queen's Bench on circuit, take the most serious offences, with a jury. The famous Central Criminal Court at the Old Bailey is, in fact, the Court of Assize for Criminal Business for London, Middlesex, and part of the Home Counties. A Court of Criminal Appeal hears appeals from Quarter Sessions and Assizes, without a jury. Very rarely, appeals may go further to the House of Lords.

For civil cases the County Courts hear disputes broadly involving sums of less than £500; the judge sits without a jury. The High Court, in one of its various divisions—Queen's Bench, Chancery, Probate, Divorce and Admiralty—takes any civil dispute, usually involving sums of over £500, occasionally with a jury. The Court of Appeal, without a jury, hears appeals from both County Courts and High Court. A further appeal lies to the House of Lords.

The above is a very simplified account of both criminal and civil courts. The ordinary citizen, if he becomes involved in the law at all, is most likely to be concerned with Petty Sessions, Courts of Summary Jurisdiction. The name Police Courts is rightly frowned upon; the courts are in no way adjuncts of the police, though it has been asserted that magistrates too readily accept police evidence. Petty Sessions, as well as dealing with innumerable minor offences such as driving without a licence, also perform some civil and administrative functions such as granting licenses for the sale of alcoholic liquor or the opening of betting shops, issuing separation and maintenance orders. The citizen might also be concerned with the County Court for such cases as debt, trespass, breach of contract and disputes between landlord and tenant.

There is nothing further of importance to say about Quarter Sessions in particular. But there are some points of general interest concerning J.P.s. A law periodical once suggested that 'about one-third of J.P.s are competent, about one third passable, and one-third ought not be be there at all'. It is suggested that there is too much secrecy about the appointment of J.P.s by the Lord Chancellor on the recommendation of local advisory committees. There is insufficient standardization of sentences and the granting of bail. The Home Secretary tries to avoid such defects by various circulars and by encouraging J.P.s to attend courses but he cannot, and should not, interfere with actual sentences. It is also suggested that some J.P.s are too much under the influence of the Clerk and, as we mentioned, of the police. A Royal Commission on the Justices of the Peace recommended against relying entirely upon paid full-time magistrates, but certainly ways should be found of generally raising the standard of J.P.s.

Some defects are also alleged to exist in the jury system. For instance, there is a property qualification for jurors (who are marked 'J' on the electoral register) which not only disqualifies some ninety-five per cent of women voters but a very large proportion of men who do not meet the required qualification. As a result it is suggested that there may be a class bias in jurors. Nor are exemptions from service granted for such defects as illiteracy or 'downright stupidity'. Lord Justice Parker has commented that juries are 'predominantly male, middle-aged, middle-minded, and middle-class'. In 1965, however, a Departmental Committee recommended that with certain exceptions, all registered voters should be liable for jury service; provision would also be made for half the jurors to be women and one-quarter under 30, with an age limit of 65. There is a general feeling that the jury system is 'a good thing', that it is somehow 'democratic'. This may, in fact, be one of the 'symbols' of the political culture rather than an objective appraisal of the merits of the system.

As we saw in our discussion of the attitude of judges to Acts of Parliament and administrative decisions, there are also criticisms which might be made of the approach of the judges to problems which come before them. Their decisions, whatever may be said by ultra-orthodox writers on jurisprudence, are clearly not just mechanical applications of existing law to particular cases. By their use of precedents and even more by their 'distinguishing' of precedents (finding sometimes minute or even obscure differences in order to sustain a different decision in an apparently similar case—a procedure particularly important in the House of Lords which is bound by its own previous decisions), they *make* the law, as Bentham asserted more than one hundred years ago. If they adopt a restrictive approach to the interpretation of statutes they are in danger of falling behind social needs. Certainly there is a case for insisting that, like judges in other systems, they should look at the background to legislation—at what the French call 'les trauvaux préparatoires'—to ascertain 'legislative intent'; at present they examine neither parliamentary debates nor even official reports on which legislation is sometimes avowedly based. On the other hand, if they exercise greater freedom in the interpretation of statutes they are in danger of allowing their own social background, education, and even prejudices to obtrude. Lord Denning has suggested that where the law appears to be at fault the judges should say so and suggest parliamentary action. But even the 'tidying up' of existing law may, in fact, result in subtle changes—hence the reluctance to allow the Law Commission to operate without reference to Parliament. But again, these are profound and technical problems to which we cannot do justice here.

Perhaps more important to the ordinary citizen are the problems of the cost of litigation, by no means entirely solved by the provision of legal aid; the problem of 'the law's delay' and the congestion of the courts; the problem of an excessive tendency to remand accused persons in prison—with over 30,000 normally awaiting trial though nearly half will eventually be fined, put on probation, discharged, or found not guilty. There is also the question of compensation for damage caused by *criminal* action, since punishment of the criminal is no more than psychological satisfaction to the person injured. That the law is too complex, and often appears to others besides Sam Weller to be 'an ass', is, perhaps, an irremediable disease in the modern state. It has, however, been suggested that the lawyers themselves might do more to assist in a process of at least relative simplification. The reader himself must assess the reasons for the lawyer's apparent reluctance to do just this! He might, perhaps, consider the problem in the context of current attempts to cut the costs and reduce the complexities of house purchase. Meanwhile, the tendency to keep many matters away from the courts continues. The new Rent Act of 1965, for example, provides for rent officers and rent committees to settle disputes between landlord and tenant, though it preserves the jurisdiction of the courts for criminal offences such as intimidation. Similarly, the Race Relations Act relies upon local conciliation committees rather than upon penalties.

7

Local Government

Nothing, we are sometimes told, is more calculated to raise a yawn, empty the lecture theatre, or keep people away from the polling booth, than local government. Yet apart from the Greater London Council and the thirty-two London Boroughs, there are sixty Administrative Counties which perform *some* functions in their geographical areas but not all, eighty-four County Boroughs ('all-purpose' authorities) and over thirteen hundred non-county boroughs, urban and rural districts whose functions supplement those of the Administrative Counties, not to mention rural parishes. Constant attention has been paid to the problem of local government reform since 1945 and the latest Local Government Commission is still engaged in the process of making recommendations for reform (at least of areas) despite the fact that in 1965 the Minister of Housing and Local Government saw no likelihood that the Commission would produce a satisfactory long-term solution and was preparing to establish a high-level Commission or Committee to advise on more fundamental changes. Two committees, under Sir John Maud and Sir George

Mallaby, were at the same time considering the problems of the supply of efficient and suitable councillors and officers and of the management of local authority affairs. Meanwhile, cries against increases in the rates continue to be heard, very largely, it is fair to surmise, from people who seldom trouble to read the back of their Demand Note (if, indeed, they are householders and receive one!) to see what essential services are (partly) paid for out of the rates, or from people who constantly demand better services while bemoaning their cost. Once again we shall not attempt to discuss all the details of local government which are available in textbooks, but merely to raise some important points of general interest.

We begin by asking why we want local government at all, then examine the services which it provides and, finally estimate its future prospects. The first question has been dealt with in interesting fashion by Mr L. J. Sharpe in Fabian Tract No. 361, 'Why Local Democracy?' The defenders of local government often lapse into what he calls mysticism; their justifications are more akin to incantations than explanations. For example, it is described as 'the seed-bed of democracy', 'the foundation of our liberty', 'a bastion against the depredations of majoritarian democracy'. Such defences tend to give the impression that there really is not much rational justification for it. As *The Times* remarked on 10 November, 1964, 'local government is a legacy of nineteenth century interest in democratic forms. It is beginning to look as if confidence in it and practice of it may prove to be a passing phase in British political evolution'. Nor is there much more force in the traditional defence that 'it exists' or 'it works'. As we remarked of the House of Lords, the cure for admiration is to go and look at it; moreover, to let sleeping dogs lie may eventually mean that they never wake up. Nor is local government necessarily 'the reconciler of classes' (too many sections of the community are largely excluded because of the time involved and the inadequate compensation for loss of earnings) or 'the training ground for democracy' (since relatively few participate and of these not many go on to central government). A more empirical approach is based on the grounds that some services are 'national and onerous', others 'local and beneficial', to use the terms of a long-forgotten Royal Commission which, however, did not succeed in making a satisfactory distinction between the two. Most services are 'onerous' in the financial sense and it is virtually impossible to decide which are 'national' in scope and which of purely local significance.

Yet everywhere it seems to be felt that some form of decentralization is necessary and that 'deconcentration' by providing local or regional offices of central departments does not fulfil the purposes of 'devolution' of responsibility on to elected bodies. At the level of central government, organized as we have seen into departments providing specialized services, it is felt that there must be some generalist agency for bringing these services together so as to meet the needs of the community for whom they are provided, and that, ultimately, this must be a 'political' agency. In the same way the specialists who administer the services at the local level (and who are not even brought together by generalists at the administrative level to the extent that is true of central government) require a higher placed superior located somewhat closer to their field of operations than the Cabinet. If we have doubts concerning the effectiveness of ministerial responsibility as a means of dealing with citizen grievances against central government it is even less likely that it will deal effectively with local government, especially since in many cases, for example, the police, the central Minister is able to argue that it is not his responsibility. Shall the generalist common superior at local level be elected or appointed? In a society with any claim to democracy the answer must be 'elected'.

Thus the first fundamental role of local government is to resolve the competing claims of major services on given resources through the elected representatives of the citizens who will use these services, and to co-ordinate them at the point of execution. Inevitably, there are limits to freedom of local action both because of the demand for national minimum standards and because of the growth of central control over such things as investment. But this first function is still important; the alternative is a less flexible, less responsive, non-democratic, more expensive, and more highly-bureaucratized system.

Secondly, local government provides a series of primary pressure points being upon the central bureaucracy. Elected representatives are neither appointed by a Ministry (as are, for example, members of Regional Hospital Boards and Hospital Management Committees, or Consumer Councils), nor its employees. We have discussed the importance of pressure groups and have seen that those representing the general public are less numerous and less powerful than those representing sectional interests. Local authorities or combinations of local authorities like the Association of Municipal Corporations, the County Councils Association, or even the Parish Councils Association, can represent the general interest. On the other hand we must be aware that such associations often represent the 'vested interests' in local government itself, the elected members, the officers, the small groups who fear a loss of their status and influence if local authorities are merged or destroyed. The interests of ordinary citizens are *not* necessarily the same as those of people engaged in local government. Indeed, many people are more concerned with obtaining satisfactory services than with who provides them, though the two things cannot always be separated.

What, then, are the specific services provided by local authorities? Standard works on local government list such functions as (1) police and fire protection, including 'public control' as of weights and measures, food and drugs, petroleum, motor and other licensing; (2) public health, highways, housing, town and country planning, mental deficiency, blind persons, maternity and child, welfare, midwives, small dwellings acquisition, allotments, advertisement regulations, restriction of ribbon development; (3) certain aspects of national assistance; (4) education, including libraries, museums, art galleries etc. In Administrative Counties these functions are divided between the County and County Districts, though some County services are run under schemes of delegation to the Districts; the all-purpose County Boroughs provide all the services. There is no need to emphasize that every one of these functions impinges closely on the daily lives of every citizen. But so, of course, does 'the burden of the rates' despite the fact that more than half the overall total expenditure on 'local services' is provided through various grants-in-aid from the central government.

There are, however, two broad reasons why citizens tend to overlook the importance of local government. The first is the loss of many functions since 1945. The second is the degree of central control over local authorities. Both are in large part due to the inadequacy of local authorities: the lack of financial resources; the existence of too many small units quite incapable of providing modern services either economically or efficiently; the fact that even the largest authorities do not cover areas sufficiently large for the most effective provision of certain services; and the belief (not always justified) that the quality of personnel, elected and official, and of administration, at local level, is inferior to that at the central level. Some would also argue that the 'intrusion' of party politics has tended to demean local government, although there is some evidence that public interest is greater and the percentage of voters going to the polls larger where there is party rivalry and party responsibility, and that many with experience of local government have expressed the opinion that party responsibility may have a salutary effect on co-ordinated and principled administration. All these points are complicated and controversial and cannot be pursued further here.

We must, however, look briefly at the question of loss of functions. Since 1945 local authorities have lost their electricity and gas services, most of their national assistance functions, control of various agricultural services, valuation for rating, various aspects of road transport, hospitals and other health services. In some cases these functions have not been transferred to central government or to *ad hoc* bodies but from 'minor' (i.e. County Districts) to 'major' (i.e. Administrative Counties) authorities— although the terms minor and major are purely definitional; they often mean nothing in terms of area, population, financial resources or capacity. The minor authorities, besides losing some of the above listed functions like gas and electricity, have lost education, town and country planning, police, care of children, care of the old, and ambulance services, though in some cases certain powers are delegated to them. These losses have been particularly serious for the minor authorities, which have been left with few functions of real significance and interest to the average citizen— or the average councillor. It is true that many welfare and recreational services have been extended and developed—care of the disabled and aged, accommodation for the aged and handicapped, many preventive health services, home helps, community centres, youth clubs, theatres, concerts, and so on. But in so many of these services central supervision and control have seemed to reduce the opportunity for initiative and blurred the sense of responsibility. This factor needs to be examined a little more closely.

Local authorities, of course, have always derived their powers from various Acts of Parliament, either general or private. Proposals to allow them to do anything which is not forbidden rather than only those things which are permitted have never won much support. They are also under stricter judicial control than central administrative agencies and Mr Sharpe has recently suggested that the whole doctrine of *ultra vires* needs to be revised. On the other hand, allegations of maladministration and abuses of discretionary powers are so frequent that strong arguments for an Ombudsman for local government have been put forward. But executive control is felt most harshly by local authorities. It is true that no Minister has a general power to give orders to a local authority or to dismiss it. But there are default powers (exercised e.g. when Coventry refused to perform its civil defence functions). More important, many Acts of Parliament give Ministers the right to impose regulations—in Education, Fire, the Children's Services, National Health, Police. There are also 'approvals' of schemes and plans in which the Minister has the last word. Circulars and memoranda flow down in a constant stream and are expected to be accepted; inspectors are the eyes and ears of central departments. There are statutory regulations concerning the appointment and dismissal of certain local government officers and several authorities have had pressure brought to bear in respect of the appointment of Chief Constables and Chief Education Officers. In many cases appeals lie from local authority decisions to the Minister.

Behind all these techniques of executive and administrative

P

control and influence there lies the weapon of finance, the iron fist in the velvet glove. Rates are an inadequate source of local revenue and for years certain kinds of property were 'derated', paying less than their fair share of rates, by government fiat through Act of Parliament. (Agricultural land and buildings are still derated). No satisfactory additional source of revenue under *local* control has yet been found. Grants bring control and supervision and the substitution of a general grant in aid of the rates in 1958 for most of the specific or percentage grants for particular services seems to have brought little of the reduction in control which was promised. A very large part of local expenditure is subject to government audit and the district auditor has power to surcharge not only for illegal but for 'unreasonable' expenditure. Capital as well as recurrent expenditure is under central control; borrowing, of course, must be to a large extent if economic and financial management is to be effective. As we saw, the demand for national minimum standards has enhanced this tendency to central supervision and control. We must be quite clear that centralization is due neither to Whitehall's liking for power or to the preference of any political party for such centralization. But the result has been a loss of interest in local government, possibly a reluctance on the part of many able men and women to 'waste time' on it, and an increase in the power of officials over elected representatives.

Further alarm has been caused by the recent establishment of new Regional Machinery. Following upon the policy of the Conservative Government in certain selected regions the Labour Government established Regional Economic Planning Councils, consisting of representatives of industry, commerce, local authorities, universities and other bodies, 'to provide considered and informal advice'. They were not to be organs of the Government or to replace elected local authorities and would have no executive powers. Regional Planning Boards were also established, consisting of civil service representatives of the main economic and social departments, under the chairmanship of the representative of the Department of Economic Affairs. *The Times* commented: 'The Planning Boards come nearer the French system of prefectures, and the Advisory Councils nearer to nominated commissions or corporate bodies, or selection (as of magistrates) by secret consultations, than either comes to the familiar device of elected local government'. These developments, coupled with the growing feeling that economic planning cannot be separated from physical land-use planning, traffic management, overspill arrangements for growing population, the establishment of New Towns, and other functions including, very possibly, the provision of educational and social amenities, have raised new fears. In addition, other functions such as police have been candidates for 'regionalization'.

It may be that the ultimate solution lies in a smaller number of *elected* Regional Authorities, with 'second-tier' elected authorities below them, possibly to the largest extent possible based on the concept of the 'City Region'. This would necessitate root and branch reform of local government and would affect practically every local authority in the land. But it may be the only alternative to an even more rapid decay of local government as we know it and a great increase in centrally controlled official and advisory bodies. This question of the future of local government cannot be discussed further here. Many, however, feel that whatever the new set-up, 'if we shape local (or regional) government from the standpoint of convenience only we shall dissipate by an act of outstanding political folly the slow gain of centuries of political experience'. On the other hand, if resistance to sensible change takes the form of the revolt of 'gallant little Rutland,' which successfully resisted abolition as a local authority, local government will remain in the 'horse and buggy age' while the motor-car and the helicopter pass it by.

Conclusion

There is little point in trying to sum up the long argument which started with an attempt to suggest a general approach to an understanding of the political system and continued with a lengthy, though still incomplete account of the major features of the working of the British political system. We have presented little of the familiar material contained in the books of the constitutional lawyers, though their concepts, like the sovereignty of Parliament, the rule of law, the separation of powers, the conventions of the constitution and the rest, have made an appearance from time to time, perhaps for criticism.

As we explained at the outset, our purpose has been to indicate the significance of politics and of political decision-making to the ordinary man and woman. In order to play an active rather than a passive part in these processes it is not necessary to master even all the information contained in a book as slight as this. But it is important to understand how one may participate, with others, in the 'input' processes which largely determine what will be the 'outputs' of the system and to know something of the factors which influence the processes whereby the inputs are converted into outputs, and the way in which the latter, by the feedback process, influence the former.

For further study we suggest not merely that some of the more factual and orthodox books be read but that the reader return to Part I after absorbing Part II to ascertain just how the analysis and method of approach of the former assists him in further understanding the British political system in action. This system has suffered and still suffers from many kinds of stress but it has generally succeeded in responding to both the physical and human intra-societal and extra-societal environmental influences with a modicum of success. These environmental influences continue to change. Can Britain be a 'Great Power'? What is her role 'East of Suez'? Shall she give up some of her 'national sovereignty' to the European Economic Community; to the United Nations Organization, to a World Government? Can the National Plan be the basis of economic growth and of improved standards of living through public as well as private provision? Can citizens obtain better housing, education, health, recreational facilities? Is the system itself in need of reform, to 'restore' the influence of Parliament, to provide more adequate safeguards against ever more complex and ubiquitous administration, to ensure more 'grass-roots' democracy? All these questions—and perhaps even such questions as how well we can do in the Olympic Games, can we win the Ashes, or perform creditably in the World Cup—are inextricably bound up with politics. By this we do not mean that they depend solely on *State* action. Our distinction between the State and the political system was intended to emphasize that the distinction between government and governed, between 'we' and 'they', is artificial, unreal, and dangerous. So, according to proverbial wisdom is 'a little learning'. More learning and greater understanding are the essential basis of a viable democratic system.

Postscript

The General Election of 1966 seems broadly to have confirmed many of the points made in our analysis. The electors appear largely to have maintained the pattern of voting which we described. There was apparently some shift of middle and lower-middle class voters to Labour while many skilled and semi-skilled workers either shifted to the Conservative party or abstained; the turn-out of voters was lower than in 1964. Young people and the over sixty-fives, as well as women seem to have shifted somewhat to Labour. But the 'swing' of just over three per cent to Labour was fairly uniform over the whole country with no really significant regional variations.

The electors again seem to have voted largely on the basis of 'party image'. Various issues were tried—the Common Market, the Trade Unions, even Rhodesia, as well as domestic issues such as the cost of living. But there is little evidence that these issues seriously affected voting patterns. The electors seem once again to have been primarily concerned to ensure a strong government—in the sense of one party with a sound working majority. Although the Liberal vote probably had little net effect on the position of the two major parties, it may have shifted in places—of which Exeter is an example—to Labour. The Labour Party benefited from the feeling that it should be given a chance to prove what it could do over a longer period than seventeen months and from the feeling that the Conservatives could not win. The public opinion polls were believed.

Above all, the election confirmed the view that a 'Presidential type' contest was being waged; leadership was an issue. Mr Wilson consistently ran ahead of his party, Mr Heath behind his, although the latter probably improved his 'image' during the campaign. As Prime Minister, Mr Wilson was able largely to dictate the tone and pace of the campaign.

On the whole, the general conclusions which we reached about the British political system are well supported by the most recent example of its most important 'symbolic' aspect—the people choosing those who for another four or five years will constitute the 'authoritative decision-makers' in the system. As to these decision-makers themselves, the House of Commons will now contain a higher proportion than ever of university graduates, and those interested will wish to analyse the changing composition particularly of Labour M.P.s. Eighty of these had a public (or private) school education, while ninety went to Oxford, Cambridge, or both. More than another ninety attended other universities. On the other hand, while 269 of them had an exclusively state schooling, this was true of only 27 Conservatives. Has Michael Young's 'meritocracy' made further gains? Political sociology has some useful tasks yet to perform.

Select Bibliography

The following works are recommended for *student reading*. A useful beginner's book with ample facts and some suggestions for critical thinking is *Westminster Workshop*, R. K. Mosley, Pergamon. Still a first-rate standard introductory work is *The Government of Britain*, 9th Edition, W. Harrison, Hutchinson's. As a start with Sir Ivor Jennings's classical writings students should look at *The Queen's Government*, Pelican. For 'inputs', the following are essential:—*Voters, Parties and Leaders*, J. Blondel, Pelican; *Anonymous Empire* (pressure groups), S. E. Finer, Pall Mall; *British Political Parties*, R. McKenzie, Heinemann. For the 'conversion processes' a representative selection of introductory texts includes: *The House of Commons at Work*, E. Taylor, Pelican; *What's Wrong with Parliament?* Hill and Whicklow, Penguin Special; *The English Constitution*, W. Bagehot (especially the Introduction by R. H. S. Crossman), Fontana Books; *A Primer of Public Administration*. S. E. Finer, Muller; *The Civil Service in Britain*, G. Campbell, Duckworth; *The Queen's Courts*, P. Archer, Pelican; *Local Government in England and Wales*, E. Jackson, Pelican. For further material on the Commonwealth, which is scarcely dealt with in this volume, a useful up-to-date introduction is *Britain and the Commonwealth*, H. Victor Wiseman, Allen and Unwin. Students who wish to look further at public policy, and especially partly policies, should read *Why Conservative?* T. Raison, Penguin Special; *Why Labour?* J. Northcott, Penguin Special; *Why Liberal?* H. Cowie, Penguin Special. Two original and stimulating books which will for long be used as the basis for intelligent discussion about British Government are *Modern British Politics*, S. Beer, Faber and *Politics in England*, R. Rose, Faber. For further study of political systems in general, although its illustrations are mainly American, *Modern Political Analysis*, Robert E. Dahl, Prentice-Hall, is an extremely stimulating work. For those who wish to pursue their studies to a greater depth the bibliographies in the above books should be consulted.